Flying Blind

The **ISEAS – Yusof Ishak Institute** (formerly Institute of Southeast Asian Studies) is an autonomous organization established in 1968. It is a regional centre dedicated to the study of socio-political, security, and economic trends and developments in Southeast Asia and its wider geostrategic and economic environment. The Institute's research programmes are grouped under Regional Economic Studies (RES), Regional Strategic and Political Studies (RSPS), and Regional Social and Cultural Studies (RSCS). The Institute is also home to the ASEAN Studies Centre (ASC), the Singapore APEC Study Centre and the Temasek History Research Centre (THRC).

ISEAS Publishing, an established academic press, has issued more than 2,000 books and journals. It is the largest scholarly publisher of research about Southeast Asia from within the region. ISEAS Publishing works with many other academic and trade publishers and distributors to disseminate important research and analyses from and about Southeast Asia to the rest of the world.

"This is a uniquely well-informed account of Vietnam's serious internal debates leading to the decision to join ASEAN in 1995. The story starts with a probing analysis of Hanoi's regional diplomacy and relations with the Soviet Union, China and the United States from the 1970s onward. Entering the 1990s, the narrative shows how Vietnamese policymakers struggled to reconcile ideological and pragmatic considerations as they navigated complex great-power and regional environments. Professor Tung dispels conventional balance-of-power explanations for Hanoi's embrace of ASEAN, and argues persuasively that the decision to join grew out of a shift from a revolutionary national identity to an identity centred on developmental state model of the Southeast Asian type. This honest and close-up view of policy debates offers a rare opportunity for readers to understand the logic of policy-making in one of the world's most complex diplomatic environments."

Andrew J. Nathan,
Class of 1919 Professor of Political Science, Columbia University

"This book is a remarkable account of why Vietnam joined ASEAN and what happened to Vietnam's world view, neighborhood policy and national identity from that membership. It is based on non-public official documents, rare personal interviews and analytical research. A fascinating picture of ASEAN's early developments and the relationships between Vietnam and China as well as with Japan, the then Soviet Union and the USA emerged from these pages. It is a valuable insight into the thinking process and ideological underpinning of Vietnam's decision-making which will definitely benefit those learning about the country's adaptive capacity and innovative resilience for survival."

Ambassador Ong Keng Yong,
Executive Deputy Chairman, S. Rajaratnam School of International Studies,
Nanyang Technological University, Singapore,
former Secretary-General of ASEAN (2003–7)

"*Flying Blind: Vietnam's Decision to Join ASEAN* is a seminal work as it presents the first comprehensive analysis of Vietnamese foreign policy decision-making based on unprecedented access to transcripts of Politburo meetings and resolutions of the Vietnam Communist Party Central Committee, internal files of Vietnam's Ministry of Foreign Affairs, and interviews with senior diplomats. The author expertly interrogates his sources through the lenses of realism, liberalism and constructivism."

Carlyle Thayer,
Emeritus Professor, UNSW Canberra, The University of New South Wales,
School of Humanities and Social Sciences at the
Australian Defence Force Academy, Canberra, ACT Australia

"This is a superb analysis of Vietnam's 1995 *jump* into ASEAN! The book's timing is perfect now that Vietnam served as ASEAN Chair in 2020."

Stein Tonnesson,
Peace Research Institute, Oslo, Norway,
author of Vietnam 1946: How the War Began
(University of California Press, 2009)

"A wonderful history of the turnaround in Vietnam's foreign affairs during the 1980s by a Vietnamese senior scholar and diplomat. The book explains how it was possible for Hanoi to move from a staunch Soviet ally to full membership in the ASEAN within only a few years after the Cold War ended.

Odd Arne Westad,
Professor of History at Yale University,
author of The Cold War: A World History
(Penguin Book, 2018)

Flying Blind

Vietnam's Decision to Join ASEAN

NGUYEN VU TUNG

 YUSOF ISHAK INSTITUTE

First published in Singapore in 2021 by
ISEAS Publishing
30 Heng Mui Keng Terrace
Singapore 119614
E-mail: publish@iseas.edu.sg
Website: http://bookshop.iseas.edu.sg

All rights reserved. No part of this publication may be reproduced, stored in a retrieval system, or transmitted in any form or by any means, electronic, mechanical, photocopying, recording or otherwise, without the prior permission of the ISEAS – Yusof Ishak Institute.

© 2021 ISEAS – Yusof Ishak Institute, Singapore.

The responsibility for facts and opinions in this publication rests exclusively with the author and his interpretations do not necessarily reflect the views or the policy of the publisher or its supporters.

ISEAS Library Cataloguing-in-Publication Data

Name(s): Nguyen, Vu Tung, author.
Title: Flying blind : Vietnam's decision to join ASEAN / Nguyen Vu Tung.
Description: Singapore : ISEAS – Yusof Ishak Institute, 2021. | Includes bibliographical references.
Identifiers: ISBN 9789814881951 (paperback) | ISBN 9789814881968 (pdf) | ISBN 9789814881975 (epub)
Subjects: LCSH: ASEAN. | Vietnam—Foreign relations—Southeast Asia. | Southeast Asia—Foreign relations—Vietnam. | Vietnam—Politics and government—1975–
Classification:

Classification: LCC DS525.9 V5N57

Illustration on front cover reproduced courtesy of the ASEAN Department, MOFA Vietnam.

Typeset by Superskill Graphics Pte Ltd
Printed in Singapore by Markono Print Media Pte Ltd

CONTENTS

Acknowledgements ix

Glossary x

1. Introduction 1

2. The Paris Agreement and Vietnam: ASEAN Relations in the Early 1970s 9
   New Priorities Given to Regional Policy 10
   Constraining Factors 16
   The Stagnating Relationship 23
   Conclusion 29

3. 1978 to 1985: Coexistence Between Two Opposing Groups 40
   The Structural Context 41
   Engraving the Differences 43
   Dialogue with ASEAN 47
   Wedge Driving 52
   The Soviet Factor 57
   Conclusion 63

4.	Joining ASEAN: Political and Strategic Factors	76
	The Internal Debates	76
	ASEAN in the Overall Foreign Policy under Renovation (*Doi Moi*)	78
	A New Basis For Sino-Vietnamese Relations and the Implications for Vietnam-ASEAN Cooperation	87
	Reduced Commitments to World Revolution	92
	Improved Vietnam-ASEAN Relations and Implications for Hanoi's Relations with Major Powers	94
	China Factor in Vietnam's Decision to Join ASEAN	98
	ASEAN and the US as Helpers: The South China Sea Disputes Connection	102
	The American Connection	114
	Conclusion	119
5.	Jumping on a Moving Train: Vietnam Joins ASEAN	134
	The Chronology of Joining ASEAN	135
	Hasty Preparations	140
	Post-Admission Awareness and Adjustments of Domestic Institutions	145
	Conclusion	160
6.	ASEAN Membership and Vietnam's Shifting National Identity	169
	More About the Internal Debates	170
	Similarity in Political Structures and Practices	170
	Common Foreign Policy Objectives	180
	The "Association Mentality" and the Question of State Identity in Vietnamese Foreign Policy	185
7.	Conclusion	201
References		213
Index		227
The Author		236

ACKNOWLEDGEMENTS

This book is adapted from my PhD dissertation submitted in 2003 at Columbia University. During my years working on this subject, I was fortunate to receive valuable support and encouragement from many people and institutions. It goes without saying that I take full personal responsibility for all the analysis and findings as well as the shortcomings in this book.

GLOSSARY

AFTA	ASEAN Free Trade Area
AMM	ASEAN Ministerial Meeting
ANC	ASEAN National Committee
ANS	ASEAN National Secretariat
APEC	Asia-Pacific Economic Cooperation Organization
ARF	ASEAN Regional Forum
ARF SOM	ARF Senior Official Meetings
ASA	Association of Southeast Asia
ASEAN	Association of Southeast Asian Nations
ASEAN SEOM	ASEAN Senior Economic Senior Officials Meetings
ASEAN SOM	ASEAN Senior Officials Meetings
ASEM	Asia-Europe Meeting
CCP	Chinese Communist Party
CEPT	Common Effective Preferences Tariffs
CERC	Commission for External Relations of the CPV
CMEA	Council for Mutual Economic Assistance
COC	Code of Conduct in the South China Sea
CPV	Communist Party of Vietnam
DOC	Declaration of Code of Conduct in the South China Sea

DRV	Democratic Republic of Vietnam
FMC	Foreign Ministers Conference (among Indochinese Foreign Ministers)
ICK	International Conference on Kampuchea
MAPHILINDO	Malaysia, the Philippines, and Indonesia
MCP	Malaysian Communist Party
MOF	Ministry of Finance
MOFA	Ministry of Foreign Affairs
MOT	Ministry of Trade
MPS	Ministry of Public Security
NAM	The Non-Aligned Movement
NCIEC	National Committee for International Economic Cooperation
NLF	National Liberation Front
PRC	People's Republic of China
PRG	Preliminary Revolutionary Government
SEAC	Southeast Asian Command
SEATO	Southeast Asian Treaty Organization
TAC	Treaty of Amity and Cooperation in Southeast Asia
USA	United States of America
WTO	World Trade Organization
ZOPFAN	Zone of Peace, Freedom, and Neutrality

1

INTRODUCTION

In late 2019 Vietnam assumed the ASEAN Chairmanship and introduced the theme of a "Cohesive and Responsive ASEAN". On this occasion, Vietnam's Prime Minister Nguyen Xuan Phuc stressed,

> Throughout its twenty-five years of ASEAN membership, Vietnam has always made active and responsible contributions to ASEAN cooperation. The growth of the ASEAN community bears the hallmarks of Vietnam's work. In 2020, Vietnam will assume major responsibilities at the regional and international level, most notably the ASEAN Chairmanship. Such a responsibility gives Vietnam an opportunity to contribute more substantively to the building and growth of a harmonious, resilient, innovative, cohesive, responsible and adaptive ASEAN Community.[1]

Such an upbeat tone about ASEAN reflected a general consensus in Vietnam that the decision to join ASEAN in 1995 had been a right foreign policy

---

This chapter was adapted from the article "Vietnam-ASEAN Cooperation after the Cold War and the Continued Search for a Theoretical Framework", *Contemporary Southeast Asia* 24, no. 1 (April 2002): 106–20. Reproduced with permission of the ISEAS – Yusof Ishak Institute.

decision of great strategic importance.² Moreover, Hanoi has attached greater importance to ASEAN. On 27 August 2019, Nguyen Xuan Phuc told ASEAN Secretary General Lim Jock Hoi that Vietnam always considered ASEAN as one of the most important pillars of its foreign policy.³ A draft of the Political Report to be introduced at the Communist Party of Vietnam Congress in first quarter of 2021 confirmed the established policy line that Vietnam will be "proactive and responsible with other ASEAN members in the building a strong ASEAN Community and maintaining the central role of ASEAN in regional security architectures".⁴ In short, in retrospect, after twenty-five years, Hanoi's decision to join ASEAN was recognized as the vintage one.⁵

But it had taken almost the same amount of time for Hanoi to change its attitude towards the organization. From the policy of denial, Hanoi gradually adopted the one of peacefully coexisting with, and ultimately embracing ASEAN. Following the open-door reforms programme introduced in 1986 (widely known as *Doi Moi*), Vietnam began to develop relations with ASEAN. The process of Vietnam-ASEAN rapprochement culminated with Vietnam's signing the ASEAN Treaty of Amity and Cooperation in 1991 and its admission to membership of the organization in 1995—the only formal international organization that the country entered since the end of the Cold War. Myanmar and Laos entered ASEAN in 1997 and Cambodia in 1999. It was acknowledged that after East Timor gained full independence, it too would seek membership in ASEAN. The mode of ASEAN cooperation now covers the entirety of Southeast Asian region. These developments were a contrast with what had happened earlier in Southeast Asia: the relations between Vietnam and ASEAN had, in general, reflected the patterns of amity and enmity among regional states along the ideological divide during the Cold War and especially the Vietnam War, the 1975 victory of the revolution in Indochina brought about the emergence of two opposing groups of countries in Southeast Asia, and when Vietnam intervened in Cambodia in 1979, relations between Vietnam and ASEAN became hostile.

Why did Vietnam decide to join ASEAN in 1995? Why did it attach a great significance to the peace and cooperation in Southeast Asia after the Cold War ended? And what prevented Vietnam from doing so earlier? This work will study Vietnam-ASEAN relations from early 1970s to provide a background to a discussion on a period from 1986 (when the reforms in Vietnam officially started) to 1995 (when Vietnam became an ASEAN member). Considerable efforts were made to explain the shift towards a cooperative posture by Vietnam with regard to the Southeast Asian course of peace and cooperation—defined as the process of policy coordination in which goal-oriented actors adjust their behaviours to the actual or anticipated preferences of others.[6] Yet, while more adequate and satisfactory answers to these questions have not yet been found, new developments in Vietnam and the rest of Southeast Asia, not to mention those in the rest of the world, keep adding new dimensions to the study of Vietnam's foreign relations.

The end of the Cold War also changed the context of Vietnam's foreign relations with major powers. The Soviet Union collapsed in 1991, effectively terminating the Soviet-Vietnamese alliance officially formed in 1978 with the conclusion of the Treaty of Friendship and Cooperation between Hanoi and Moscow. Relations between Vietnam and China were normalized in 1991 with the two states agreeing not to return to the type of alliance that had existed in the past and was broken by the border war between the two countries in 1979. Besides, the relations between Vietnam and the United States started to improve in the early 1990s. The two countries normalized diplomatic and trade relations in 1995 and 2001 respectively although ideological differences and legacies of the Vietnam War still complicated this bilateral relationship.

The impacts on Vietnam's foreign relations in Southeast Asia were curious. On the one hand, Vietnam no longer enjoyed any alliance-type of relations with any major power. On the other hand, it enjoyed a greater freedom in the design and conduct of foreign policy. The absence of constraints imposed by great powers confrontation and détente on smaller states and the relaxation of ideological constraints in world politics following the end of the Cold War suggested that Vietnam and other Southeast Asian states could be freer to follow their nationalist agenda. The region, therefore, would be "ripe for rivalry"[7] because the regional states had traditional suspicions about, and territorial disputes with, each other. But as instability and even hostility became more evident elsewhere, Vietnam acceded to the Treaty of Amity and Cooperation in Southeast Asia (TAC), while the process of ASEAN enlargement starting from Vietnam's membership did facilitate a Zone of Peace in the entirety of Southeast Asia. Since international relations are often about cooperation and conflict, and in general, it has been agreed that states find it difficult to cooperate with one another, the shift of Vietnam to a foreign policy committed to peace and cooperation with its Southeast Asian neighbours in the early 1990s is worth studying. To borrow Milner's words, why nations cooperate with each other is always "the particular empirical puzzle".[8]

The specific puzzle about Vietnam's new cooperative behaviour towards ASEAN also has a theoretical aspect: explanations provided by established international relations theories do not seem totally applicable. Liberals often claim that peace is more likely possible among states with domestic democratic institutions. Vietnam and other Southeast Asian states, however, were not democracies, by Western standards. At the same time, as some of the regional states had been undergoing democratic transformation, the prospect of interstate conflicts in Southeast Asia should become more likely, as critics of democratic peace theory would suggest.[9] Any non-democratic Zone of Peace should, therefore, be an anomaly for democratic peace theorists. What factors have contributed to a "non-democratic" peace in Southeast Asia?

Realists have long argued that cooperation is an anomaly and, if cooperation is materialized, ideology is a weak cause, and balancing power (or common external threat) is the main reason. Therefore, Vietnam-ASEAN cooperation and the non-liberal peace in the region would be justified because the threat of the post-Cold War China looms large. Yet, also from a rational point of view, it would be, historically and practically, too provoking for a small state like Vietnam to consider the giant neighbour as a threat, especially when the very notion of Chinese threat was still problematic. Besides, ASEAN was not a security alliance in the traditional sense; economic cooperation among the members was always modest, and the combination of capabilities of ASEAN as a collective entity was not matching those of China. But Vietnam chose to become a member of ASEAN and found a long-term link between its national security, regime legitimacy, and economic welfare with the cooperative relationship within ASEAN. There must, therefore, be other factors for the country to decide with whom it should align itself and cultivate cooperative relations. I try to seek ways to find these factors.

This book discusses relations between Vietnam and ASEAN from the early 1970s, and the reasons behind the decision made in Hanoi according to which Vietnam joined ASEAN in 1995. Based on Vietnamese documentation, this book attempts to give a fuller account of how leaders in Hanoi had constructed realities, changed their perceptions, and designed foreign policies to establish better relationship with ASEAN and then to join the regional organization in the wake of the collapse of the Soviet Union and the socialist bloc. The central argument of this book is simple: There is a strong linkage between the search for a new state identity in the aftermath of the Cold War and the making of foreign policy in Hanoi as well as the linkage between an improved understanding of ASEAN on the part of Hanoi and resultant better Vietnam-ASEAN relations. The search for a new state identity—which was believed to be compatible to that of ASEAN states—informed Hanoi's efforts to forge a closer cooperative relationship with ASEAN states; and similarly, the membership in ASEAN would inform Hanoi's present and future foreign policy.

Process tracing is the main method for this study. By tracing the actual process of decision-making, this method focuses on the collection of evidences showing the actual thinking by the decision-makers in Hanoi about Vietnam's foreign policy, differences (or congruencies) between rhetoric statements on, and actual practices of, Vietnamese foreign policy with regard to ASEAN. In other words, a historical inquiry focusing on process and discourse is central to the method for this study.[10]

Conducting the research, I gained access to various sources that include the followings:

- Secondary sources: published party documents, officials' memoirs; other secondary sources including books, monographs, newspaper and journal articles, etc.
- Primary sources: unpublished documents such as memorandum, political reports, talking points, transcripts of talks, cables sent to or received from Vietnamese embassies abroad, works and situation analyses by foreign ministry's researchers and officials.
- Personal interviews with officials from Ministry of Foreign Affairs, Communist Party of Vietnam Central Committee for External Relations, and Prime Minister's Office.

Access to sources was essential in the research for this book. Although difficulties remain, there has been some progress with regard to access to sources. Both academic and bureaucratic circles in Vietnam have been, for more than three decades, engaged in various types of exchanges with their foreign counterparts. These exchanges will be most important for Vietnamese foreign policy watchers to have a relatively good opportunity to access various kinds of sources. Besides, being a researcher at the Diplomatic Academy of Vietnam (DAV)—which serves as a main teaching and researching body and a think-tank for the Vietnam's Ministry of Foreign Affairs (MOFA)—I could have a relatively good chance of accessing various kinds of sources, thanks to my working connections with both academic and official circles who generally considered Vietnam's joining ASEAN a successful case of its foreign policy. Especially for this study, I was indebted to those who were willing to share with me documents of primary sources from the MOFA archives, several MOFA departments' files, and personal collections which were inaccessible to the public.

Apart from gathering data, the research also included a close reading of the available data, comparisons between public records and unpublished documents, and a careful reading of available historical events. I also tried to balance the personal and the widely accepted historical accounts and analysis. Especially, I focused on interviewing officials who were involved in Vietnam-ASEAN relations. These people helped me to interpret the real meaning of documents as well as introduce some of the "behind-the-scene events" that may not be documented as well as to close some possible gaps between what had been said and done.

In fact, as I learned during the course of research, collecting non-public documents and carefully reading them as well as interviewing relevant officials really helped me to get close to the actual thinking of decision-makers. These indeed revealed the perceptions and motivations of the leadership when they made decisions. For example, the data provided clues to Hanoi's perceptions and concerns over external and internal threats, actual thinking about Vietnam as an ASEAN member state, about other ASEAN members, and ASEAN as an organization, thus making it easier to determine how leaders in Hanoi attached importance to Vietnam-ASEAN relations while designing their policy towards ASEAN, how real "the sense of belonging" to the region was, how important ASEAN was in Hanoi's foreign policy, and what role ASEAN played in the overall mode of political and political developments of Vietnam. In short, this book represents an attempt for a more rigorous search for sources and their interpretation that helps provide a more detailed story of Hanoi's decision to join ASEAN and the Vietnam-ASEAN relationship from which theoretical generalizations may be possible.

It has been widely acknowledged that analysts of international relations and states' foreign policies should employ four independent variables, namely autonomy, welfare, security, and regime maintenance.[11] Findings in this book suggest that state identity should also be another variable to better explain and compare the foreign policy of different states in specific time and space settings.

Notes

1. Keynote speech by PM Nguyen Xuan Phuc at the launching ceremony of Vietnam's 2020 ASEAN Chairmanship on 6 January 2020, at http://news.chinhphu.vn/Home/Keynote-speech-by-PM-Nguyen-Xuan-Phuc-at-launching-ceremony-of-VNs-2020-ASEAN-Chairmanship/20201/38445.vgp
2. Nguyen Manh Cam, "Vietnam's Membership in ASEAN: A Right Decision of History-Making Significance" (Việt Nam tham gia ASEAN – một quyết sách đúng đắn có ý nghĩa lịch sử quan trọng), *Vietnam and the World* (Báo Thế giới và Việt Nam), July 2010.
3. "Prime Minister Phuc Receives ASEAN Secretary General", *People's Daily* (Báo Nhan Dan), 27 August 2019.
4. Communist Party of Vietnam, Drafts of Documents to be submitted to the Thirteenth Congress (Hanoi: Office of the CPV Central Committee, April 2020), p. 52. CPV, *Documents of the Xth, XIth, and XIIth Party Congresses* (Hanoi: National Politics Publishing House, 2001, 2006, and 2011).
5. Dang Cam Tu, "Vietnam in ASEAN: The Past 25 Years and the Way Forward" (Việt Nam trong ASEAN: 25 năm qua và chặng đường phía trước", *Communist Review* 7, no. 321 (July 2020): 8–17. See also Pham Binh Minh, "Việt Nam tham gia ASEAN: 20 năm qua và con đường đi tới" [Vietnam's Participation in ASEAN: The Past 20 Years and Beyond], in *Ngoại giao Việt Nam: Quá trình triển khai đường lối đối ngoại đại hội toàn quốc lần thứ XII của Đảng [Vietnamese Diplomacy: On the Process of Implementation of Foreign Policy Adopted by the Party's XIIth Congresss]*, by Pham Binh Minh (Hanoi: Nhà xuất bản Chính trị Quốc gia, National Political Publishing House 2015),

pp. 149–58, and Nguyen Hung Son, "Việt Nam sau 15 năm là thành viên ASEAN: Hướng tới một Việt Nam chủ động, tích cực, và có trách nhiệm trong ASEAN" [Vietnam after 15 Years in ASEAN: Toward a Proactive and Responsible Member], in *Vietnam's Foreign Policy Orientations toward 2030*, edited by Pham Binh Minh (Hà nội: Nhà xuất bản Chính trị Quốc gia, National Political Publishing House, 2010), pp. 223–36.
6. Robert Keohane, *After Hegemony* (Princeton, NJ: Princeton University Press, 1984), pp. 51–52.
7. Aaron Friedberg, "Ripe for Rivalry: Prospects for Peace in a Multipolar Asia", *International Security* 18, no. 3 (1995): 5–33.
8. Helen Milner, *Interest, Institutions, and Information: Domestic Politics and International Relations* (Princeton, NJ: Princeton University Press, 1997), p. 5.
9. Jack Snyder, *Voting for Violence: Democratization and Nationalist Conflict* (New York: Norton, 2000).
10. Theoretically, this approach is more sympathetic to constructivism. While realists claim that history does not matter (states have similar interests defined in terms of power, regardless of times and space), constructivists argue, among other things, that history does. See Sorpong Peou, "Realism and Constructivism in Southeast Asian Security Studies today: A Review Essay", *Pacific Review* 15, no. 1 (2002): 121–23.
11. K.J. Holsti, *Change in the International System: Essays on the Theory and Practice of International Relations* (Brookfield, VT: Edward Elgar, 1991), pp. 17–18.

2

THE PARIS AGREEMENT AND VIETNAM-ASEAN RELATIONS IN THE EARLY 1970s

The Paris Agreement, which was signed on 27 January 1973, was the outcome of a fierce military struggle and an effective and creative negotiating strategy. By providing for the complete withdrawal of US troops from South Vietnam, the Agreement seriously weakened the Saigon regime and created favourable conditions for North Vietnam and the Provisional Revolutionary Government (PRG) to strengthen their position, thus creating the potentials for a final victory.[1] Against this background, this chapter deals with relations between Vietnam ASEAN from roughly 1972 to 1978 and examines how the Paris Agreement and other factors influenced the worldview of Hanoi, and as a result, its policies towards ASEAN in a crucial period.

This chapter was adapted from "The Paris Agreement and Vietnam-ASEAN Relations in the Early 1970s", in *The Third Indochina War: Conflict between China, Vietnam and Cambodia, 1972–79*, edited by Odd Arne Westad and Sophie Quinn-Judge, pp. 103–25 (Abingdon: Routledge, 2006). Republished with permission of Taylor & Francis Informa UK Ltd (Books); permission conveyed through Copyright Clearance Center, Inc.

NEW PRIORITIES GIVEN TO REGIONAL POLICY

Following the Paris Agreement, a number of countries, including ASEAN member states, proceeded towards establishing diplomatic relations with the Democratic Republic of Vietnam (DRV) and the PRG. This gave rise to changes, still embryonic, in Hanoi's perception and subsequent policy directions with regard to Southeast Asia.

Firstly, there was a new perception of a higher stature of Vietnam in its relations with other countries in the region. A report of 1973 said that "the stature and influence enjoyed by the DRV and the status and prestige of the PRG have never been stronger",[2] and analysed this prestige in a number of aspects: Vietnam became a new model for local revolutionary movements as its performance and its experiences

> were extremely valuable for the revolutionary movement in the region, strongly encouraged and supported the national independence spirit of regional countries, communist parties, progressive forces, and patriotic movements fighting for national independence, democracy, and social progress in the region.[3]

Moreover, it was thought that Vietnam had become an important actor in the regional politics. According to one of the documents, "many states have considered Vietnam 'a superpower', with 'a great stature' and influence in Asia and the Pacific; peace-loving countries consider that Vietnam is in a unique position to help ease world tensions; and the countries that hold great ambitions regard us as a political opponent." As a result, "activities at the regional level will be meaningless without the participation by Vietnam."[4]

Hanoi also contrasted its new posture with the weakened positions of other regional countries. One report said,

> The Vietnamese victory and the American defeat have seriously weakened governments in the region that are lackeys of and dependent on the US. These governments are very much worried. [Governments of Indonesia, Malaysia, and Philippines] are even horrified, because their positions and prestige have been shaky as a result of following and supporting the aggressive policies of the US; their capabilities do not allow them to cope with their own domestic economic and political problems by themselves, let alone to fill the [power] "vacuum" in this region.[5]

Obviously, with the Paris Agreement, Hanoi perceived that it had an enhanced stature in Southeast Asia and could influence the future trends in Vietnam-ASEAN relations. Vietnam thought that as it was becoming stronger, ASEAN would grow more interested in developing cooperative relations with it. A report covering the first half of 1971 concluded that: "The neutralization proposal put forward by Malaysia reflected the objective reality in the region which has been increasingly influenced by the socialist bloc, the victory of Vietnam, the competition for influence by major powers, and the defeat of the US aggressive policies."[6] A report in 1974 further stated:

> In fact, for many years, Southeast Asian states including Malaysia, Singapore and the Philippines had little and distorted information about Vietnam. They have now come to see our important role and stature; they have also started to understand that their policies towards Vietnam in the past were wrong, and therefore want to change and correct these policies, to enhance understanding and proceed towards establishing friendly relations.[7]

Thus, with the signing of the Paris Agreement détente was perceived to emerge in Vietnam-ASEAN relations. And the root cause of détente, according to Hanoi, was its enhanced posture, and perhaps power, as compared with other states in the region. In 1974, a report provided a policy suggestion: "We should develop relations with other Southeast Asian states to show the goodwill of a victorious country."[8]

Secondly, the idea of developing relations with ASEAN member states following the Paris Agreement was designed to ensure security and development for Vietnam in the future. But the immediate and main objective was to "force the US and Saigon to strictly observe the Agreement and preserve peace, to bring into full play the political advantages of the PRG, and to limit the material and spiritual support by the ASEAN states to the Saigon regime".[9]

Geographical proximity as a factor of great importance, in term of security and development, had started to influence Hanoi's thinking. While not forgetting the involvements by some ASEAN states in the US war efforts in Vietnam, Hanoi began to see ASEAN members as regional states with which it was natural to develop relations. A report in 1974 wrote, "Developing relations with neighboring countries is a task of primary importance in the foreign affairs of any state, for neighbouring countries are closely linked with the security and development of the state concerned. For us, this task is even more urgent."[10] Developing relations with ASEAN states was specifically designed to "create a security belt around Vietnam consisting of the neighbouring Southeast Asian countries, thus facilitating the task of seeking long-term security and strengthening national defense and serving other revolutionary purposes".[11] As far as economic development was concerned, Hanoi perceived that ASEAN states could "contribute to the healing of the wounds of war, restoring and developing the economy, and enhancing our national defense capability, because we could take advantage of the favourable geographical and natural conditions that ASEAN states could offer".[12] While Hanoi's fresh approach to ASEAN states did take geo-political and geo-economic elements into consideration, its immediate design seemed to focus more on the implementation of the Paris Agreement. Indeed, a report in 1974 wrote,

> If we develop relations with other Southeast Asian countries, we will be able to create favourable conditions for causing the governments in these countries to have more appropriate relations with the PRG, and thereafter, discard Saigon's influence [in the region]. This would create opportunities for better relations, which could serve our country's needs in economic reconstruction and development.[13]

Also in 1973, the Vietnamese Prime Minister took the decision to establish the Institute for Southeast Asian Studies as a unit of the State Committee for Social Sciences.[14]

Thirdly, Hanoi was aware of a growing tendency of ASEAN states to promote peace and neutrality. An internal document provided the following analysis:

> While taking advantage of contradictions among superpowers and relying on their political and economic power, the ruling classes in many regional countries are raising the banner of national independence, showing their independent positions and declaring a foreign policy of peace and neutrality. Therefore, these countries have acted, and will act, in a way to prove their independent and neutral policies, and will seek

ways to establish relations with all superpowers, including those in the socialist camp.[15]

At the ASEAN Foreign Ministers' Meeting (AMM) held on 12 and 13 March 1971, Malaysia put forward a formal proposal to establish a Zone of Peace, Freedom, and Neutrality (ZOPFAN) in Southeast Asia. On 26 and 27 November 1971, ASEAN adopted the Kuala Lumpur Declaration officially endorsing ZOPFAN. *Nhan Dan* newspaper soon gave a positive reaction. The commentary by Quang Thai wrote: "This is a noteworthy development, because these countries, which have been extremely dependent on the US, have adopted a policy which runs counter to that of the US." Such a policy, according to the author, was "another testimony to the weakness of the US," (as on 25 October the US had to agree to the replacement of Taiwan by the PRC at the United Nations) and reflected "the struggle by Southeast Asian peoples to get rid of the US control and to strive for peace, freedom, and neutrality, which is in accordance with their national interests and the trends of history".[16] Similar assessments can also be detected in official political reports. Apart from the impact of "rapid and complicated developments in the détente among the superpowers," the ASEAN policy aimed at neutralization was encouraged by the developments in Vietnam.[17] Hanoi held that many world developments, and especially the détente among superpowers, were related to the Vietnam War, and the success of the war of liberation in Vietnam had helped ASEAN states to realize that small states, who did not want to be the victims of superpowers' compromises, must "take advantage of détente, must conduct a policy of balanced acts with regard to the superpowers, and must not adopt a lean-to-one-side strategy in order to protect their interests and their independence".[18] In 1973, a report stated that,

> Bourgeois governments of Southeast Asia have developed oil and gas exploitation, opened the door to investments from capitalist countries. But at the same time, they have also expanded trade with socialist countries and increased regional cooperation to cope with the precarious economic situation with a view to implementing the doctrine of national and regional resilience.[19]

These assessments are important, because they show that their authors could foresee new developments and directions in the foreign policies by the ASEAN states towards further distancing themselves from the US and advocating normal or better relations with states with a different ideology. In this sense, Hanoi expected that the ASEAN states would take moves to improve relations with Vietnam.

Indeed, during this period, ASEAN states started to improve relations with Vietnam, introducing a new framework in international relations in Southeast Asia. Since early 1970s Hanoi had documented the emergence of "a distancing tendency" by the ASEAN states with respect to the US war efforts in Vietnam. This trend had a new impetus in late 1972 and early 1973 as the Paris Peace Talks achieved good progress. About a month after the signing of the Paris Agreement, an informal ASEAN AMM released a statement welcoming the Agreement, calling for increased mutual understanding, better relations among regional states, and expanding ASEAN new membership. In addition, Indonesia, which had diplomatic relations with the DRV since 1964, sent back its ambassador to Hanoi in early 1973.

Other ASEAN states began in 1972 to enter into formal relations with Hanoi. As documented, after three attempts to contact Hanoi, partly by using Sweden as a mediator, Malaysia started talks on the establishment of diplomatic relations with Vietnam, which finally achieved a success on 30 March 1973. Singaporean officials met the representatives of Vietnamese trading companies in Singapore to talk about upgrading economic and political relations. According to reports by the representatives concerned, in private, these officials showed their respect and admiration, and believed that Vietnam would finally win; they also showed that they were aware of the nature of the Saigon regime.[20] Diplomatic relations at the embassy level were established between Vietnam and Singapore on 1 August 1973. Another report said that on 23 February 1972 the Philippine Chargé d'Affaires in Vientiane explored with his Vietnamese counterpart the possibility of opening trade and diplomatic relations, and concluded: "In spite of political chaos, the Philippines also proposed to Vietnam to hold talks on the establishment of diplomatic relations."[21]

Thailand did the same. Two months after the signing of the Paris Agreement, in March 1973, General Chatichai Choonhavan, then Deputy Foreign Minister, stated that Thailand was considering possibilities of establishing diplomatic relations with Vietnam. The Thai ambassador in Vientiane was instructed to directly contact his Vietnamese counterpart for talks.[22] At the same time, Thailand proposed that ASEAN invite a Vietnamese observer to the AMM meeting held in Bangkok in April 1973.[23] But Hanoi declined the invitation.[24] On 31 August 1974 the Thai parliament passed a law legalizing trade with all communist states. Earlier, in March 1973, Thailand and the Philippines withdrew their military personnel from South Vietnam.

The trend towards better relations with Vietnam continued. Again, ASEAN invited Hanoi to send an observer to ASEAN AMM in 1974. In May 1975, at the Eighth ASEAN AMM Malaysian Prime Minister Tun Abdul Razak extended an invitation to the Indochinese states to join ASEAN.[25] Thailand and the Philippines established diplomatic relations with Vietnam in 1976. Vietnamese Foreign Minister Nguyen Duy Trinh and Prime Minister Pham Van Dong visited ASEAN states in 1977 and 1978 respectively.

Economic ties were also established. In the period from 1976 to the end of 1978, Vietnam signed trade and technological cooperation agreements with Malaysia and Thailand, and a civil aviation agreement with Thailand. Thailand agreed to provide Hanoi with a loan worth 100 million baht, and sold 145,500 tons of rice and 50,000 tons of maize to Vietnam and bought 27,600 tons of coal. Two-way trade between Vietnam and Singapore in 1977 reached US$62.4 million. Indonesia and the Philippines provided economic assistance to Hanoi. Hanoi acknowledged these developments, stressing that

> While having greater political implications, the above-mentioned agreements with ASEAN states, especially those involving trade and technological exchanges, would benefit our cause of economic development, and serve our long-term strategy in the region.[26]

In retrospect, many Vietnamese observers concluded that the 1973–78 period witnessed "a good start" in Vietnam-ASEAN relations.[27] The good start, however, did not lead to qualitative development. Further, from 1979, Vietnam-ASEAN relations were marked by stagnation, tension, and even hostility for roughly ten years. The conventional wisdom is that Vietnam-ASEAN relations turned sour after Vietnam had sent its troops into Kampuchea in early 1979. Yet, documents show that even in the period between 1970 and 1978, there had been elements that could harm, and actually did obstruct, better relations between Vietnam and ASEAN. Although structural variables, namely complexities in superpowers' relations in the context of the Cold War at the global and regional levels, cannot be neglected, Hanoi's perceptions and visions of its international duties, the nature of its revolution, and the perceived nature of ASEAN states and organization were also important causes.

CONSTRAINING FACTORS

The Paris Agreement provided for a complete US troop withdrawal from South Vietnam. Yet, Hanoi was still concerned about the Southeast Asia Treaty Organization (SEATO) and the continued US military presence in Southeast Asia, the possibility of a renewed US intervention in Vietnam during the process of reunification, and the possibility of a US subversive plan against Vietnam during the post-war period. Hanoi, therefore, continued to see the US as "the most basic, long-term, and dangerous enemy".[28]

With these substantial and immediate concerns, it seemed that Hanoi failed to see the 1969 Nixon Doctrine in the greater context of a US reduction of its commitments in Asia-Pacific. The Doctrine marked a substantial decrease in the US commitments abroad as Washington wanted to scale down its overseas intervention and military presence. The commitment to withdraw US troops from South Vietnam under the Paris Agreement was indeed a part of the Nixon Doctrine. In addition, US forces in Thailand and the Philippines were also reduced. But Hanoi still stressed the "wicked and cunning" nature of the Nixon Doctrine,[29] and was concerned that the Doctrine would be applied to Southeast Asia with a view to opposing the Vietnamese revolution by other means, indirect but more sinister, even in the post-Vietnam War period. Therefore, Hanoi saw ASEAN as a more important tool in this US plan.[30] This alarmist view was supported by analyses holding that ASEAN member countries were not only politically subordinated to the US but were also were totally dependent on the US economically, a neo-imperialist type of political-economic relations.[31] The nature of this relationship suggested, according to Hanoi, that

The US supported and closely controlled the lackeys who ruled ASEAN countries. At the same time, however, the US tried to provide them with a national and democratic appearance, thus trying to steal the national and democratic banner from the hands of the proletariat.[32]

Therefore, Hanoi was watchful of US power and a US comeback, possibly via ASEAN.

In this light, the Nixon Doctrine had implications for Vietnam-ASEAN relations. Hanoi perceived ASEAN as part of "a regional rally of forces in accordance with the Nixon Doctrine whose aim is to use Asians to fight Asians," and "the ASEAN objectives of economic and cultural cooperation is a new formula for the regional rally of military forces".[33] In this new rally, Indonesia "will serve as the spearhead in the fight against communism and revolutionary movements".[34] While the Philippines, Malaysia, Singapore and Thailand were involved in one way or another in the Vietnam War, Indonesia had maintained a neutral position. Yet, Hanoi came to see this record of Indonesia as a factor that would be beneficial for the implementation of the Nixon Doctrine, because Indonesia would enjoy "conditions favourable for initiating anti-revolutionary activities, forming military alliances, thus realizing the Nixon Doctrine in Asia". The Indonesian policy of maintaining relations with the Soviet Union was also regarded as designed to "conceal the reactionary face of the spearhead of the Nixon Doctrine".[35]

Against that perceived background, one of the main tasks of Hanoi's foreign policy following the Paris Agreement was aimed at

> Defeating the US efforts to implement the Nixon Doctrine in the region as well as the political and military schemes of the US, other imperialist states, and their henchmen in the region; and actively contributing to the removal of US bases in the Philippines and Thailand as well as defeating the US plot to use Indonesia in its capacity as a member of the International Commission to oppose revolution in Vietnam and in other Indochinese countries.[36]

Hanoi started to think about "participating in a number of regional organizations, but with the clearly defined objective to encourage positive neutral trends, to expose sham neutrality and to unmask aggressive military organizations in disguise."[37]

In Hanoi's view, ASEAN is both an offshoot and a disguise of the US-led SEATO that serve the US interests and this explained the "insincerity of ASEAN proposal of neutrality". Thus, in Hanoi's future relations with ASEAN the opposition aspect would be greater than the cooperation aspect. Moreover, cooperation should serve to drive a wedge among ASEAN member states, that is "to exploit contradictions among those in the opposite side", which had become one of the guiding principles of the Vietnamese foreign policy with respect to ASEAN.[38] Hanoi therefore did not focus much on relations with ASEAN. Instead, it attached greater importance to relations with individual ASEAN member states, with the purpose of "winning to our side the ones that are sitting on the fence, distancing them from the US, and isolating the reactionary lackey governments in ASEAN".[39] In this connection, the US military presence in Southeast Asia was the main issue in Vietnam-ASEAN relations. On the one hand, Hanoi stated that it was "ready to cooperate with regional countries, to contribute to joint efforts for the establishment of a region of peace, independence, and prosperity". On the other hand, the cooperation was limited only

> to countries, which were independent, not influenced by outside powers, had no military bases for outside powers, did not allow outside powers to use the local people to fight against the people of other regional states, did not interfere in other regional states' internal affairs, peacefully coexisted and cooperated with other regional countries on the basis of mutual benefit.[40]

This shows that Hanoi in fact was not fully ready to accept détente and peaceful relations with ASEAN member states, perceiving that many of them were reactionary and not neutral. Of course, the fact that some ASEAN member states were involved in the US war efforts did help to strengthen this perception of ASEAN. Frost quoted a Vietnamese high-ranking diplomat as saying: "since the end of the war in Indochina, a new situation exists in Southeast Asia. Why should we get absorbed into an already existing organization whose past is known?"[41] The notion that ASEAN member states were not genuinely independent and neutral could be found in documents written in the early 1970s.[42] Hanoi subsequently viewed the ASEAN proposal for neutralization in late 1971 as "old wine in a new bottle".[43] And in the four-point position relating to the development of relations with ASEAN issued in 1976, Hanoi officially advocated genuine peace, independence, and neutrality for all Southeast Asian countries. In short, ASEAN's foreign policy, in the eyes of Hanoi leaders, was designed to serve the interests of the US.

The above statement also reflected Hanoi's readings of the domestic politics of ASEAN countries, and the reactionary nature of their governments. Because Hanoi equated genuine independence and neutrality with association with the socialist bloc and not association with the US, the ASEAN countries had failed the litmus test.[44] But more importantly, the ASEAN proposal of peace and neutrality was seen as a tool for suppressing revolutionary and democratic forces in the region and strengthening the rule of the capitalist class in ASEAN states.[45] In Hanoi's view the Sino-Soviet rift, the Sino-US rapprochement, and the US-Soviet Union détente had "most harmfully affected the revolutionary movements and communist parties in the region by causing them to lose orientations and putting an end to all material support from socialist countries".[46] The ASEAN proposal of peace and neutrality was aimed at promoting the international and regional détente and taking advantage of it to suppress the mass and the revolutionary movements in their countries by "ruthless and fascist means".[47]

ASEAN's call for increased cooperation among its member states for "national and regional resilience" was viewed by Vietnam as a scheme to build up military capability in order to crush people's uprisings, and a project for greater bilateral military cooperation for suppressing revolutionary forces and preventing the penetration of external (revolutionary) forces.[48] Cooperation within ASEAN was therefore, seen as serving counter-revolutionary purposes.[49] Therefore, Vietnam should not develop relations with ASEAN states because, as Hanoi understood the situation, ASEAN states wanted to enjoy increased external stability to individually and collectively wipe out local communism.[50] What should be done instead was to promote "in a proactive and urgent manner" the political and diplomatic activities in the ASEAN countries because "the banner, the voice, and the presence of the DRV in each of the other Southeast Asian nations will be in accordance with the wishes of the local people and will enhance their anti-imperialist spirits."[51] And if formal relations were established at all, "we should not let the ASEAN governments to exploit it for harming the local revolutionary movements."[52]

The above perception of nature of the governments in ASEAN led to the perceived task of supporting the revolutions in ASEAN countries. Hanoi believed that the successful strategy employed in the Vietnam War "was helping to solve the policy impasse for the local communist parties and was encouraging the revolutionary movements to develop".[53] Another document of the Foreign Ministry also stated: "in developing relations with the [other] Southeast Asian governments, we must uphold the principle of actively supporting and assisting Southeast Asian communist parties and revolutionary movements, considering it a task of proletarian internationalism that has been entrusted to our Party, State, and people by history and that we have to fulfill."[54] General Secretary Le Duan formally stated in early 1976

> The Vietnamese people fully support the just and victorious cause of the peoples of the countries of Southeast Asia for peace, national independence, democracy and social progress and contribute actively to the efforts of the nations in Southeast Asia to really become independent, peaceful and neutral…. The Vietnamese people fully support the Thai people's struggle for a really independent and democratic Thailand without US forces and military bases.[55]

Yet, it is also obvious in these documents that Hanoi did not have any specific plans to export revolution to the whole Southeast Asian region and indeed only gave limited assistance to local communist movements. In other words, there was a gap between rhetoric and action. A document pointed out: "We actively support [local] communist parties and revolutionary movements, realizing our international responsibility towards them. Yet, we only provide our experience, help train their cadres, and material assistance should be given only in accordance with our capability." And, "we should mainly share with them our experiences in drafting strategies and policies for the revolutions. This is the task of the offices and units in Vietnam. Our representatives abroad only are 'the eyes and ears' and should not act without instructions."[56] In addition, Hanoi also set the task of persuading ASEAN countries that Vietnam was not a threat to them. A policy document written right after the signing of the Paris Agreement said,

> We should reassure regional countries that the successes of the Vietnamese revolution will only benefit their independence and the regional peace. They therefore should not be concerned and apprehensive of the threat of the "domino theory" as invented by the USA. We should also help them to recognize that the threat to regional security is in fact the USA and the Nixon Doctrine, not the Vietnamese revolution.[57]

In 1976, Hanoi put an end to its relations with the Malayan Communist Party while establishing formal diplomatic relations with Malaysia. And in 1978, before sending troops to Cambodia, Vietnam and Laos ceased all support to the Thai Communist Party.

Foreign observers, too, have acknowledged that Hanoi was long on rhetoric, but gave very little material assistance to communists of Southeast Asia.[58] Huxley noticed that while openly stating its support for the local revolutions, possessing a large arsenal of fire arms, and enjoying geographical proximity to ASEAN countries, Hanoi maintained relations with the communist parties that followed the path of armed struggles, at potential not actual levels.[59] But these statements were bound to cause alarm among ASEAN countries and reduce their eagerness to improve relations with Hanoi.[60]

Hanoi's perception that ASEAN was not neutral and independent was also reinforced by ASEAN's policy of non-recognition of the PRG. Following the Paris Agreement, ASEAN countries still maintained relations with the Saigon government, and Hanoi interpreted this as indications of ASEAN countries strictly following the US line. Also, Indonesia, Malaysia, and Singapore did not recognize the PRG as the official member of the Non-Aligned Movement (NAM) and did not approve the participation of the PRG delegation in the NAM Summit held in George Town in 1972 while the majority of the NAM members did. ASEAN was positive about the Paris Agreement. But in Hanoi's view "the end of the war and restoration of peace were something that everyone must welcome. But they [ASEAN countries] were unhappy with the contents of the Agreement, because the Agreement represented the failure of the USA and the victory of Vietnam."[61] Hanoi was also unhappy with ASEAN's claim that "both sides violated the Agreement," and when ASEAN countries refrained from criticizing either side, this did not impress Hanoi, which stated that

They actually maintain close relations with the governments in Saigon, Phnom Penh, and Vientiane, thus helping them to consolidate their positions. Although ASEAN governments try to give the impressions that they have reduced commitments to Saigon, Phnom Penh, and Vientiane and have been more attentive to our reactions, as far as the PRG is concerned, the ASEAN governments' attitude remained what it was prior to the conclusion of the Agreement, although some slight changes have been detected such as attempts to contact with and grant visas to PRG officials.[62]

After some time, Hanoi concluded that ASEAN countries could not recognize the PRG, for "this is for them a matter of principle in view of their domestic politics: if they recognize the PRG, they will set a dangerous precedent for Indonesian, Malaysian, and Philippines governments that are resisting demands for international recognition by anti-government forces in exile."[63] Hanoi was clearly unhappy with the ASEAN position regarding the implementation of the Paris Accords and the recognition of the PRG, which in its view was biased and in favour of the US and Saigon. According to Hanoi, ASEAN countries were "trying to show that they are impartial, but in fact they are pro-US and pro-Saigon".[64] Surprisingly, Indonesia was seen as having the worst behaviour, for it had "distorted our Spring-Summer Offensive, supported the US escalation of war efforts, received many Saigon delegations, and taken advantage of its role in the International Commission to carry out schemes designed to contain the Vietnamese revolution".[65] (That also partly explains Hanoi's perception of Indonesia as the "spearhead" in the implementation of the Nixon Doctrine in the region as discussed above.) The post-Paris Agreement period, which was marked by political and military stalemate for about a year, also made Hanoi more sensitive to the ASEAN attitude. In Hanoi's view, ASEAN countries believed that Hanoi and the National Liberation Front (NLF) had little chance of achieving ultimate victory and therefore they were in no hurry to improve relations with Vietnam. One MOFA document said, "ASEAN countries now consider that the situation in Vietnam is more or less the same [as compared with the pre-Paris Agreement period] and therefore, their desire to establish relations with us is not as strong as it was in 1973."[66]

Last but not least, Hanoi was very critical of the perceived "opportunism and self-seeking attitude of ASEAN countries" when they expressed the wish to develop relations with Vietnam. The Sixth ASEAN AMM held in Pattaya (Thailand) between 16 and 18 April 1973, called on international community to provide the Indochinese states with aid for reconstruction and at the same time established an ASEAN Coordinating Committee to seek ways for ASEAN to "contribute to the reconstruction of Indochina". An annual report in 1973 analysed: ASEAN countries could not ignore the role of Vietnam in the region and therefore they saw the need to improve relations with us. Yet, "as they want to take advantage of the US war reparations, they seek ways to improve relations with us."[67]

In short, Hanoi's overall assessment of ASEAN's standing was very negative. And the perception of ASEAN as being not independent and neutral pervaded the thinking in Hanoi about ASEAN and its member states' domestic and foreign policies. In Hanoi's view, ASEAN countries were dependent and non-neutral because they relied politically and economically on the capitalist bloc, allowed US military presence in their territory, crushed local revolutionary movements, and put Hanoi and Saigon on the same footing. With the euphoria of victory in May 1975, suspicion and doubt about the nature and policy of ASEAN states were codified into the four-point position of 1976 demanding that Southeast Asia be turned into a region of genuine peace, independence, and neutrality, which strongly offended the ASEAN countries.

THE STAGNATING RELATIONSHIP

As a matter of fact, this perception had harmed the Vietnam-ASEAN relations. The following part will show how this perception was responsible for Hanoi's inflexibility towards ASEAN's moves and its lack of creativeness in developing a new type of relations with ASEAN member states.

Hanoi negatively assessed ASEAN's invitations to the AMM meetings. An internal document wrote,

> Indonesia knows clearly our attitude towards ASEAN, but insists on inviting us because it did not want to be accused [of partiality] as it also invited Saigon, Phnom Penh, and Vientiane regimes to join ASEAN. At the same time, these countries want to show that ASEAN is an organization for broad regional cooperation and does not serve the US and the Nixon Doctrine. [In responding to the invitation] we have made clear to ASEAN countries that our policy towards states of different regimes is based on

the five principles of peaceful co-existence, that many of the ASEAN member states are US lackeys, who have given assistance to the US in the war of aggression in Vietnam and Indochina, and that ASEAN's invitations to Saigon, Phnom Penh, and Vientiane are designed to legalize the US lackeys in Indochina and to oppose the Indochinese people.[68]

It is remarkable that Hanoi was silent on the fact that ASEAN was not eager to grant ASEAN membership to the Saigon regime as shown by one of the accounts of Saigon. In 1969, 1971 and 1972, Saigon sent observers to ASEAN AMM and on 22 January 1970 Saigon submitted an official application for ASEAN membership, which was, however, rejected on various grounds. Singapore held that ASEAN was still in its infancy, and therefore was not ready to accept new members; Indonesia and Singapore wanted to treat Hanoi and Saigon on an equal basis, and therefore thought that if Saigon were admitted, ASEAN "would be politicized and vulnerable to collapse"; the Philippines, Thailand and Malaysia supported the idea of admitting Saigon but invoked the principle of forging consensus among ASEAN members to defer the final decision.[69]

Thereafter, ASEAN invited Hanoi to send an observer to the Sixth AMM in Pattaya (1973), and to the Seventh AMM in Jakarta (1974). A report mentioned these moves and made the following comment:

> We have not only rejected the invitations, but we have also taken the opportunity to criticize the ASEAN proposal on neutralization and criticize ASEAN itself ... Our rejection involves two objectives: one, to step up the struggle for the total withdrawal of US troops and US military bases from Southeast Asia; two, to step up the struggle so that ASEAN would adopt a proper attitude towards the PRG, also to expose the ASEAN member states which pay lip service to neutrality and peace but continue to act as lackeys of the USA, allowing the US to use their territories as bases for aggression and intervention in the Indochinese countries.[70]

Hanoi also lobbied Burma to do likewise. Another report also suggested that efforts should be made to change the policy of ASEAN, and to even paralyse the organization. Identifying the tasks for the coming period, this departmental report holds that Hanoi should coordinate with Kampuchea and Laos, and other states, to influence ASEAN with a view to (1) turning it into an organization for genuine economic and cultural cooperation, independent from the control of imperialism and any superpower, and (2) (if we cannot do so) paralysing it so that ASEAN cannot contain the Indochinese revolutions.[71]

There was little change in Vietnam's perception after the 1975 victory. In this period, ASEAN held several meetings to discuss ways to ensure peaceful coexistence with the Indochinese states. The ASEAN Summit held on 25 February 1976 adopted the Treaty of Amity and Cooperation in Southeast Asia (TAC), known as the Bali Treaty, and invited Vietnam to accede to it, but did not renew the invitation for Vietnam to join ASEAN. Hanoi turned down the offer. At the same time, *Nhan Dan* carried a commentary, accusing the US of using ASEAN as a means to support all the reactionary and pro-US forces against revolutionary movements in Southeast Asia. And when the Summit ended, *Nhan Dan* wrote that a new round of confrontation had started in the region between the Indochinese and the reactionary countries supported by the US. Hanoi also openly, although only verbally, supported the local revolutions. *Nhan Dan* wrote,

> The time is very good for the struggle of the Southeast Asian people. By stepping it up, the peoples of Southeast Asia will certainly thwart all schemes of US imperialism and the reaction, and wrest back independence and sovereignty and the right of Southeast Asians to be the absolute masters of the region.[72]

The climax was the four-point position announced on 5 July 1976. In an interview given to *Vietnam News Agency*, the Vietnamese Foreign Minister Nguyen Duy Trinh stated that: In view of the total victories by Vietnam, Laos, and Kampuchea and the weakness of the US, "the present situation is very favourable for the states in Southeast Asia to become genuinely independent, peaceful, and neutral states." Moreover, "the Vietnamese people entirely support the just cause of the Southeast Asian peoples for national independence, peace, democracy and social progresses; we also support the Southeast Asian states to become genuinely independent, peaceful, and neutral, without imperialist military bases and armed forces on their soil." In the same interview, the Foreign Minister also introduced the four-point position on Vietnam-ASEAN relations. In principle, the position was based on the broadly recognized five principles of peaceful coexistence that include peaceful coexistence, respect to independence and sovereignty, equality, mutual benefit, non-intervention and interference, and peaceful solutions to disputes. Yet, the statement clearly implied that ASEAN countries were not neutral, were dependent, and aggressive. The second point stressed that: "The regional states should not allow outside countries to use their territories as military bases for the purpose of direct aggression and intervention in other regional countries." The fourth point proposed that: "Regional states should develop cooperation among themselves in accordance with the specific conditions of each state and in the interest of genuine independence, peace, and neutrality in Southeast Asia, thus contributing to the cause of world peace."[73] It is noteworthy that during his visit to five ASEAN countries in July 1976, Deputy Foreign Minister Phan Hien put forward the four-point position. In Manila, he tried to insert the four-point position into the Joint Declaration of the establishment of diplomatic relations between Vietnam and the Philippines. Earlier, giving an interview to *Bangkok Post*, he said: "At this moment, Vietnam is not interested in joining ASEAN nor supporting ZOPFAN, although this does not mean Vietnam will not be interested in the organization at a later period."[74]

The phrase "genuine independence, peace, and neutrality" caused ASEAN states to conclude that although small improvements had been detected in the relations between Vietnam and ASEAN countries, Hanoi in reality still held a hostile attitude towards ASEAN, refusing to consider them as independent and neutral.[75] Speaking at the NAM Summit held in Colombo, the Singaporean Prime Minister referred to this phrase and asked, "Is this a precursor of the kind of double definition of independence which will classify a Marxist state as being genuinely independent and the others as being not genuine … and hence subject to overthrow?"[76]

Added to this, there were apprehensions about military capability of a unified Vietnam, and its verbal support to local revolutions. As a result, ASEAN countries were inclined to view Vietnam as an immediate threat.[77] While certain ASEAN countries had the tendency to inflate the Vietnamese threat for their own internal purposes, they recognized in private that Vietnam was too war-exhausted and too preoccupied with national reconstruction tasks in the post-war period to be able to substantially assist local communist parties. Developments in the period between 1970 and 1976 show that both Vietnam and ASEAN wished to develop bilateral relations based on their own perception and their own terms, failing to iron out the differences among them and forge a common denominator to improve relations.[78] A Singaporean observer commented that the question of Vietnam joining ASEAN in this period was purely hypothetical, for both sides did not recognize each other and even the understandings by two sides of basic terminologies such as independence, freedom, and neutrality were too far to be bridged.[79] Ambassador Trinh Xuan Lang, one of the principal officials who helped to draft the four-point position, acknowledged in 1995 that Hanoi's perception and attitude contributed to one of the "misopportunities" in the relations with ASEAN.[80] Earlier, a MOFA report also stated: "We missed the opportunity to cooperate with ASEAN in establishing a zone of peace and peaceful coexistence in Southeast Asia in keeping with the proposal forwarded by the ASEAN Summit in February 1976."[81]

CONCLUSION

Vietnam had a mistaken perception concerning ASEAN after 1967 mainly because of the SEATO connection and the involvement in the Vietnam War of some of its members, the ambivalent attitude of ASEAN towards North Vietnam, the NLF, and the Saigon regime during the post-Paris Agreement period, and also because of poor research and little political contacts with ASEAN countries. But the euphoria of victory also served to reinforce these views and make them inflexible, seriously elevating ideological differences to the level of ideological superiority. As a result, Hanoi failed to see that behind ideological differences lie great similarities among Southeast Asian countries that include eagerness to defend their independence from major powers, preoccupation with nation-building and economic development, similar challenges in both domestic and international settings. While looking at its relations with ASEAN states through the lens of its relations with the US and its association with the Soviet bloc, Hanoi failed to see that by 1973 most ASEAN countries had less faith in US credibility and therefore wanted to promote relations with socialist countries, and that the attempt to neutralize Southeast Asia was quite sincere. In assessing too highly its own nationalistic credentials and its own socialist identity, Hanoi failed to appreciate the will to independence of other countries of Southeast Asia, which is a permanent feature in the politics of Southeast Asian states in spite of the different ways chosen to achieve this national objective. On balance, while some developments reflecting new perceptions of and priorities in Vietnam-ASEAN relations were detected, they were overwhelmed by orthodox mainstreams and a new hubris in Hanoi. Moreover, they also reflected the fact that Hanoi lacked an overall strategy and foreign policy for the post-unification period. Later, MOFA acknowledged:

> When the national independence revolution ended, we entered the socialist revolution without having an opportunity to thoroughly discuss and assess the characteristics of the Vietnamese and Indochinese revolutions as well as the struggles in the global scale. We therefore did not have a good grasp of the trends, advantages, and disadvantages of the new era. Neither did we understand the enemy-friend question in the new era, nor strategic and tactical matters in the course of strengthening the peace and security of our country.[82]

The key and sensitive question was independence and neutrality. Both Vietnam and ASEAN uphold independence and neutrality. According to Deputy Foreign Minister Phan Hien if ASEAN proposed ZOPFAN, Hanoi supported "the 6-word motto of independence, neutrality and prosperity (*độc lập, trung lập, phồn vinh*)."[83] Yet, by criticizing the ASEAN countries as not being genuinely committed to independence and neutrality, Hanoi was seen as trying to impose its own world-view on ASEAN. On the other hand, this also meant setting a very high entry barrier for regional cooperation, implying that ASEAN states should reject their own models of political, security, and economic development if they wanted to improve relations with Hanoi, and that another regional organization should be set up. The same attitude was applied to the bilateral relations between Vietnam and individual ASEAN states. In March 1976, a commentary in *Nhan Dan* wrote:

> The continued presence of US military forces in Thailand and the previous acts of aggression [during the Vietnam War] perpetrated by the US imperialists from Thailand are both the root and immediate causes that obstruct and damage the relations between Vietnam and Thailand. Therefore, completely abolishing the US military presence in every

aspect would open a new period of very good, friendly and cooperative relations between the two countries.[84]

Hanoi recognized the desirability of developing relations of friendship and good neighbourliness with ASEAN countries and promoting regional cooperation for the sake of security and development. Yet, on the other hand, it overstressed the ideological differences, a self-defeating approach indeed. In other words, Hanoi was not eager to cooperate with ASEAN on the ground that the ASEAN member states were simply different from it! A MOFA document written in 1976 clearly pointed out: "To normalize and develop relations with us, ASEAN states pretend to show that they are not different from us and even spread the rumour that we are ready to cooperate with them. But the differences exist and must be clearly perceived."[85] These differences, according to one senior official, stemmed from the political and economic systems and patterns of foreign relations that the two sides were following. "We adopted the socialist path and they adopted the capitalist path, and accordingly, both sides have two opposed strategies and policies; ours is revolutionary, progressive, and just; and theirs is reactionary, unjust, and anti-revolutionary." On a higher level, "the world-views are 80 per cent similar in terms of terminologies, but totally different in terms of philosophies," according to the same official.[86]

Some observers may point out that Hanoi's perception on the "war-winning image and status" in its relations with ASEAN states bears evidence of the realist approach with Hanoi seeing itself as having an upper hand and hence better leverage in forming frameworks for future relations. Gilpin, for example, has posited that image and role are in fact based on the capabilities that a state possesses. For him, power is the currency in international relations and definitive to "the hierarchy of prestige".[87] If this is true, a possible explanation would be the following: Since Hanoi thought that it possessed more military capability and a better fighting spirit, it wished to have a final say in the establishment of an order and framework for international relations in Southeast Asia which should be in accordance with its preferences. Kissinger asserted that during the Paris negotiations, Le Duc Tho, his interlocutor, did not hide his conviction that "it was Vietnam's destiny to dominate not only Indochina but all of

Southeast Asia."[88] In another discussion, Vietnam's Prime Minister Pham Van Dong allegedly told Kissinger, "We are the Prussians of Southeast Asia. We are a people of greater zeal, greater energy, greater intelligence than our neighbours, and we don't have to take military action to expand our sphere of influences."[89]

The truthfulness of Kissinger's account is subject to doubt. Further, it is important to remember the serious preoccupations of Hanoi with economic recovery and development tasks and its real concerns about US and Chinese schemes, all of which would check any inclination towards expansionism in Southeast Asia and hostility towards the rest of the region. The task of "doing our best to ensure most favourable conditions to quickly heal the war wounds, reconstruct and develop the economy, develop culture, technology, and science, strengthen national defence, and build the material and technological foundation for socialism" ranked first in the order of importance among the tasks for the post-war Vietnam spelled out at the Fourth Party Congress.[90] There is a sense of hubris in the rhetoric, but this did not indicate any concrete threat towards ASEAN or any intention on Hanoi's part to impose a new order in Southeast Asia.

In the early 1970s, Hanoi perceived potential economic and security benefits in developing relations with ASEAN countries. Then, when differences arose concerning the implementation of the Paris Agreement and ASEAN attitude towards the PRG, Hanoi, which still remembered the involvement of some ASEAN countries in the Vietnam War, soon reverted to the view of ASEAN as a hostile group of states. This was subsequently further reinforced by ideological considerations about antagonisms between socialism and capitalism and the hubris of victory. All these conspired to cause Hanoi to take a hardline attitude towards ASEAN, which was quite different from its initial views of the organization. Further, having seen its relations with China deteriorate steadily in the late 1960s over negotiations to end the Vietnam War, the Sino-US détente in the early 1970s, and the Chinese seizure of the Paracels, Hanoi should have formulated a policy designed to improve relations with ASEAN, as a fall-back position. In addition, Hanoi did not know about Thailand's new policy from 1968 aimed at strengthening relations with China in order to oppose Vietnam's possible future expansion in Indochina and Southeast Asia. If Hanoi had known about that, it should have taken care to discourage Thailand from forming a de facto alliance with China against Vietnam in case Vietnam had to take action over Cambodia. Some other observers would, therefore, believe that a heavy dose of ideology had influenced both the crafting and the implementation of Vietnamese foreign policy in this period. Lacking a complex and subtle world-view and rigorous research on world and regional politics, especially the foresight on the real importance of Vietnam-ASEAN relations (perhaps because it had focused most of its diplomatic resources on the struggle against the US for national reunification), Hanoi had not freed itself from being "a prisoner of communist ideology".[91] In short, the combination of ideological blinkers and intellectual limitations helped to contribute to the missed opportunities of the Vietnam-ASEAN relationship in this period.

Notes

1. On the decisions and military activities in this period, see Gen. Vo Nguyen Giap, *The Headquarters in the Spring of Great Victory* (Hanoi: National Politics Publishing House, 2000); Nguyen Phuc Luan et al., *Contemporary Vietnamese Diplomacy for Independence and Freedom* (Hanoi: National Politics Publishing House, 2001), pp. 300–10; SRV Ministry of Foreign Affairs, *Vietnamese Diplomacy, 1945–2000* (Hanoi: National Politics Publishing House, 2002), pp. 267–77. For a discussion on how Hanoi formed that strategy, see Nguyen Vu Tung, "Coping with the United States: Hanoi's Search for an Effective Strategy", in *The Vietnam War*, edited by Peter Lowe (London: Longman, 1998), pp. 30–61.
2. The Asia-3 Department, MOFA, Biannual Report for the First Half of 1973, p. 3. (If not indicated otherwise, all the (bi)annual and quarterly reports are prepared by the Asia-3 Department, MOFA). (Vụ Châu Á 3, Bộ Ngoại giao, Báo cáo Sáu tháng đầu năm 1973).
3. Ibid., p. 3.
4. Ibid. The 1974 Annual Report (Báo cáo Tổng kết năm 1974) adds (p. 11): "Other Southeast Asian countries have recognized the DRV's important position and role in the region; they have also recognized that regional problems cannot be solved without our participation. Therefore, all of them want to have relations with us."
5. Biannual Report for the First Half of 1973, p. 4. In addition to this, the report (pp. 1–2) provides analyses of the economic situations in ASEAN countries as follows: "ASEAN economies are still bogged down in difficulties, which

have been aggravated by food shortages and the international monetary crisis." The Annual Report of 1972 (Báo cáo tổng kết năm 1972) wrote among other things: "economic difficulties are common and chronic for capitalist governments in the region. The situation in 1972 has been even more serious. And failing to find solutions, existing contradictions among the ruling ranks and files have become deeper." (pp. 1–2).

6. Biannual Report for the First Half of 1971 (Báo cáo Sáu tháng đầu năm 1971), pp. 1–2.
7. Biannual Report for the First Half of 1974 (Báo cáo Sáu tháng đầu năm 1974), p. 28.
8. Ibid.
9. The Annual Report of 1972 (Báo cáo tổng kết năm 1972), p. 23.
10. Biannual Report for the First Half of 1974 (Báo cáo Sáu tháng đầu năm 1974), p. 27.
11. The Annual Report of 1972 (Báo cáo tổng kết năm 1972), p. 23.
12. Ibid, pp. 23–25. The Annual Report of 1974 (Báo cáo tổng kết năm 1974), mentions favourable conditions for economic cooperation related to tropical plantation and technologies suitable for tropical conditions, (p. 15).
13. Biannual Report for the First Half of 1974 (Báo cáo Sáu tháng đầu năm 1974), p. 29.
14. The Southeast Asian Studies Division of the Institute of International Relations under MOFA supervision was established in 1977.
15. The Annual Report of 1970 (Báo cáo tổng kết năm 1970), p. 4Q.
16. Quang Thai, "On the Neutralization of Southeast Asia" (Về vấn đề Trung lập hóa Đông nam Á), Nhan Dan (People's Daily), 1 December 1971. The commentator, however, still considered that the root cause of the ASEAN move was "the Vietnamese victory, which had contributed in an important way to the aggravation of the existing contradictions in the US capitalist society, to the increase of the difficulties experienced by the US imperialists, to the exposure of fatal weaknesses of the US, thus strongly encouraging the peoples of the world to struggle for national independence, peace, democracy, and social progress".
17. Biannual Reports for the First Half of 1972 (Báo cáo Sáu tháng đầu năm 1972), pp. 1–7 and 1973, p. 6.
18. Biannual Report for the First Half of 1972 (Báo cáo Sáu tháng đầu năm 1972), pp. 3–4k.
19. The Annual Report of 1973 (Báo cáo tổng kết năm 1973), p. 6.
20. Biannual Report for the First Half of 1972 (Báo cáo Sáu tháng đầu năm 1972), p. 7k.

21. The Annual Report of 1973 (Báo cáo tổng kết năm 1973), p. 16.
22. Noordin Sopiee, "The 'Neutralization' of Southeast Asia", in *Asia and the Western Pacific: Toward a New International Order*, edited by Hedley Bull (Canberra: Thomas Nelson Publisher, 1975), p. 148. Thai Deputy Foreign Minister Chatichai Choonhavan also used other channels to contact Hanoi. The document dated 10 July 1974 by the Saigon Embassy in Vientiane enclosed a letter dated 6 July 1974 sent to Vietnamese Prime Minister Pham Van Dong by Thai congressman Naisaing Marangkoun, who had been entrusted by Deputy Foreign Minister Chatichai Choonhavan, proposing that both sides "open secret contacts at the ministerial level at anytime and anywhere to exchange views for advancing toward peace and security on the basis of equal footing".
23. Noordin Sopiee, "The 'Neutralization' of Southeast Asia", p. 149. The IIR monograph entitled "Vietnam-ASEAN Relations and the Prospects" (September 1995) holds that Thailand lobbied other ASEAN states to invite the DRV to send an observer to the AMM held in Pattaya on 18 April 1973.
24. Asia-3 Department Annual Report of 1973 (Báo cáo tổng kết năm 1973), p. 20.
25. See Shee Poon Kim, *The ASEAN States' Relations with the Socialist Republic of Vietnam* (Singapore: University of Singapore, 1980), p. 8.
26. Asia-3 Department, MOFA, A Research Document (Tài liệu nghiên cứu tổng hợp).
27. See Luu Van Loi, *50 Years of Vietnamese Diplomacy, Vol. II, 1975–1995* (Hanoi: Public Order Publishing House, 1998), p. 247; MOFA, *The Vietnamese Diplomacy, 1945–2000* (Hanoi: National Politics Publishing House, 2002), p. 300.
28. Luu Van Loi, *50 Years of Vietnamese Diplomacy, Vol. II*, p. 65.
29. Asia-3 Department, MOFA, A Themed Report entitled "On Neo-Imperialism in Some of the Southeast Asian Countries" (Về chủ nghĩa thực dân mới ở một số nước Đông nam Á), dated 4 June 1973, p. 17.
30. See Trinh Xuan Lang, "Some Reflections on Our Policies toward ASEAN Countries and the USA from 1975 to 1979", *Proceedings of the Seminar on 50 Years of Vietnamese Diplomacy* (Hanoi: The IIR, 1995), p. 51. See also Biannual Report for the First Half of 1970 (Báo cáo sáu tháng đầu năm 1970), p. 1. In a commentary entitled "Toward Friendly and Cooperative Relations among Southeast Asian Countries", *Nhan Dan Daily* wrote about the Ford Administration's Foreign Policy: "The Ford Administration's New Pacific Doctrine, which is extremely wicked, is designed to maintain the US

military presence and prolong its neo-imperialist policy in the region under new circumstances."

31. Asia-3 Department Annual Report of 1973 (Báo cáo tổng kết năm 1973), p. 11. Asia-3 Department Biannual report for the first half of 1975 (Báo cáo sáu tháng đầu năm 1975, p. 3) said that ASEAN economies were dependent on the West, especially the US and Japan. Another MOFA report entitled "Carrying out Our International Tasks in Southeast Asia" (Triển khai nhiệm vụ quốc tế của chúng ta ở Đông nam Á), dated March 1972 wrote (p. 2): Vietnam is the only socialist country in the region. The rest are capitalist. The capitalist mode of development in these countries is basically dependent on investments, aid, and loans from abroad."
32. The Themed Report "On Neo-Imperialism in Some of the Southeast Asian Nations" (Về chủ nghĩa thực dân mới ở một số nước Đông nam Á), p. 15.
33. Ibid.
34. The Annual Report of 1972 (Báo cáo tổng kết năm 1972), p. 28.
35. Biannual Report for the First Half of 1972 (Báo cáo sáu tháng đầu năm 1972), p. 11k.
36. The Annual Report of 1972 (Báo cáo tổng kết năm 1973), p. 28.
37. Ibid. See also Trinh Xuan Lang, "Some Reflections on Our Policies toward ASEAN Countries and the US", (Một số suy nghĩ về chính sách của chúng ta đối với ASEAN và Mỹ), p. 50.
38. Biannual Report for the First Half of 1974 (Báo cáo sáu tháng đầu năm 1974), (p. 28) laid out the rationale for developing relations with countries such as Thailand, Malaysia, and the Philippines: "we cannot give Saigon a free hand in some parts of Southeast Asia to distort and slander the revolutionary cause of our people and to destroy the friendship between our people with the peoples in these countries; we cannot let Indonesia, the 'US-appointed balancer' in Southeast Asia, the 'spearhead of the Nixon Doctrine' to solely enjoy formal relations with us and to take advantage of this situation to carry out reactionary activities and rally forces along the line of the Nixon Doctrine. We must divide the enemies, because comrade Le Duan has said that to exploit internal contradictions among the enemies is one of the matters of strategic significance for the proletarian revolution."
39. Biannual Report for the First Half of 1973 (Báo cáo sáu tháng đầu năm 1973), p. 28. See also Shee Poon Kim, *The ASEAN States' Relations with the Socialist Republic of Vietnam*, pp. 10–15.
40. The Annual Report of 1972 (Báo cáo tổng kết năm 1972), p. 4L.
41. Frank Frost, *Vietnam's Foreign Relations: Dynamics of Change* (Singapore: Institute of Southeast Asian Studies, 1993), p. 59.

42. Biannual Report for the First Half of 1970 (Báo cáo sáu tháng đầu năm 1970), p. 7.
43. Biannual Report for the First Half of 1975 (Báo cáo sáu tháng đầu năm 1975), p. 6.
44. MOFA Report, "To Carry out Our International Tasks in Southeast Asia and South Asia" (Báo cáo của Bộ Ngoại giao về Triển khai nhiệm vụ quốc tế của chúng ta ở Đông nam Á và Nam Á), p. 5.
45. The Annual Report of 1970 (Báo cáo tổng kết năm 1970), p. 5Q.
46. Biannual Report for the First Half of 1972 (Báo cáo sáu tháng đầu năm 1972), p. 5k.
47. The Annual Report of 1972 (Báo cáo tổng kết năm 1972), p. 2, and the Biannual Report for the First Half of 1973 (Báo cáo tổng kết năm 1973), p. 5.
48. The Annual Report of 1973 (Báo cáo tổng kết năm 1970), p. 8.
49. The Annual Report of 1973 (Báo cáo tổng kết năm 1973), (p. 11) points out, "ASEAN states have tried to iron out contradictions and shelve disagreements with each other in order to reach an agreed assessment of the situation and make joint efforts to cope with revolutions. In military terms, they coordinate with each other to destroy the communists, control the border areas, conduct joint military exercises, training programs, and harmonize logistical and strategic matters. Their doctrines of national and regional construction and defense totally rely on the US, Japan and other countries in the West. In 1973, there was an increase in ASEAN relations with the West."
50. Deputy Foreign Minister Phan Hien also said: "One of the ASEAN principles is security cooperation. Security cooperation is anti-communist by nature. How can you agree with such a principle?". Phan Hien's speech at the closing session of the meeting for Vietnamese diplomats posted in the ASEAN states on 7 December 1978, p. 36.
51. The Annual Report of 1974 (Báo cáo tổng kết năm 1974), p. 34.
52. Ibid.
53. The Annual Report of 1973 (Báo cáo tổng kết năm 1973), p. 4.
54. Asia-3 Department, MOFA, Report "On the Tasks in 1974 and 1975" (Về các nhiệm vụ trong hai năm 1974 và 1975), p. 5.
55. Speech by Le Duan on 7 February 1976 as reported by BBC on 11 February 1976.
56. The Annual Report of 1972 (Báo cáo tổng kết năm 1972), p. 28, and Report "On the Tasks for 1974 and 1975" (Về các nhiệm vụ trong hai năm 1974 và 1975), pp. 5–6. The policy suggestions laid out in Asia-3 Department Annual Report of 1972 (Báo cáo tổng kết năm 1972), (p. 34) stated: [we should]

actively support local communist parties by presenting, through published articles and broadcast commentaries in local languages our experiences in struggles; we should take the initiative in sending delegations to these countries, especially the ones we have never sent delegations to; we should timely and appropriately disseminate and express our views on hot issues of revolutionary struggles in regional countries; and assist them in effective but discrete ways."

57. Asia-3 Annual Report of 1972 (Báo cáo tổng kết năm 1972), p. 26. One senior Vietnamese diplomat relayed a remark by General Secretary Le Duan that Hanoi should assist revolutions in Laos and Kampuchea only (March 2003).
58. Reports indicate that Hanoi only used *Nhan Dan Daily* to express its support for, and imply its relations with, local communist parties. For example, on 30 April 1975, *Nhan Dan* carried a congratulatory message on the 45th anniversary of the founding of the Malayan Communist Party and on 23 May 1975 it carried a congratulatory message on the 55th anniversary of the founding of the Indonesian Communist Party (Asia-3 Department Annual Report of 1975 (Báo cáo tổng kết năm 1975), p. 5).
59. Tim Huxley, *Indochina and Insurgency in the ASEAN States, 1975–1981*, Working Paper No. 67 (Canberra: Research School of Pacific Studies, The Australian National University, 1983), p. 56. Overall, Hanoi did not provide material assistance to communist parties in the Third World. Odd Arne Westad, who has had access to many documents of Asian, African, and Latin American communist parties, has indicated that some of the representatives of these parties went to Vietnam and asked Hanoi to provide them with material assistance, thinking that Hanoi meant what it had said about international responsibility. Yet, they did not get such assistance. And some internal documents even described Hanoi as selfish and uninterested in the common revolutionary movement. Talks by the author with Odd Arne Westad in March 2001, New York City.
60. See Trinh Xuan Lang, "Some Reflections on Our Policies toward ASEAN Countries and the USA from 1975 to 1979", p. 50. On 7 March 1976, Malaysian Prime Minister stated that he regretted that Hanoi openly announced its continued support for "national independence movements" in regional states. He also stressed that ASEAN did not have any intention to turn itself into a military grouping.
61. The Annual Report of 1973 (Báo cáo tổng kết năm 1973), p. 17.
62. Biannual Report for the First Half of 1973 (Báo cáo sáu tháng đầu năm 1973), p. 11; and The Annual Report of 1973 (Báo cáo tổng kết năm 1972), p. 17.

63. The Annual Report of 1973 (Báo cáo tổng kết năm 1973), p. 16.
64. Biannual Report for the First Half of 1974 (Báo cáo sáu tháng đầu năm 1974), p. 22.
65. The Annual Report of 1972 (Báo cáo tổng kết năm 1972), p. 9x.
66. Biannual Report for the First Half of 1974 (Báo cáo sáu tháng đầu năm 1974).
67. The Annual Report of 1973 (Báo cáo tổng kết năm 1973), p. 15.
68. Biannual Report for the First Half of 1971 (Báo cáo sáu tháng đầu năm 1974), p. 8T.
69. Documents by Saigon Foreign Ministry cited in the IIR Research Paper "ASEAN: Establishment, Development, and Prospects" (ASEAN Hình thành, phát triển và triển vọng), (December 1990).
70. The Annual Report of 1974, (Báo cáo tổng kết năm 1974), p. 36. The report "On the Tasks for 1974 and 1975" (Về các nhiệm vụ trong hai năm 1974 và 1975), (pp. 7–8) suggested that: in case they invite us to join ASEAN, we will take advantage of the opportunity to demand that they must not allow the US to use their territories to oppose us, that they must recognize the Paris Agreement and the reality of the existence of two governments in South Vietnam, that they must adopt appropriate attitudes towards the PRG, and must not intervene and interfere in the internal affairs of the people in South Vietnam.
71. Biannual Report for the First Half of 1975 (Báo cáo sáu tháng đầu năm 1975), p. 19. Hanoi still supported peaceful coexistence with the ASEAN states, but not in the ASEAN framework. Deputy Foreign Minister Phan Hien said: "Through negotiations, both bilateral and multilateral, we will identify the principles for relations. Negotiations will be the main thing. We shall not talk about forms of organizations, as this problem is very complicated and we need to do thorough research ... If in our proposal we mention something leading them to misunderstand that we propose a certain formal organization, we must correct it right away: we mention the region, not any regional organization. We agree on participation in principle, but not on participation in any specific organization and in any form. There should be no misunderstanding about this. We have a lot of other ways, such as holding annual or biannual meetings to review the developments of relations." (Phan Hien's speech on 7 December 1978, pp. 35–36).

Note should be taken of the changes in Saigon's attitudes towards ASEAN. Following the signing of the Paris Agreement, Saigon no longer highly valued ASEAN. The official document No. 227-BNG/ACTBD/TM on 19 March 1973 writes: "from now on, we will not send representatives to the AMM, nor request aid and discuss possibilities of receiving aid from ASEAN; we will closely examine the ASEAN membership if invited." The document also gives reasons for the change: "(i) ASEAN does not have funds enough to finance projects; (ii) the EEC states insist that talks on trade and tariffs between EEC and ASEAN must include the Indochinese states. Therefore, ASEAN will need us more than we need them; (iii) the ASEAN reconstruction program for Vietnam is designed to exploit US and Japanese aid to Indochina. This is an impertinent attitude on the part of ASEAN." (The IIR research paper, "ASEAN: Establishment, Development, and Prospects".)

72. Shee Poon Kim, *ASEAN States' Relations with the Socialist Republic of Vietnam*, p. 8.
73. "The SRV Four-Point Position on Relations with Southeast Asian Nations", *Nhan Dan Daily*, 6 July 1976.
74. *Bangkok Post*, 1 July 1976, cited in "ASEAN: Establishment, Development, and Prospects".
75. Carl Thayer, "ASEAN and Indochina: The Trends toward Dialogue", a monograph dated 13 May 1998.
76. Sheldon Simon, "China, Vietnam, and ASEAN: The Politics of Polarization", *Asian Survey* XIX, no. 12 (1979), p. 1172.
77. Shee Poon Kim, *ASEAN States' Relations with the Socialist Republic of Vietnam*, p. 6.
78. Tim Huxley commented "Hanoi was unwilling to become involved in a new regional order on ASEAN's terms". See Tim Huxley, *ASEAN and Indochina: A Study of Political Responses, 1955–1981* (Canberra: Department of International Relations, The Australian National University, 1985), p. 85.
79. Shee Poon Kim, *ASEAN States' Relations with the Socialist Republic of Vietnam*, pp. 6 and 10.
80. Trinh Xuan Lang, "Some Reflections on Our Relations with the ASEAN Countries and the US from 1975 to 1979", p. 50. Trinh Xuan Lang, however, said that in the process of drafting the four-point position, some diplomats, including him, tried but failed to soften the tone in the English version in order not to harm the relationship with ASEAN. Another senior diplomat, in retrospect, did not hesitate to call that attitude "an arrogant one". The author's interviews in Hanoi, February 2003.
81. The MOFA Annual Report of 1986, p. 31.
82. MOFA Annual Report of 1986, "On the World Situation and Our Struggle in the Foreign Affairs Front" (Báo cáo của Tổng kết năm 1986 của Bộ Ngoại giao "Tình hình thế giới và Cuộc đấu tranh của chúng ta trên mặt trận đối ngoại", p. 30.

83. Phan Hien's speech of 7 December 1978, p. 5.
84. "The Heated Struggle before the Elections Day in Thailand" (Cuộc đấu tranh nóng bỏng trước ngày bầu cử ở Thái lan), *Nhan Dan* (*People's Daily*), 3 March 1976.
85. The Annual Report of 1976 (Báo cáo tổng kết năm 1976), p. 8.
86. Phan Hien's speech of 7 December 1978, pp. 9 and 34. He also said (p. 35): "You [ASEAN] said that your version of peace contains no war, no ideological struggles, no conflicts and no disputes. What kind of peace is this? There is no such peace even in the heavens. The same is true about your version of neutrality. Can you stand neutral in all issues, all wars, and all disputes in the world? How can you call this neutrality?" Hanoi, however, was less confrontational in open dialogues with ASEAN. One Talking Point (p. 1) dated 12 December 1978 that suggests what should be said in formal exchanges with ASEAN states writes, "We want to say clearly that our concepts and principles are not contrary to those of ASEAN on the region and ASEAN itself. For our part, we have not expressed our ideas about regional organizations in Southeast Asia." The Annual Report of 1976 (Báo cáo tổng kết năm 1974), stresses: "We are the only socialist state in Southeast Asia."
87. Robert Gilpin, *War and Change in World Politics* (New York: Cambridge University Press, 1983), p. 14.
88. Henry Kissinger, *The White House Years* (Boston: Little, Brown, 1979), p. 441.
89. Thai Quang Trung quoted *The Hearings before the Senate Committee of Foreign Affairs, 97th Congress*, October 1981, p. 141. Thai Quang Trung, "The Ties that Bind", in *Military Basing and the US-Soviet Military Balance in Southeast Asia*, edited by George K. Tanham and Alvil Bernstein (New York: Crane Russak, 1989), p. 29.
90. Political Report by General Secretary Le Duan at the First Session of the VI National Assembly, carried in *The People's Daily*, 3 July 1976.
91. The author's discussions with senior researchers in Hanoi, March 2003.

3

1978 TO 1985: Coexistence between Two Opposing Groups

In what was termed the first round of reconciliation, there were improvements in the Vietnam-ASEAN relationship in the 1975–78 period.[1] Yet, they were not enough to construct a cooperative relationship between Vietnam and ASEAN. What was missing were mutual trust, Vietnamese non-recognition of ASEAN, and in particular its view about a new role in regional politics.

The previous chapter has analysed the reasons for Hanoi's hardening attitude towards ASEAN. As a result, from 1975 to early 1977, Hanoi adopted a less than friendly attitude towards ASEAN and its member states, in spite of various advances by the latter, and specifically a proposal for Vietnam to accede the TAC. But from the end of 1977, Hanoi took the initiative in improving its relations with ASEAN as witnessed by the July 1977 visit by Deputy Foreign Minister Phan Hien to ASEAN countries and the start of negotiations with Indonesia on sea boundaries in November 1977. In addition, the December 1977 visit by Foreign Minister Nguyen Duy Trinh to ASEAN countries was marked by the conclusion of several economic agreements and the agreement for the establishment of Thai and Vietnamese embassies in Hanoi and Bangkok. Further, in September

1978, Prime Minister Pham Van Dong visited some ASEAN countries and promised to refrain from supporting local rebellions, interfering in their internal affairs, and using force against them. All these actions should not be seen as a breakthrough in Vietnam-ASEAN relations as there was still an absence of trust on both sides and Hanoi sought improvement in relations mainly because of the rising tension and hostility in its relations with Beijing and the Khmer Rouge.

Indeed, during the visit of Prime Minister Pham Van Dong, there was no frank and extensive exchange of views on the Khmer Rouge issue and how it should be solved. Instead, Hanoi offered a Friendship Treaty, a move to which ASEAN countries were not eager to respond, to forestall possible reaction from ASEAN towards its action in Kampuchea. Thereafter, as soon as Vietnamese troops entered Kampuchea, Thailand allied itself with the PRC to oppose the Vietnamese move and could subsequently rally the support of all other ASEAN countries to its cause. As a result, for more than ten years, confrontation took place between Vietnam and ASEAN countries and Southeast Asia was divided into two opposing blocs.

THE STRUCTURAL CONTEXT

Vietnam-Kampuchea relations had been deteriorating since May 1975. Phnom Penh took the initiative in launching repeated armed attacks on Vietnam while purging pro-Hanoi elements in the Khmer Rouge regime. A MOFA document acknowledged that from April 1977, Vietnam-Kampuchea relations had "worsened day by day".[2] A departmental research paper provided a brief chronology: since 1977 Phnom Penh openly carried out a hostile foreign policy towards Hanoi and had been preparing for a war against Vietnam. In September 1978, Pol Pot officially included Vietnam in the list of enemies of the Khmer Rouge regime, putting Hanoi and Washington on an equal footing. In October 1978, Phnom Penh officially declared war against Vietnam.[3] Towards the end of 1978, Vietnamese troops were sent to Kampuchea in order to overthrow the Khmer Rouge regime, eliminating the probability of the Khmer Rouge launching a large-scale military attack against the southern part of Vietnam in coordination with predicted China's military attacks from the North. On 7 January 1979, a pro-Vietnamese government was set up in the country.

Sino-Vietnamese tension, which had been rising since the early 1970s, took a turn for the worse in 1978, with Beijing ending aid to Hanoi and launching nationwide political campaigns over the issue of Hanoi's maltreatment of ethnic Chinese in Vietnam, a move which was soon perceived by Hanoi as a psychological preparation for forthcoming war against Vietnam.[4] The CPV Fourth Central Committee Plenum held on 6 July 1978 identified China as "the direct and dangerous enemy of the Vietnamese people" and laid out the following tasks for the Party, the State and the people:

> To step up the cause of constructing socialism and defending the socialist state, to accelerate the construction of economic and national-defence capability, to defeat the enemies' strategies aimed at weakening and invading our country, as well as to win the border war [with Kampuchea], consolidate the defensive posture and be ready to defeat the war of aggression on a large scale if China wages it.[5]

Further, against this background, Hanoi concluded a Treaty of Friendship and Cooperation with Moscow in November 1978. In February 1979, the Sino-Vietnamese border war broke out.

In spite of the initiative taken by the Carter administration in early 1977, talks on normalization of Vietnam-US relations could not get off the ground because of Hanoi's insistence on the US contribution to healing the wounds of war which Washington interpreted as war reparations and aid as a condition.[6] Between September and October, normalization talks took place. Hanoi and Washington even discussed the location of the US Embassy in Hanoi. But a legislation passed by the US Congress prevented any funds for reparations, thus cutting off the discussions on normalization. Besides, Washington became more critical to Hanoi as the boat people crisis worsened.[7] In 1978, partly because of rising tension in its relations with Beijing and Khmer Rouge, Hanoi shifted to unconditional normalization of relations. But the move failed because of the prevailing view in the Carter administration, propounded especially by Brzezinski, that priority should be given to Sino-US normalization, and because of the US suspicion of Hanoi's motive in connection with the conclusion of the Soviet-Vietnamese Treaty of Friendship and Cooperation.[8] Subsequently, in receiving Deng Xiaoping in Washington, President Carter gave his approval to the war which Beijing intended to launch against Hanoi.⁹ Then on 17 February 1979 Beijing launched a large-scale military offensive against Vietnam, which was followed by a low-level war in the Sino-Vietnamese border areas lasting for over ten years. These developments helped to consolidate the perception that the US remained the "common enemy of mankind" and "the archenemy of Vietnam".¹⁰ According to a MOFA analysis, "Washington takes advantage of our difficulties caused by border clashes with Kampuchea; it digs deeply into Vietnam-Kampuchea and Vietnam-China contradictions, and postpones normalization of relations with us."¹¹ Consequently, Hanoi decided to lean further on the Soviet side while its action in Kampuchea was condemned by many countries with concomitant isolation and cessation of aid. Earlier, Hanoi joined the Council on Mutual Economic Assistance (CMEA) in the summer of 1978 and signed the Treaty of Friendship and Cooperation with the Soviet Union in November 1978. How did Vietnam-ASEAN relations evolve in this period?

ENGRAVING THE DIFFERENCES

Having considered ASEAN in the previous period as an offshoot of and a disguise for US-led military organizations, Hanoi now described it as an integral part of a new alliance that included Hanoi's implacable enemies, namely the US and China. Vietnam-ASEAN relations had been seen through the lens of Hanoi's relations with Washington. What was new in this period was the Chinese connection, which caused Hanoi to take a more negative view of ASEAN. A MOFA document stated, "China supports ASEAN while we oppose it; China supports the US presence in Southeast Asia while we oppose it."¹² The MOFA Annual Report of 1981 stressed, "China, the US, and ASEAN continue to collude with each other to oppose the revolutions in Indochina."¹³ ASEAN, therefore, was considered hostile towards Vietnam and was put into the list of "Chinese expansionists and hegemonists in their collusion with the US imperialists and other reactionary forces."¹⁴ This phrase became a common usage for both internal and public discourse in Vietnam. Therefore, in this period, inherent differences between ASEAN and Vietnam were further reinforced by changes in the patterns of foreign relations of the two sides, with the former developing ties with the US,

China, and the anti-Phnom Penh Kampuchean forces and the latter with the Soviet bloc and other Indochinese states.

Initially, Hanoi had hoped that in view of Prime Minister Pham Van Dong's visit in September 1978, ASEAN states would show understanding or even sympathy for Hanoi's intervention in Kampuchea. Furthermore, Hanoi misread a number of diplomatic signals from ASEAN, some of which were due to lack of consensus among ASEAN countries during the initial period or were deliberate attempts on the part of Thailand to lull Vietnam into complacency at the very time when Thai Deputy Prime Minister Sunthorn Hongladarom was engaged in high-level talks in Beijing, requesting China to take firm measures against Hanoi.[15] One MOFA report, as a result, said that ASEAN did not see any force being able to change the situation in Kampuchea, and therefore, did not want to confront Hanoi and was willing to accept the new status quo.[16] In January 1979, Thai Deputy Minister of Foreign Affairs Wong Polnikorn told Vietnamese ambassador Hoang Bao Son that Thailand "will recognize the new government in Kampuchea. But we will do it a little bit late; we hope that Vietnam will understand [the lateness]." Deputy Minister Wong also asked the Ambassador to help Bangkok to get in contact with the new government in Phnom Penh.[17] On 8 January 1979, receiving Vietnamese Ambassador Vu Tien in Manila, Mrs Marcos "congratulated Vietnam on the liberation of Phnom Penh". Hanoi thus believed that "the ASEAN states tended to accept the situation in Kampuchea."[18]

Yet eventually, ASEAN strongly opposed the Vietnamese intervention. From September 1979, ASEAN collectively demanded the withdrawal of foreign troops from Kampuchea together with the recognition of the right to self-determination of Kampuchea. In November the same year, ASEAN initiated the UN resolution demanding that Vietnam withdraw troops from Kampuchea and allowing the Khmer Rouge government to keep Kampuchea's UN seat, which after June 1982 was given to the Government of the Democratic Kampuchea that had been established following an ASEAN-sponsored agreement among the three anti-Phnom Penh factions. ASEAN also openly criticized Hanoi at other multilateral fora, including the Non-Aligned Movement (NAM). In addition to these moves, ASEAN was successful in requesting most Western countries to cut economic and humanitarian aid to Hanoi. A MOFA report therefore said, "From mid 1979, ASEAN countries became hostile to Vietnam."[19]

Hanoi ascribed this joint ASEAN attitude to the Chinese connection. The normalization of Sino-US relations and the Sino-Vietnamese border war contributed to the changed position by ASEAN. One MOFA document analysed, "within a month, the war of aggression by China in the border areas and the climax of the Sino-US collusion caused the total change in the ASEAN attitude. It now openly opposes Vietnam and other Indochinese countries on the Kampuchea issue."[20] A MOFA report said:

> After China had mobilized 600,000 troops to launch the border war with Vietnam, ASEAN seized the opportunity to rely on China in order to exert pressure on Vietnam. That explains why ASEAN countries, especially Thailand, colluded with China to oppose Vietnam. Therefore, the reason is not our liberation of Phnom Penh. The decisive factor [for the collusion] is the war of aggression by China. The fact is that only after the border war had broken out on 17 February 1979, the US, China, and ASEAN formed a united front to oppose the three Indochinese countries.[21]

In short, as was the case previously, Hanoi viewed ASEAN's attitude and action as being dependent on other actors as a new expression of the reactionary nature of ASEAN countries. To Hanoi, the axiom "a friend of our enemies is also our enemy" also applied to ASEAN. That "ASEAN follows the US and China in opposing the Indochinese revolution" became the official narrative by Hanoi.[22]

At the same time, Hanoi was certain that it could withstand the challenge in Kampuchea, where Khmer Rouge troops suffered big losses and had to regroup outside Kampuchean border or were reduced to small pockets of resistance inside the country. Hanoi also believed in the effectiveness of its pacification of Kampuchea and thought that the alliance between Vietnam, Laos, and Kampuchea would enhance Vietnam's strength.[23] Deputy Foreign Minister Phan Hien offered his own analysis: "If the victory in 1975 gave rise to a strong country of Vietnam which ASEAN must take into consideration then the formation of a bloc including the Indochinese states further enhanced Hanoi's posture in its relations with ASEAN countries. The intervention by Hanoi in Kampuchea was to bring the country back to the genuine revolutionary course and to strengthen the Indochinese strategic solidarity, which existed as an objective fact of history."[24] He then stressed:

> Now that the Kampuchean revolution has succeeded and Kampuchea has returned to the fold of solidarity with Vietnam and Laos, this solidarity has acquired a quality that is higher than ever before. That three Indochinese countries unite in an association of such a high quality will strongly affect revolutions in Southeast Asia; as a result, the regional revolution will develop into a higher stage, thus exerting a greater influence on the trend towards peace and neutrality in Southeast Asia.[25]

An Asia-3 Department report in 1980 also wrote, "In 1979, although experiencing severe challenges, the revolutions in Vietnam, Laos, and Kampuchea continued to grow. The situation in Kampuchea has increasingly been stable and irreversible."[26]

Close cooperation between the Indochinese countries and the Soviet Union also added to Hanoi's perception of strength. According to a MOFA report, "the militant alliance, the special relationship, and the all-sided cooperation among Vietnam, Laos, and Kampuchea, alongside coordination with the Soviet Union and other socialist countries have made the forces and the posture of the Indochinese countries unprecedentedly stronger."[27] In the view of Hanoi, the signing of the Treaty of Friendship and Cooperation with the Soviet Union represented a close linkage between the national independence and socialist movements, which were seen as leading forces in the post-Vietnam War era. Therefore, the Treaty was "an important contribution to peace and stability in Southeast Asia and the rest of the world".[28] In short, victories by Vietnam and other Indochinese countries as well as the mode of international relations among them, which Hanoi believed to be "exemplary and decisive for regional peace and stability,"[29] was a factor behind the "irreversible trend towards peace and neutrality in Southeast Asia".[30]

Hanoi, therefore, believed that it still had leverage in relations with ASEAN. It assessed that "ASEAN countries are very much afraid of the powerful and victorious posture of the revolutionary forces of Vietnam, Laos, and Kampuchea".[31] Because of this fear, ASEAN "on the one hand reacted negatively to our action in Kampuchea by ending bilateral agreements and criticizing us at multilateral fora. But on the other hand, ASEAN still had to maintain relations with us."[32] The MOFA Report of 1981 said:

After the victory in January 1979 that toppled the Pol Pot–Ieng Sary clique, the three Indochinese countries advanced towards socialism. Coming second only to Europe, Southeast Asia is the region where there is coexistence between two opposing systems, namely the Indochinese socialist system and the ASEAN capitalist states. The former is clearly stronger than the latter.[33]

Hanoi also believed, "Because of their military weakness and unstable domestic politics especially after the US defeat in Vietnam and withdrawal from Southeast Asia, ASEAN countries are afraid of confronting us by military means."[34] The same report also predicted, "Because of the fact that the Government in Kampuchea can increasingly control the situation and China cannot teach Vietnam a second lesson, ASEAN will have to accept our position that the situation in Kampuchea is irreversible and will have to re-accept the trend of détente and dialogue with the Indochinese countries."[35] Hanoi judged that ASEAN countries "had the illusion that they could rely on Chinese military pressure, exploit Kampuchea's political weakness and Vietnam's economic difficulties to demand us to withdraw [troops from Kampuchea]". But, "the illusion was not well founded because Phnom Penh could increasingly manage the situation" and Beijing "had limits in using force against Vietnam and in teaching Vietnam another lesson."[36] On 14 May 1979, Foreign Minister Nguyen Co Thach said, "China is unlikely to launch a second border war against Vietnam. As a result, ASEAN will see that we are strong and that resorting to military means to oppose us is not productive. Subsequently, ASEAN will see that it will be better to enter into a peaceful dialogue with Vietnam."[37] In 1983, Hanoi predicted future trends in ASEAN foreign policy: "When the two mainstays of ASEAN policy, namely imperialism and China, have been weakened, ASEAN has to accept détente with the socialist Indochinese states."[38] To put in other words, Hanoi continued to underestimate the spirit of independence, the strength, and the real role of ASEAN.

DIALOGUE WITH ASEAN

Believing in the irreversibility of the Cambodian situation, Hanoi now set about holding talks with Thailand and other ASEAN countries with a view to convincing them to accept the status quo in Cambodia. After

1980, Vietnam, Laos and Kampuchea began a series of Foreign Minister Conferences to discuss various proposals. And talks were held by Foreign Minister Nguyen Co Thach with his ASEAN counterparts.

The first Foreign Ministers' Conference (FMC) among the three countries, held on 7 January 1980 put forward a proposal on the conclusion of a non-aggression treaty between the two groups of countries in order to "establish long-term friendship and cooperation with other countries in Southeast Asia".[39] The Foreign Ministers also stated that the governments of Vietnam, Laos, and Kampuchea "are ready to discuss and sign, on a bilateral basis, a non-aggression treaty" and "to discuss the establishment of a Southeast Asian region of peace, independence, freedom, neutrality, and prosperity" with the governments of ASEAN countries and Burma.[40] On other occasions around that time, Hanoi also stated that it was ready to join the ASEAN countries to build the Southeast Asian region into a zone of peace and stability, using the ZOPFAN proposal by ASEAN as a starting point for further discussions.[41] This proposal was considered a "de facto recognition of ZOPFAN".[42] The proposal to sign bilateral treaties of non-aggression and peaceful coexistence was put forth again in the second FMC held in Vientiane on 17 and 18 July 1980.[43]

Hanoi also tried to turn the FMC into a counterpart institution to ASEAN AMM. During the third FMC held on 27–28 January 1981, it was agreed that the Foreign Ministers would hold regular meetings twice a year and that the location of these meetings would alternate between each country.[44] According to a MOFA report, the purpose of the FMC was to "further expand the cooperation in diplomatic matters into other fields, thus strengthening the combatant alliance among the three countries".[45] Further, in the same FMC, the Foreign Ministers of Laos, Kampuchea and Vietnam proposed that "a regional conference be held between the two groups—the Indochinese countries and the ASEAN countries—to discuss the problems of mutual concerns", and "to conclude a treaty of peace and stability in Southeast Asia". They also proposed that an international conference be convened "with the purpose of recognizing and guaranteeing that treaty".[46] In the Sixth FMC held on 7 July 1982, the proposal for an international conference on Southeast Asia to guarantee regional peace was considered as a new initiative by the Indochinese countries.[47] Hanoi continued to lobby for the initiative to organize an international conference on Southeast Asia in subsequent FMCs. For example, in the Tenth FMC in January 1985, the Foreign Ministers of Laos, Kampuchea and Vietnam proposed that apart from countries that had taken part in the Geneva Conferences on restoration of peace in Indochina in 1954 and on neutralization of Laos in 1961–62 respectively, and the Paris Conference in 1973, other countries such as Sweden and Australia, which "have contributed to peace in Southeast Asia", would also be invited.[48]

Clearly, these proposals showed Hanoi's efforts to build counterpart institutions with those of ASEAN. From the first meeting in January 1980 to the last one in August 1986, thirteen FMCs were held. Besides, some other forms and frameworks for international relations of the region were even initiated. MOFA introduced two projects to promote relations with ASEAN on a multilateral basis. The first project, entitled "Regional Consultations", was designed to materialize the proposal by the third FMC to convene a Regional Conference. According to a MOFA document, the Conference was to be scheduled before the date of the annual ASEAN AMM in 1981.[49] The second project was designed to promote economic relations between the CMEA and ASEAN and to "create a certain level of economic interdependence between ASEAN and Indochinese countries."[50] In short, by trying to win the regional and international recognition of the existence of a bloc of the three Indochinese countries, Hanoi hoped that ASEAN countries would accept the status quo in Kampuchea and in Southeast Asia.

But the efforts to build a counterpart institution to ASEAN also showed that Hanoi accepted ASEAN as an organization, although did not see it representing the whole region, and that Hanoi's regional ambitions were indeed limited. By late 1978, it was clear that Hanoi had a more refined idea of its revolutionary goals. For example, in December 1978, Deputy Foreign Minister Phan Hien said that Vietnamese diplomats posted in the region should help ASEAN countries to recognize that "Vietnam makes revolution only within Kampuchea, and no more. Our troops will stay there and will not enter your countries."[51] This statement, which reflected the view of the supreme leadership, constituted a firm veto against the view of certain Vietnamese commanders in Kampuchea who considered Thailand as the next target.[52] In 1980 and beginning of 1981, the Vietnamese Ambassador to Thailand reported to Hanoi about a possible coup d'état by the Thai "Young Turks" officers. These officers, through intermediates, contacted the Vietnamese Embassy and asked Vietnam to help facilitate the coup by increasing military activities along the Thai-Kampuchean borders. The Ambassador, however, warned: "This may be provocation. Even if the coup attempt is real, it will not be beneficial for Vietnam to interfere into Thai domestic politics." He added, "I have instructed the Embassy staff to state clearly our consistent policy not to meddle into Thai internal politics even though we welcome the trend in Thailand towards genuine national independence and neutrality as well as friendship with Vietnam. Our Embassy will not contact with them on this issue."[53]

Another cable from Vietnamese Embassy in Bangkok in 1982 offered a similar policy suggestion:

> The struggle by Thai revolutionary and progressive forces to take Thailand along the path of genuine independence, peace, and neutrality and socialism will be a long one. Therefore, in state-to-state relations with Thailand, we should adopt a long-term policy of peaceful coexistence and try to build up relations of good neighborliness with it.[54]

In addition, Hanoi was categorically against supporting the communist parties in ASEAN countries, a trend that started in 1978 and was further strengthened in subsequent years, not only because of lack of resources but mostly because of the pro-China character of these parties and the necessity for Vietnam to reduce ASEAN's countries opposition to its Kampuchea project. The MOFA annual report of 1978 stated:

> One of the most important guidelines with regard to the ASEAN countries is to declare that we do not support the Maoist communist groups in Southeast Asia. Southeast Asian communist Parties have been around for a long time, but the Chinese-majority leadership leads them; they are following Maoist policies, and dependent on China in many other aspects. They are not genuine communists and have turned into tools for Beijing to interfere into domestic politics of the local countries and carry out its expansionist policies in Southeast Asia. Recently, these parties have even implemented policies aimed at harming the Indochinese revolutions, running counter to their people's interests. If these parties grow and seize power in Southeast Asia, they will unleash disasters for the Southeast Asian peoples. We should not, therefore, support nor have any contacts with these parties in any form whatsoever.[55]

Thus, from 1978, the verbal support to revolutions in Southeast Asia came to an end.

Further, in a meeting with Vietnamese diplomats in 1982 to discuss foreign policy issues in preparation for the Fifth CPV National Congress, the President of the State Council Truong Chinh stated: "We have severe difficulties. You will be worried when our Party mentions them. But if we are not aware of these difficulties, how can we overcome them? The economy is seriously imbalanced; there have been acute contradictions between production and consumption, between saving and spending.... I can say that the present situation is too dangerous to be allowed to deteriorate further."[56] Referring to the debates within the leadership on the strategic tasks to be discussed at the coming National Party Congress, he said:

> There is unanimity on the two tasks, namely to successfully build up socialism and to defend the socialist fatherland. But some comrades wish to add a third strategic task, namely to fulfil our international duties, that is to contribute to the struggle of the peoples of the world for peace, national independence, democracy, and socialism. These views have not been accepted, because, in terms of tactics, such an approach will be counter-productive as far as our relations with ASEAN countries are concerned.[57]

The proposals on the signing of a non-aggression treaty with ASEAN countries, the unwillingness to meddle in Thailand's domestic affairs, the cessation of all aid to communist groups in ASEAN countries, the construction of a bloc of Indochinese countries as a counter grouping alongside with ASEAN, and initiatives to start dialogues between the two groups of Indochinese and ASEAN countries, therefore, suggest that Hanoi had accepted peaceful coexistence with ASEAN. By the end of 1978, a MOFA report stated:

> We should help ASEAN states understand that we respect their organization, that our concept about the region does not imply the replacement of ASEAN, and if ASEAN does not oppose Vietnam, we will be ready to develop relations with it on the basis of mutual benefit.[58]

Further, a MOFA document in 1983 provided a policy suggestion, "At this juncture, our strategic objective is to strive step by step for the construction of the basis for the peaceful coexistence between the two opposing systems in Southeast Asia, namely the system of the Indochinese socialist states and that of the ASEAN capitalist states."[59]

While economic conditions did have a certain impact on Hanoi's policymaking, in this initial period, political and strategic considerations continued to play the most important role. The main aim of the above peaceful overtures was to make ASEAN countries realize the peaceful intentions of Vietnam towards them in order to convince them to accept the status quo in Kampuchea and in Southeast Asia. Hanoi's posture vis-à-vis ASEAN was still based on the perception that it had leverage to exert influence on the construction of regional order, although it was increasingly clear that Hanoi wanted the socialist international order to be applied only in Indochina.

WEDGE DRIVING

Equally important, if not more, was the pressing necessity to loosen the de facto alliance between China and ASEAN, and particularly Thailand, over Kampuchea, to neutralize ASEAN in the Sino-Vietnamese conflict, and also to drive a wedge between Indonesia, Malaysia (believed to be anti-China) and Thailand (thought to be pro-China).

In mid-1979, Foreign Minister Nguyen Co Thach said,

> We have not done a number of things well. Our diplomatic efforts have not focused on attacking the principal enemy and isolating it. Instead, we have picked quarrels with too many countries. We should no longer do that. We should focus on the US and China only. As far as ASEAN countries are concerned, we have caned them a little bit too much. Now we have to caress them a bit. Caning and caressing should go together. Otherwise, we will drive them closer to the Chinese side, and this will be an extremely bad scenario.[60]

The MOFA Annual Report of 1983 also stressed, "We considered China as the principal enemy and ASEAN as the object for division. But since 1979, at times, our position towards ASEAN countries, especially Thailand, has been too inflexible. This created confusion, causing people to think that ASEAN countries were in fact the main target of our criticism."[61]

Hanoi believed that wedge driving would be possible because of several factors. In the first place, Hanoi continued to think that ASEAN would eventually acquiesce to the status quo in Kampuchea. A policy suggestion in 1982 noted that:

> After three years of intense struggles, the international and regional situations are favourable for our struggle on the diplomatic front. The military, economic, and political measures used by China, the US, and ASEAN to force us to withdraw troops from Kampuchea and reverse the situation there have failed. These countries are facing a policy impasse, which in part explains why some factions in Thailand, Indonesia, and Malaysia have started to ponder a policy of distancing themselves from China and opening dialogues with Vietnam.[62]

Another document concluded: "After understanding that all the policy options, including collusion with China, have failed, ASEAN states are likely to adapt to the new situation, improve relations with Vietnam, and accept the status quo in Indochina."[63]

Hanoi also thought that ASEAN countries were increasingly concerned about the China threat. A MOFA document claimed that since 1981, contradictions between ASEAN and China "had come to the fore".[64] In 1982, Hanoi and Jakarta came to the understanding that "the main and long-term threat is China."[65] Hanoi, therefore, hoped that improving relations with ASEAN would encourage the latter to loosen its ties with China.

The Soviet factor was also used to encourage ASEAN to have better relations with Vietnam. Foreign Minister Nguyen Co Thach said, "ASEAN is worried that if it presses Vietnam too hard, we will let the Soviet Union use the Cam Ranh Bay base. So it is better for them to reduce the pressure on us, improve relations with us, provide us with aid so that we will not tilt further towards the Soviets."[66] Hanoi further believed that Sino-Soviet détente might worry ASEAN countries and cause them to readjust their position. ASEAN, according to a MOFA report, "was concerned that the betterment of Sino-Soviet relations will harm ASEAN and benefit Vietnam,"[67] and that "China will directly negotiate with Vietnam, ignoring ASEAN and the coalition government of the Kampuchean reactionaries."[68]

Indeed, after the early 1980s, separate dialogues began to be held between Vietnam and Malaysia, and Indonesia and Thailand. Laos also held exchanges of views with Thailand, Indonesia, Malaysia, and the Philippines. In July 1982, Foreign Minister Nguyen Co Thach visited Singapore, Malaysia and Thailand. The visit was considered by MOFA as "a success that contributed to the common victory of the three Indochinese countries on the diplomatic front and was likely to open a new stage for dialogues between the two sides."[69] At a special AMM held on 8 May 1984, ASEAN reached a consensus on allowing Indonesia to represent the organization in seeking "substantive dialogues" with Vietnam.

In the broader context of designing and implementing foreign policy, Hanoi always categorized its relations with ASEAN as "those with the enemies" and attached great importance to driving a wedge among them. Phan Hien provided the following rationale: "It is appropriate to group imperialist countries in the West and capitalist countries in Southeast Asia in the same category because they are identical in nature and they are our rivals and opponents. Yet, they have conflicts of interest among them and hold different attitudes towards us." He then concluded: "In principle, if we focus on the contradictions among the opponents, we can identify opportunities for the trend towards peace, independence, and neutrality to grow."[70] A MOFA document also suggested that Hanoi should further encourage the trend towards dialogues between Indochina and ASEAN "but to serve the goals of "winning over public opinion, dividing our enemies, and entirely isolating China."[71] In essence, Hanoi did not seriously think about developing a cooperative relationship with ASEAN as long as the ASEAN states improved relations with the countries that were hostile to it. Moreover, ASEAN foreign policy served to strengthen Vietnam's perception that it differed from the ASEAN states, because of their political and social systems. For example, the MOFA files on the NAM meetings between 1981 and 1986 always described Malaysia and Singapore as "bad countries", or "followers of imperialists" and "lackeys of imperialists".[72] Therefore, according to Hanoi, if it could take advantage of ASEAN's incentives to enter dialogues with Vietnam for a settlement of the Kampuchea problem, the united front among the enemies would be weakened.

Yet, the outcomes fell short of what Hanoi had desired. While talks took place in a friendly atmosphere, Hanoi could not reach even a modest understanding with ASEAN about Kampuchea because ASEAN continued to consider the unconditional withdrawal of Vietnamese troops from Kampuchea and an international political settlement in that country as the prerequisite for any talks about a framework for international relations in Southeast Asia. At the UN, ASEAN states continued to sponsor each year a resolution to that effect on Kampuchea, which gained an ever-increasing number of votes. Perhaps having in mind Hanoi's attempts at wedge driving, Malaysia Foreign Minister Ghazali Shafie proposed to Nguyen Co Thach that Vietnam should "consider ASEAN as one entity".[73]

But why did Vietnam fail to do so? The failure of Hanoi's diplomacy was due to the following reasons. In the first place, while some ASEAN countries might have seen China as a potential challenge, others, in particular Thailand, viewed Vietnam's military occupation of Kampuchea as an immediate threat to their national security. And all ASEAN countries, out of ASEAN solidarity and consensus principle, felt obliged to support Thailand, the frontline state. In addition, not only did ASEAN countries oppose aggression as a matter of principle, some of them were afraid that the Kampuchean episode might create a dangerous precedent for them in view of the uncertain relationships among Indonesia, Malaysia, and Singapore. Being authoritarian regimes, they attached little importance to Pol Pot genocidal policy per se, and more importance to national independence and territorial integrity. Therefore, the strong opposition to Vietnam served as a rallying point for ASEAN, and Kampuchea became "the glue" for the organization's increased cohesiveness.[74] Further, ASEAN countries suspected that Vietnam's military action in Kampuchea was designed to set up an Indochina federation or bloc dominated by Hanoi for confrontation with ASEAN. Singaporean Foreign Minister Dhanabalan was telling Nguyen Co Thach, "The recent statement by the Indochinese Summit Meeting is an additional step towards turning the three Indochinese states into one country. If any state stresses national independence, you will accuse it of upholding narrow nationalism."[75] Therefore, as long as Hanoi approached ASEAN states on a bilateral basis, its efforts at dividing ASEAN and neutralizing it on the Kampuchea problem could not succeed.

As a result, ASEAN countries were determined to continue the political and diplomatic struggle against Hanoi, including the provision of political and logistical support to Khmer Rouge and other anti-Phnom Penh factions.

While ASEAN countries were not strong enough to impose a political solution on Vietnam—and indeed Beijing did prevent a similar attempt by ASEAN in the form of an International Conference on Kampuchea (ICK) in 1979—but they could rally anti-Phnom Penh factions, many countries in the world, including major powers, to tie down Vietnam and prevent Vietnam from consolidating its success in Kampuchea. Hanoi was wrong in not foreseeing this. Further, Hanoi was wrong in thinking that it could compel and convince ASEAN countries to accept Vietnam's *fait accompli* in Kampuchea, and could fully pacify Kampuchea.

Yet, they refrained from entering into military confrontation with Hanoi. In addition to tough statements and diplomatic démarches to bring pressure to bear on Hanoi to agree on an unconditional withdrawal of its troops from Kampuchea, ASEAN countries at the same time adopted certain friendly gestures towards Hanoi. For the entire period after 1979, Thailand continued to maintain the air links between Bangkok and Hanoi. Singapore remained the biggest trade partner of Vietnam and the bilateral trade actually recorded growth in this period.[76] Besides, Indonesia and Malaysia continued to hold political dialogues with Hanoi. As noted above, in May 1984, Indonesia was allowed to represent ASEAN to conduct "substantive dialogues" with Vietnam. These gestures were designed to show Hanoi that as and when Hanoi agreed to an international settlement on Kampuchea, ASEAN countries would be ready to normalize relations with Vietnam and discuss regional cooperation.

In short, a Vietnam-ASEAN cooperative relationship was not feasible in this period. From the beginning, Hanoi disregarded the ASEAN code of conduct among the regional states by refusing to accede to the Bali Treaty, joining the Soviet bloc, and intervening in Kampuchea. Subsequently, Hanoi formed an Indochinese bloc to counter ASEAN in Southeast Asia. Therefore, in retrospect, during this period, Vietnamese diplomacy showed several major weaknesses including failing from December 1978 to March 1979 to approach ASEAN countries to explain to the latter about its action in Kampuchea; the absence of diplomatic démarche which was a serious shortcoming as ASEAN countries might construe it as a gesture of defiance; overestimating its own strength and underestimating that of ASEAN countries; and misreading diplomatic signals by ASEAN countries. In other words, while the rule should always be to make more friends and fewer enemies, Hanoi did the opposite, which was a serious mistake in policymaking.

Hanoi might have been adept in the diplomatic struggle for national liberation. But it did not have a contingent of well-trained diplomats for diplomacy in the nation-building period that followed. Further, Hanoi had insufficient knowledge on Southeast Asia, and its diplomatic research work was weak. On the contrary, ASEAN countries were very rich in knowledge, experience, and resources, as most of them had some thirty years of nation-building in a peaceful environment while Thailand's modern diplomacy was nearly 200 years old. As a result, an intellectual weakness and ideological blinkers continued to influence Hanoi's policy towards ASEAN countries, which was basically founded on the continued perception that ASEAN belonged to the capitalist bloc (and since 1979 to the alliance that included the US and China), thus differing from Vietnam by its very nature. On the other hand, Hanoi also believed that ASEAN had interests different from those of the US and China and that some individual ASEAN states had interests which were not identical with those of other member states. Therefore, the principle of "exploiting contradictions among the enemies' ranks" still guided Hanoi's policy with regard to ASEAN. And this policy, for the most part, failed.

THE SOVIET FACTOR

Some observers of Vietnamese foreign policy might argue that Hanoi did not find it beneficial to improve relations with ASEAN because of its alliance with the Soviet Union and other socialist countries. These countries shared the same ideology with, gave reconstruction aid to, and helped strengthen security of Vietnam. After 1975, Moscow proposed a treaty of friendship to Hanoi. Hanoi was, however, reluctant to accept the offer. In June 1978, Hanoi joined the CMEA. Yet, not until July 1978, did Hanoi set about negotiating such a treaty in earnest, in view of the rapidly deteriorating relations with Beijing and the Khmer Rouge and the deadlock in negotiations on normalization of US-Vietnamese relations.[77] Hanoi thought that such a treaty would provide deterrence against any retaliation attack by Beijing in case it sent troops to Kampuchea. Nayan Chanda observed, "Hanoi had postponed the signing of the treaty with the Soviet until it recognized that the chance for normalize diplomatic relations with the US had gone."⁷⁸ Steven Morris even argued that Hanoi was "paranoid" when relations with China and Kampuchea suddenly and concurrently deteriorated, a situation which Hanoi had never experienced and with which it found difficult to deal. The alliance with the Soviets, therefore, was a natural and logical step to ensure its security.⁷⁹ This realistic rationale can be seen in the MOFA Annual Report of 1978 which, among other things, explained the Treaty of Friendship and Cooperation with Moscow:

> The Treaty is the most essential element in the whole strategy for our foreign relations in the new situation. After the Beijing reactionary cliques have openly betrayed the socialist revolution and Marxism-Leninism, the Soviet Union increasingly proves to be the main pillar for world peace and revolution. Previously, we have cultivated solidarity with both China and the Soviet Union. Now that China has turned out to be our direct and dangerous enemy, it is inevitable that we should strengthen the ties with the Soviet Union, our most strategic ally, which is most capable of assisting us to reconstruct the economy and strengthen our national defence. Consolidating the long-standing and close relationship with the Soviet Union and other socialist countries is the number-one task of strategic importance for the course of building and defending socialism in our country. The signing of the Treaty has contributed to strengthening our economic and military capability, thus reinforcing our strategic posture in international relations, especially in Southeast Asia. The Treaty is of great importance, directly contributing to the realization of our strategic goals in Kampuchea; it has also become a form of deterrence to the Chinese reactionary forces and the Pol Pot–Ieng Sary cliques. Therefore, the Treaty is an important contribution to regional as well as global peace and stability.⁸⁰

In this context, Hanoi's emphasis on the choice of socialism in domestic settings and on the socialist nature of its foreign relations were aimed at proving its loyalty to communism to ensure more aid from the Soviet Union. If Hanoi's conviction—that it enjoyed a "stronger position" in its relations with ASEAN as a result of national unification, the strengthening of the Indochinese solidarity, and the strategic association and alliance with the Soviet bloc—is taken into account, one might argue that Vietnam felt no pressing need to develop relations with ASEAN either to promote economic reconstruction or to enhance national security. Sections of the Vietnamese media even felt free to engage in rhetoric about the revolutionary nature of Vietnamese activities and advertise its support for local revolutionary movements regardless of the consequences, including increased suspicion on the part of ASEAN and deepening perceptions about the essential differences between the two sides.[81] A document acknowledged, "The ASEAN concern over our stronger posture has turned into an increasing doubt about our intentions."[82]

Yet, Vietnam's complacency was ill founded. This was because during his visit to the US in early 1978, Deng Xiaoping had succeeded in securing Carter's support for a Chinese war against Vietnam. Following the visit of the Chinese paramount leader, Washington reportedly warned Moscow against taking military action to support its Vietnamese ally if Beijing launched an offensive against Hanoi.[83] In its military planning, Beijing did make preparations to counter a hypothetical Soviet attack, but the Chinese leadership was almost certain that such an attack would not take place. Thus, not only did the Soviet-Vietnamese Treaty of Friendship and Cooperation fail to prevent Beijing from launching a war against Hanoi but Moscow also refrained from any military action on the Sino-Soviet border when Chinese aggression against Vietnam took place. The war, however, was rather short partly because of Beijing's desire not to provoke Moscow too much.

However it may be, the disappointment among Vietnamese officials and people was great. The Treaty did serve Moscow's purpose of bringing additional pressure to bear on China (by surrounding China from the south) and using Vietnam as a base for further expansion into Southeast Asia. But it did not serve Hanoi's immediate goals with respect to Kampuchea and China. Foreign Minister Nguyen Co Thach offered various explanations to soothe the feeling of disappointment that swept the nation. Acknowledging that, "Many comrades wonder why the Soviet Union did not implement the Sixth Article of the Treaty,"[84] he stated:

> We can say that the decision not to ask the Soviet Union to intervene is a correct one. In the first place, if the Soviet Union intervened, the victory would belong to the Soviet Union. Secondly, when we have not used

regular forces, why do we need the Soviet Union to jump in? Thirdly, if the Soviet Union jumped in, the conflict would turn into a Sino-Soviet war, which would unite the whole of China as well as accelerate the Sino-US collusion. As a result, the [Soviet Union's] task to oppose the US—"the common enemy of the mankind"—would be neglected. Therefore, while China represented "the most dangerous enemy of Vietnam," the Soviet intervention is not desirable, because if it happened, the nature and the scope of the war would change.[85]

He went on to stress that both Hanoi and Moscow did not want to interpret the Treaty as laying the groundwork for a military alliance, declaring, "About the Treaty with the Soviet Union, we should understand that it does not constitute a military alliance."[86]

When the storm had passed, Hanoi gradually realized that the need for military cooperation with the Soviet Union had become less urgent. China had been unable to secure a military victory against Vietnam, and Beijing no longer wanted to teach Hanoi "a second lesson". Subsequently, China became "busy with the Four Modernization".[87] Vietnam's confidence vis-à-vis its great northern neighbour grew. A document entitled "On the Situation in Southeast Asia and Guidelines for Our Diplomatic Struggle" in October 1981 stated, "China is big, but it is not strong. Internally, it is not stable; externally, it has contradictions with most of the countries in the world, especially in Asia and Southeast Asia. Therefore, China's scope for action, especially in the military field, will be limited in nature and will take place only in very specific conditions."[88] The MOFA Annual Report of 1981 wrote, "The possibility that China would teach a second lesson is increasingly limited."[89] Moreover, in 1982 when signs of a Sino-Soviet rapprochement became apparent, MOFA claimed, "Relatively peaceful and stable conditions in Southeast Asia already exist."[90] The Soviet security role might therefore be of reduced importance.

Was the Soviet-Vietnamese cooperation mainly intended to serve Vietnam's economic needs? It is difficult to sustain this argument, for in fact Moscow was not instrumental in providing Hanoi with reconstruction aid (see Table 3.1).

Hanoi attached great importance to economic reconstruction and development in the post-1975 period. Vietnam's foreign policy, therefore, was designed mainly to serve that end. According to a 1982 MOFA

TABLE 3.1
Soviet Aid to Vietnam, 1976–86
(US$ million)

Year	1976	1977	1987	1979	1980	1981	1982	1983	1984	1985	1986
Economic Aid	560	560	700	800	1,000	1,050	1,175	1,250	1,400	1,600	1,800
Military Aid	450	630	720	1300	960	800	940	1,150	1,250	1,360	1,440
Total	1,010	1,190	1,420	2,100	1,960	1,850	2,115	2,400	2,650	2,960	3,240

Source: The Soviet Strategic Reach In Southeast Asia, Indochina Report, Oct 1986, p. 14. See also Thai Quang Trung (1989), p. 26.

document, "To seek aid from and cooperation with foreign countries in order to contribute to the course of economic reconstruction and development is the principal diplomatic task, against the background of an economy that has experienced through thirty years of successive wars." Yet the context had changed, because "The Soviet Union has ceased to provide us with non-refundable aid. All the new aid by the Soviet Union is now on a loan basis. In addition, China has not fulfilled its aid commitments for the pre-1975 period. Worse still, it has refused to provide new aid."[91] The document then suggested, "While trying to ensure aid by the Soviet Union and other socialist countries, we should seek aid from the West and international organizations. This is a correct policy, which is built on necessity, although we should not have illusions about capitalist countries giving aid to us."[92] Another MOFA document also provided details of the situation when Hanoi drafted the second five-year plan,

> 50 per cent of the total funds for capital construction depends on external sources. If civil consumption is also taken into account, we have to raise from external sources an amount of about VND35 billion, which is equivalent to 18 per cent of our GDP. So far, socialist countries have accounted for 53.6 per cent of Vietnam's total external economic relations while capitalist and nationalist countries for 37.9 per cent and 8.5 per cent respectively.[93]

The amount of aid in terms of cash also revealed the limits of Soviet assistance. In his study of Vietnamese diplomacy, Luu Van Loi quotes the report read at the Third Diplomatic Conference held in October 1976 to show that by the end of 1975, Moscow had promised aid worth of US$4.275 billion. Yet, Hanoi still needed an additional amount of US$5.5 billion for both production and consumption. Luu Van Loi commented: "This represented a very heavy task for diplomatic activities."[94] This figure was very close to what foreign observers had estimated of Hanoi's demand for aid would be. For example, Douglas Pike mentioned an amount of US$10 billion, half of which was promised by Moscow.[95] But by 1983, Hanoi had mobilized about US$7.5 billion, of which US$5.4 billion constituted of loans and US$2.1 billion constituted of non-refundable aid.[96] It is noteworthy that the non-refundable aid from non-socialist countries almost quadrupled that by the socialist states. Out of the US$2.1 billion of non-refundable aid, non-socialist states contributed US$0.412 billion while the Western countries gave US$1.7 billion.[97] In short, the Soviet Union could not satisfy the economic needs of Vietnam. The MOFA report at the Sixteenth Diplomatic Conference held in 1984 was candid about this:

> Economic relations between Vietnam and other socialist countries continue to grow, but not in accordance with good political relations ... The Soviet Union is the main pillar for us, but she has not met our most urgent needs for raw materials and energy; on the other hand, the major infrastructure projects, which she helps to build, upon their completion, will still fail to meet our expectations. By the end of the 1980s, we still see no prospect for major improvements in key sectors including oil and gas, and metallurgy. The main reasons include: we fail to prove to the Soviet Union that we can effectively use the Soviet aid as well as fulfil our economic obligations and responsibilities on the basis of mutual interest; and the Soviet Union has certain limitations in terms of funds, technologies, and materials.[98]

In short, besides security needs, Hanoi wanted to obtain Soviet aid for construction of its economy. It indeed did receive from the Soviet Union machinery and equipment for building industries. Yet its needs in consumer goods could not be met because the Soviet Union itself did not produce such goods in sufficient quantity and quality. On balance, the Soviet connection was not fully able to satisfy the security and economic needs of Hanoi. Strained relations with non-socialist countries, including ASEAN, therefore, was not serving the developmental needs for Hanoi in the post-war period. Even so, a more realistic foreign policy strategy was not seriously initiated during this period.

CONCLUSION

With hindsight, one can see that Vietnam's changing policies towards ASEAN countries during this period were based less on solid ideological principles than on expediency. At first, Hanoi did have in mind the aim of promoting relations with ASEAN for the sake of future peace and development. Subsequently, because of the ASEAN countries' failure to satisfy Hanoi's requirements on the implementation of the 1973 Paris

Agreement, notably with regard to the recognition of the PRG, Hanoi regarded them as reactionaries, and increased its rhetoric about solidarity with communist movements in the region. Then, when Hanoi's relations with Beijing and the Khmer Rouge seriously deteriorated, Hanoi set about improving relations with ASEAN. Later, when planning decisive action against the Khmer Rouge in 1977, Hanoi put its trust in the Soviet Union instead of discussing the issue with ASEAN countries. The failure to take due account of ASEAN's importance was perhaps due to an ideological residue and/or due to Hanoi's poor knowledge of the history and actual situation in Southeast Asia. For example, Hanoi did not seem to have been aware of the historical Thai-Vietnamese contention for influence in Laos and Kampuchea which had been evident since the sixteenth century, the then Thai strategic concern about Kampuchea, about Bangkok's policy of using Pol Pot's Kampuchea as a shield against Vietnam's perceived expansion and of allying with China, if necessary, to cope with Vietnam in case this shield was destroyed. Nor did Vietnam seem to have been aware of the rule of ASEAN solidarity and consensus.

If Hanoi had understood that the Kampuchean problem was not only a problem for Indochina but also for Southeast Asia as a whole, if it had been conversant with the history of Thai-Vietnamese disputes over Laos and Kampuchea and grasped the necessity of taking into account Thai sensitivities concerning any move vis-à-vis Kampuchea, it would have taken care to engage in wide-ranging and patient discussions with Thailand and other ASEAN countries, and to convince them that the removal of Khmer Rouge from power would not necessarily endanger Thai security, and that the new Cambodian government would be friendly to both Vietnam and Thailand. If a consensus could be reached with ASEAN countries and particularly with Thailand, which might have taken considerable time and involved great difficulties, before making a decisive move over Kampuchea, it would have been impossible for Beijing to manipulate the issue.

Theoretically, a good knowledge of history and of the importance of ASEAN's position on the Kampuchean issue would have mitigated the impact of purely ideological considerations. However, a poor knowledge of history and ASEAN *did* allow simplistic ideological interpretations (socialism versus capitalism) to have an undue impact on Hanoi's foreign policy design and conduct. Hanoi, therefore, continued to seek quick and simple answers to complicated questions of international affairs, using the convenient ideological lens, while nationalist calculations were dominant, yet unarticulated.[99] As a result, the Vietnam-ASEAN relationship was seen until 1986 as one latent rivalry between two opposing ideologies.[100]

There are certain difficulties in explaining Vietnam's foreign policy in general and that related to ASEAN from 1973 to 1986 in particular within the framework of realist approaches. If Hanoi had adhered to the logic of realism it would have diversified its foreign relations to develop ties with non-socialist states including those with ASEAN during this period. Certainly thoughts about possible diversification could be detected in a MOFA Report in 1977 that suggested,

> While developing by different laws, the socialist and capitalist systems have increasingly expanded the scope of economic exchanges to cooperate (*hợp tác*) and struggle (*đấu tranh*) in the single world economic system. Our policy, therefore, is to do our best to maximize economic relations with the socialist countries. But at the same time, we should develop economic ties with capitalist countries as much as we can, because it is beneficial to the course of national construction.[101]

And in the brief period from 1975 to 1977, some efforts were made towards this end. Yet, development of relations with states of different political and economic systems still had to overcome the ideology-influenced perception in Hanoi, which saw socialist and capitalist states as being different in nature.

Yet, at a deeper level, the stress on ideological differences perhaps reflects what constructivists have in mind when they speak of the effect of "socializing experiences"[102] among states: when the perceptions are so focused on dissimilarities, one can fail to see the other side in terms of similarities. Further, no institutional frameworks can be agreed upon to help facilitate durable interactions so that misunderstandings could be dispersed and ideas of common identity given opportunities to develop. During the early 1970s, Hanoi began to perceive the potential economic and security benefits of developing relations with ASEAN. Despite the conventional ideological rhetoric, Hanoi developed no concrete plans of actions aimed at excluding the ASEAN states or forcing them to accept Vietnam's preferences. Yet, it was largely Hanoi's perception of a post-war

Vietnam with a communist identity and its perception of the ASEAN states as possessing anti-communist and reactionary identities, together with its rhetoric along these lines, that actually obstructed the opportunities for and initial efforts at a better relationship between Vietnam and ASEAN.

Patterns of international relations subsequently reinforced these perceptions on different identities, thus further worsening Vietnam-ASEAN relations in the period from 1978 to 1986. That Vietnam and ASEAN countries joined different camps in the Cold War in this period greatly influenced the way Hanoi viewed ASEAN. In other words, Hanoi saw ASEAN through the lens of its relations with other actors rather than with ASEAN states themselves. In this period, the alliance with the Soviet Union and the "traditional and special relations" with Laos and Kampuchea based on the "guiding principles of revolutionary sentiments and international duties" greatly influenced the Vietnam-ASEAN relations. Hanoi accepted peaceful coexistence between the Indochinese and ASEAN countries. Yet, for Hanoi, it was the coexistence between two opposing systems. To put in another way, if economic and security needs perhaps represent necessary conditions for improving relations among ASEAN states and Vietnam, the lack of a sufficient condition—namely the absence of an internalized consciousness of common identity, to say nothing about the stress on different identities—obstructed the improvement of this relationship. It even led to tensions and hostility. The lack of this sufficient condition also suggested that even if relations could have been improved, they would not have been sustained. Improvements in this relationship at the time were aimed at realizing short-term objectives—namely to divide and neutralize the organization on the Kampuchean problem, and to reduce Chinese pressures. Hanoi's perception of ASEAN did not change: ASEAN was still in the enemies list.

On balance, however, the process of struggle from 1979 to 1986 did serve to enhance Hanoi's awareness of the above-mentioned issues, including the understanding that ASEAN countries wanted to be friends with Vietnam provided the latter agreed to an international settlement of the Kampuchean issue involving, among other things, the unconditional withdrawal of Vietnamese troops from that country. As a result, following Vietnam's withdrawal of troops from Kampuchea, Vietnam-ASEAN relations started to improve. In January 1989, Foreign Minister Nguyen

1978 to 1985: Coexistence between Two Opposing Groups 67

Co Thach expressed Hanoi's desire to join ASEAN.[103] Implicitly, however, this represented Vietnam's acceptance of the ASEAN mode of international relations for regional countries in general and the ASEAN mode of conflict management in specific.[104] Therefore, when the Agreement on Cambodia was concluded in Paris on 24 October 1991, "the last obstacle to the normalization of relations" with ASEAN countries was removed.[105] For Hanoi, the lessons had been learned, but at a great cost, and in a hard way.

Notes

1. Asia-3 Department, The Annual Report for 1976 (Báo cáo tổng kết năm 1976), (p. 12) said, "Many Southeast Asian countries wish to contribute to the healing of war wounds and economic reconstruction in our country. We have initially taken advantage of economic and trade relations with them to serve the cause of socialist construction. We also have studied possibilities for further economic cooperation with individual countries in the later stage."
2. MOFA, "On the World Situation in 1977" (Về tình hình thế giới năm 1977), p. 18. Asia-3 Department Report on the First Half of 1977 (Báo cáo tình hình sáu tháng đầu năm 1977), (p. 24) said: "Kampuchea's domestic and foreign policies have shown many negative aspects that have caused new difficulties and complexities in relations with Vietnam."
3. MOFA, Asia-2 Department Research Paper, "Vietnam-Cambodia Relations: History, Present, and Prospects", Hanoi, November 2001, pp. 78–79.
4. See Ramses Amer, *The Ethnic Chinese in Vietnam and Sino-Vietnamese Relations* (Kuala Lumpur: Forum, 1991); Ramses Amer, "Sino-Vietnamese Relations: Past, Present, and Future", in *Vietnamese Foreign Policy in Transition*, edited by Carlyle Thayer and Ramses Amer (Singapore: Institute of Southeast Asian Studies, 1999); William Duiker, *China and Vietnam: Roots of Conflict* (Berkeley: Institute of East Asian Studies, University of California, 1986); MOFA, *The White Book on the 30 Years of Vietnam-China Relations* (Hanoi: The Truth Publishing House, 1980); MOFA, "On the World Situation in 1977", p. 18.
5. MOFA Report "On the Characteristics of the World Situation since from Early 1970s to the Present" (Về đặc điểm tình hình thế giới từ đầu những năm 1907s đến nay), (April 1982), p. 9.
6. See Desaix Anderson, *An American in Hanoi: American's Reconciliation with Vietnam* (New York: East Bridge, 2002), pp. 97–111.
7. "United States Policy towards Revolutionary Regimes: Vietnam (1975–1983)",

in *U.S. Foreign Policy: Adjusting to Change in the Third World*, edited by Dick Clark, No. 85-W441 (Wye Plantation, Queenstown, MD: Aspen Institute for Humanistic Studies, 1985) pp. 121–28.
8. See Nayan Chanda, *Brother Enemy: The War after the War* (New York: Collier Book, 1986); Desaix Anderson, *An American in Hanoi*, pp. 98–100; Patrick Tyler, "The (Ab)Normalization of US-Chinese Relations", *Foreign Affairs* (September/October 1999).
9. Cecil Menetrey-Monchau, "The Changing US Strategy in Indochina", paper presented at the London School of Economics and Political Science Cold War Study Program Conference entitled Tripartite Diplomacy and the Third Indochina War, Cumberland Lodge, London, 14–16 May 2003. See also Cécile Menétrey-Monchau, *American-Vietnamese Relations in the Wake of War: Diplomacy after the Capture of Saigon, 1975–1979* (Jefferson, NC: McFarland & Co. Inc., 2006).
10. Transcripts of Foreign Minister Nguyen Co Thach's Talk to a Journalists' Conference, Hanoi, 14 May 1979, p. 3.
11. Asia-2 Department, First Quarter of 1978 Report (Báo cáo quý 1 năm 1978), p. 2.
12. MOFA, "On the World Situation in 1977" (Về tình hình thế giới năm 1977), p. 18.
13. MOFA, The Annual Report of 1981 (Báo cáo tổng kết năm 1981), p. 31.
14. Transcripts of the speech by President Truong Chinh at the Fifteenth Diplomatic Conference, Hanoi, 25 May 1982, p. 4.
15. Luu Doan Huynh's Personal Notes on Sino-Thai Relations and the Cambodian Issue, p. 9.
16. Asia-3 Department Report, "On the Evolution of ASEAN Positions on Solutions to the Kampuchean Problem between 1979 and 1986" (Về diễn biến lập trường của ASEAN liên quan đến giải pháp cho vấn đề Campuchia trong các năm 1979–1986), p. 2.
17. Luu Doan Huynh's Personal Notes on Sino-Thai Relations and the Cambodian Issue, p. 3. Some documents of the Asia-3 Department, however, incorrectly indicated that Thai Prime Minister Kriangsak made such a statement to Ambassador Hoang Bao Son. See Asia-3 Department Report, "On the Evolution of ASEAN Positions on Solutions to the Kampuchean Problem between 1979 and 1986", p. 2.
18. Asia-3 Department Report, "On the Evolution of ASEAN Positions on Solutions to the Kampuchean Problem between 1979 and 1986", p. 2.
19. Ibid., p. 3.
20. Ibid.

21. MOFA Report "On Situation in Southeast Asia and Our Policy" (Về tình hình Đông nam Á và chính sách của chúng ta), (1983), p. 14.
22. MOFA, The Annual Report of 1981 (Báo cáo tổng kết năm 1981), p. 32.
23. Asia-3 Department Annual Report of 1976 (Báo cáo tổng kết năm 1976), (p. 8) wrote: "During the war, ASEAN countries, because of their anti-communist nature, followed the US to oppose us and were nonchalant towards us. Therefore, when the war has ended, they are concerned that enjoying greater influence in the region, we will be more critical to them, and support revolutionary movements in their countries through training local communists and supplying them with weapons. On the other hand, however, they show the willingness to establish relations with us in order to prevent us from supporting local communist parties. At the same time, they wish to do business on a long-term basis with us. The reason is that they cannot afford to have no relations with a country that has the population of 50 million people, strong military capabilities, huge political prestige, and great potentials for rapid economic development."
24. Transcripts of Deputy Foreign Minister Phan Hien's Talk, p. 10.
25. Ibid., pp. 12–13.
26. Asia-3 Department Report for the First Half of 1980 (Báo cáo sơ kết sáu tháng đầu năm 1980), p. 8.
27. MOFA Annual Report of 1981 (Báo cáo tổng kết năm 1981), p. 30.
28. MOFA Annual Report of 1978, "On the World Situation and Our Foreign Policy" (Báo cáo tổng kết năm 1978 về tình hình thế giới và chính sách đối ngoại của chúng ta), p. 17.
29. MOFA, The Annual Report of 1981 (Báo cáo tổng kết năm 1981), p. 30. The Asia-3 Department Annual Report of 1983, "On the Situation in Southeast Asia and Our Policy" (Báo cáo tổng kết năm 1983 về tình hình Đông nam Á và chính sách của chúng ta), (p. 21) predicted that Southeast Asia would only be stable after questions related to regional revolutions have been solved.
30. MOFA Report "On the World Situation and Our Foreign Policy" (Về tình hình thế giới và chính sách đối ngoại của chúng ta) (presented at the Sixteenth Diplomatic Conference on 12 May 1983), p. 45. In January 1980, the Joint Communiqué issued by the Foreign Ministers of Vietnam, Laos, and Kampuchea after their meeting in Phnom Penh stated: "the biggest, most significant common victory of the three peoples has been their militant solidarity. This solidarity, closely linked to the Soviet Union and the other socialist countries, has become invincible. It can completely defeat any aggressors and change the balance of forces more in favor of peace, national independence, and social progress in Southeast Asia." See MOFA,

"Joint Communiqué of Vietnam, Kampuchea, and Laos Foreign Ministers' Conference", *Conferences of Foreign Ministers of Vietnam, Laos, and Kampuchea: 1980–1981* (Hanoi: MOFA Information and Press Department, 1981), p. 11.
31. Asia-3 Department Report for the First Quarter of 1979 (Báo cáo tổng kết quý 1 năm năm 1979), p. 4.
32. Ibid., pp. 1–2.
33. "On the Situation in Southeast Asia and Our Policy", p. 7.
34. MOFA Report "On the World Situation and Our Foreign Policy", (presented at the Sixteenth Diplomatic Conference on 12 May 1983), p. 50.
35. Ibid., p. 45.
36. MOFA Report, "On the Situation in Southeast Asia and Our Policy" (1983), p. 14.
37. Transcript of Foreign Minister Nguyen Co Thach's Talk to a Journalists' Conference, p. 21.
38. MOFA Report "On the Situation in Southeast Asia and Our Policy", p. 15.
39. MOFA, "Joint Communiqué of Vietnam, Kampuchea, and Laos Foreign Ministers' Conference", *Conferences of Foreign Ministers of Vietnam, Laos, and Kampuchea: 1980–1981* (Hanoi: MOFA Information and Press Department, 1981), p. 17.
40. Ibid., p. 18.
41. Asia-3 Department Report for the First Half of 1980 (Báo cáo tổng kết quý 1 năm 1980), p. 14.
42. MOFA, "On the Emergence and Transformation of ASEAN and Vietnam-ASEAN Relations" (Về sự ra đời và chuyển hóa của ASEAN và quan hệ Việt nam – ASEAN) Appendix to the MOFA, 8 July 1992 Memo to CPV Politburo entitled "On the Relationship between Vietnam and ASEAN" (Về mối quan hệ giữa Việt nam và ASEAN).
43. MOFA, "Statement of the Conference of Foreign Ministers of Laos, Kampuchea, and Vietnam", *Conferences of Foreign Ministers of Vietnam, Laos, and Kampuchea*, pp. 24–25.
44. MOFA, "Communiqué of the Conference of Foreign Ministers of Vietnam, Laos, and Kampuchea", *Conferences of Foreign Ministers of Vietnam, Laos, and Kampuchea*, p. 46.
45. Asia-3 Department, "Drafts for the Indochinese Foreign Ministers' Conference on New Diplomatic Offensives", (Dự thảo văn kiện phục vụ hội nghị bộ trưởng ngoại giao ba nước Đông dương liên quan đến các đòn tấn công ngoại giao mới), p. 3.
46. MOFA, "Statement by the Conference of Foreign Ministers of Vietnam, Laos,

and Kampuchea on Peace, Stability, Friendship and Cooperation in Southeast Asia", *Conferences of Foreign Ministers of Vietnam, Laos, and Kampuchea*, pp. 42–43.
47. MOFA, *Sixth Conference of Foreign Ministers of Laos, Kampuchea, and Vietnam*, "Communiqué of the Sixth Conference of Foreign Ministers of Laos, Kampuchea, and Vietnam", p. 8, and "VNA's Interview with Foreign Minister Nguyen Co Thach", p. 13.
48. Foreign Minister Nguyen Co Thach's interview given to *Nhan Dan*, 4 January 1985.
49. Asia-3 Department Report "On Regional Consultations" (Báo cáo về các cuộc tham vấn khu vực).
50. Asia-3 Department Report "On the ASEAN-CMEA Economic Relations" (Về quan hệ kinh tế giữa ASEAN và COMECON), p. 3.
51. Transcripts of Deputy Foreign Minister Phan Hien's Talks, p. 19. He also said: "The tasks for comrade Hoang Bao Son, as our ambassador to Thailand, are very heavy. You should make them aware that we are restrained and committed to our promise not to go beyond Kampuchea." Transcripts of Phan Hien's Talks, p. 20.
52. Luu Doan Huynh's Personal Notes on Sino-Thai Relations and the Cambodian Issue, p. 11.
53. Cable from Vietnamese Embassy in Bangkok to MOFA.
54. Vietnamese Charge d'Affaires Ambassador to Thailand Do Ngoc Duong's Report "On the Situation in Thailand: Thailand's Policy towards Vietnam and Our Policy towards Thailand, 1978–1982" (Về tình hình Thái lan: Chính sách của Thái lan đối với Việt Nam và chính sách của chúng ta đối với Thái lan), (16 September 1982), p. 13.
55. MOFA, the Annual Report of 1978, "On the World Situation and Our Foreign Policy" (Báo cáo tổng kết năm 1978 về tình hình thế giới và chính sách đối ngoại của chúng ta), p. 24.
56. Transcripts of President Truong Chinh's Speech at the Fifteenth Diplomatic Conference, pp. 9–10. He further explained (pp. 4 and 26): "In the text of the Political Report for the V National Party Congress, we will only state that "Vietnam is loyal to its international obligations, unites itself with revolutionary and progressive forces and supports the struggle by the peoples in the world for peace, national independence, democracy, and social progress." He also said, "We will not declare that fulfilling the international obligations is one of the strategic tasks."
57. Ibid., pp. 4–6.
58. Asia-3 Department Annual Report of 1978 (Báo cáo tổng kết năm 1978),

pp. 22–23. Deputy Foreign Minister Phan Hien also said at that time: "The Indochinese reunion (implying the effort to bring Phnom Penh back to Hanoi's fold) does not mean we put the Indochinese bloc and ASEAN against each other to cause a new round of confrontation. We simply influence the growth of revolution in Kampuchea." Transcripts of Phan Hien's Talk, p. 13.

59. Asia-3 Department Annual Report of 1983, "On the Situation in Southeast Asia and Our Policy", p. 21. During a visit to Indonesia in October/November 1982, Foreign Minister Nguyen Co Thach stated that Hanoi respected the ASEAN solidarity because this was the matter of life and death for ASEAN countries, which was equal to the importance that the Indochinese countries attach to their solidarity." A MOFA Report on Nguyen Co Thach's visit to Indonesia, p. 3.
60. Transcripts of Foreign Minister Nguyen Co Thach's Speech, p. 22.
61. MOFA Annual Report of 1983 (Báo cáo tổng kết năm 1983), p. 20.
62. MOFA 10 June 1982 Memo to Le Duc Tho "On the Diplomatic Activities for the Coming Period" (Về các hoạt động ngoại giao trong thời gian tới), p. 2.
63. MOFA August 1981 Draft "On the Strategic Thinking by ASEAN" (Về tư duy chiến lược của ASEAN), p. 15.
64. MOFA Report at the Sixteenth Diplomatic Conference, "On the International Situation and Our Foreign Relations" (Về tình hình thế giới và quan hệ đối ngoại của ta), (1983), p. 51.
65. MOFA Report "On the Visit to Indonesia by Foreign Minister Nguyen Co Thach" (Về chuyến đi thăm Indonesia của bộ trưởng ngoại giao Nguyễn Cơ Thạch), (28 October–1 November 1982), p. 7.
66. Transcripts of Foreign Minister Nguyen Co Thach's Talk, p. 21.
67. MOFA Report "On the Visit to Indonesia by Foreign Minister Nguyen Co Thach" (28 October–1 November 1982), p. 1.
68. MOFA Report at the Sixteenth Diplomatic Conference, p. 54.
69. MOFA Report "On the Visit by Foreign Minister Nguyen Co Thach to Several Southeast Asian Countries" (Về chuyến đi thăm của bộ trưởng ngoại giao Nguyễn Cơ Thạch tại một số nước Đông nam Á), (July 1982), pp. 8–9.
70. Transcripts of Deputy Foreign Minister Phan Hien's Talks, p. 5.
71. MOFA Report, "On the Situation in Southeast Asia and Our Policy" (1983), p. 17.
72. International Organizations Department, Talking Points for Meetings by Vice President Nguyen Huu Tho at the Eighth NAM Summit.
73. Transcripts of Talks between Foreign Minister Nguyen Co Thach with Singaporean, Malaysian, and Sri Lankan Counterparts (New Delhi, 8 March

1983), p. 2. A report covering the month of July 1979 said, "In their relations with Vietnam, ASEAN states were positive towards our readiness to hold bilateral and multilateral dialogues with them. Yet, they want us to treat them as a group."
74. See, for example, Alison Broinowski, ed., *Understanding ASEAN* (Hong Kong: Macmillan Press, 1982).
75. Transcripts of the Meeting between Foreign Minister Nguyen Co Thach and Singaporean Foreign Minister Dhanabalan, (Singapore, July 1982), p. 2.
76. According to Asia-3 Department Report for the First Half of 1982 (Báo cáo 6 tháng đầu năm 1982) (p. 19), "Singapore continued to expand trade relations with us. The growth is 7 per cent higher than last year", The Asia-3 Department Report of 12 March 1984 "On Economic Relations between Vietnam and Southeast Asian countries" (Về quan hệ kinh tế giữa Việt nam và các nước Đông nam Á), (pp. 1–3) provided the following figures: trade turnovers between Vietnam and Singapore were reduced to US$13 million in 1979 from US$62.4 million in 1977. But in 1983, the turnovers reached US$20 million, four time higher than 1982. Asia-3 Department Report for the First Half of 1976 (Báo cáo 6 tháng đầu năm 1976) (p. 17) stated that trade turnovers between the two countries were US$12 million for the first half of the year. Other gestures include good treatment and eventual release of the crew of a Vietnamese military aircraft crash-landed in Thailand, and the return to Vietnam of a hijacked military transport plane by Singapore.
77. Negotiations on the conclusion of the Treaty was intensified following the CPV Politburo Resolution No. 9 which was adopted on 27 July 1978 and in the main set the task of removing the Khmer Rouge regime in order to cope with the threat of Chinese attacks in the North, thus avoiding the worst case scenario of fighting two wars at the same time.
78. Chanda Nayan, *Brother Enemy: The War after the War*, Ch. 10, fn 5. Pike also noted that the signing of the treaty "came after a last minute delay of several days of hard bargaining" that involved Vietnam's Minister of Defence. See Douglas Pike, *Vietnam and the Soviet Union: Anatomy of an Alliance* (Boulder: Westview Press, 1987), p. 184.
79. Stephen Morris, *Why Vietnam Invaded Cambodia: Political Culture and the Cause of War* (California: Stanford University Press, 1999).
80. MOFA Annual Report of 1978 (Báo cáo 6 tháng đầu năm 1978), p. 17.
81. Asia-3 Department Report for the First Half of 1976 (Báo cáo 6 tháng đầu năm 1976), (p. 21b) mentioned counterproductive effects of the anti-ASEAN tones by Vietnam. It wrote in part: "Our propaganda related to ASEAN has not been well managed. The guidelines and policies for Southeast Asia have

not at times been followed by the press, which as a result, caused negative reactions by several countries. This is not beneficial to the implementation of our policy with regard to the region."

82. Asia-3 Department Report for the First Quarter of 1979 (Báo cáo quý 1 năm 1979), p. 5.
83. On 17 February 1979, President Carter sent a message to CPSU General Secretary Brezhnev to request Moscow's neutrality in the coming Sino-Vietnamese conflict. A MOFA Asian-3 Department Report on Vietnam-ASEAN relations in 1978–86. See also Carlyle Thayer, "United States Policy towards Revolutionary Regimes: Vietnam (1975–1983)", in *U.S. Foreign Policy: Adjusting to Change in the Third World*, edited by Dick Clark, (No. 85-W441) (Wye Plantation, Queenstown, MD: Aspen Institute for Humanistic Studies, 1985) pp. 121–28.
84. Transcripts of Foreign Minister Nguyen Co Thach's Speech at a Journalists' Conference, p. 3.
85. Ibid., p. 3.
86. Ibid., p. 16.
87. Ibid., p. 18.
88. MOFA, 31 October 1981 Report, "On the Situation in Southeast Asia and the Guidelines for Our Diplomatic Offensives" (Về tình hình Đông nam Á và định hướng cho các đòn tấn công ngoại giao của chúng ta), p. 4.
89. MOFA Annual Report of 1981, "On the World Situation and Our Foreign Policy", p. 16. MOFA Report, "Reviewing Our Foreign Policy since 1978" (Nhìn lại chính sách đối ngoại của chúng ta từ năm 1978) for the Sixteenth Diplomatic Conference in 1983, (p. 11) wrote: "The chance of China undertaking major military operations is less likely."
90. MOFA, 10 June 1982 Memo to Le Duc Tho, "On the Diplomatic Activities for the Coming Period", p. 3.
91. MOFA, April 1982 Report, "On the Characteristics of the World Situation since from Early 1970s to the Present" (Về đặc điểm tình hình thế giới từ đầu 1970s đến nay), p. 19.
92. Ibid., pp. 4–5.
93. MOFA Draft, "On the World Situation and Our International Relations in 1977" (Về tình hình thế giới và quan hệ quốc tế của chúng ta trong năm 1977), p. 18.
94. Luu Van Loi, *50 Years of Vietnamese Diplomacy, Volume 2 (1975–1995)*, p. 56.
95. According to Douglas Pike, Soviet aid to Vietnam between 1981 and 1986 was about US$5 billion. See Pike, *Vietnam and the Soviet Union: Anatomy*

of an Alliance, p. 140. See also Carlyle Thayer with Ramesh Thakur, *Soviet Relations with India and Vietnam* (London: Macmillan Press; New York: St. Martin's Press, 1992).

96. MOFA, April 1982 Report, "On the Characteristics of the World Situation since from Early 1970s to the Present" (Về đặc điểm tình hình thế giới từ đầu 1970s đến nay), p. 5.
97. Ibid.
98. MOFA Report, "Reviewing Our Foreign Policy since 1978" (Nhìn lại chính sách đối ngoại của chúng ta từ năm 1978) for the Sixteenth Diplomatic Conference in 1983, pp. 39–40.
99. Luu Doan Huynh observed that for Hanoi, "it was ideologically comforting to describe ASEAN as SEATO in disguise". Luu Doan Huynh's remarks at the 3rd Asia-Europe Roundtable, "Peace and Reconciliation: Success Stories and Lessons in Asia and Europe", Hanoi, 20–21 October 2003.
100. ASEAN Department, MOFA, unpublished Research Paper entitled, "Five Years after Joining ASEAN: Achievements, Challenges, and Prospects", October 2001, p. 37.
101. MOFA Report, "On the World Situation and Our International Relations in 1977", p. 18.
102. Alastair Iain Johnston, "Is China a Status Quo Power?", *International Security* 27, no. 4 (Spring 2003), p. 56.
103. The IIR Southeast Asian Studies Division, A Study entitled "ASEAN, Vietnam-ASEAN Relations and Prospects" (Hanoi, 1995), p. 62.
104. Luu Doan Huynh at the 3rd Asia-Europe Roundtable, "Peace and Reconciliation: Success Stories and Lessons in Asia and Europe", Hanoi, 20–21 October 2003.
105. Speech by Foreign Minister Nguyen Manh Cam at the International Conference on Cambodia, Paris, 23 October 1991, on *Nhan Dan*, 24 October 1991.

4
JOINING ASEAN: Political and Strategic Factors

THE INTERNAL DEBATES

The Seventh CPV National Congress (July 1991) officially proclaimed, "Vietnam wants to be a friend of all members of the world community which strive for peace, national independence, and development." The Second and Third CPV Central Committee Plenums, which met in January and June 1992 respectively, focused on developing relations with major powers as well as countries in the region.[1] The Third CPV CC Plenum Resolution gave instructions on how to conduct Vietnam-ASEAN relations, "[We should] as an immediate step, accede to the Bali Treaty, take part in ASEAN consultative forums, and actively conduct research on how to expand our relations with ASEAN in the future."[2] However, immediately after the accession to the Bali Treaty, Hanoi still did not feel ready for ASEAN membership. Responding to a MOFA Southeast Asian and South Pacific Affairs (SEA/SPA) Department report on Vietnam-ASEAN relations which suggested that the Politburo should provide further instructions on the question of ASEAN membership, the Politburo held a meeting in November 1992 and concluded that "more research should be done".[3]

In February 1993, Hanoi officially stated, "Vietnam is ready to join ASEAN at an appropriate time."[4] In mid-September 1993, a meeting was convened by Hong Ha, Director of the Commission for External Relation of the CPV Central Committee (CERC), with the participation of representatives from MOFA, the Ministry of National Defence, the Ministry of Internal Affairs, and the National Borders Committee to work on a policy announcement that General Secretary Do Muoi was going to make during his visit to Malaysia in October. The question of ASEAN membership was of course brought up. Transcripts of the meeting revealed that the participants were in favour of joining ASEAN and proposed that Do Muoi should state that "Vietnam is ready to join ASEAN", thus dropping the "at an appropriate time" phrase.[5] When the visit took place, Do Muoi announced a four-point policy concerning Vietnam-ASEAN relations that stressed, "Vietnam will increase multifaceted cooperation with individual neighbouring countries as well as with ASEAN as a regional organization." Yet, the sentence of "Vietnam is ready to join ASEAN at an appropriate time" remained unchanged in the four-point policy.[6]

The question of ASEAN membership was again discussed, as preparations were under way for the official visit to Indonesia by Vietnamese President Le Duc Anh in April 1994. Hanoi had been more eager to join ASEAN by that time, which was reflected in the statement Le Duc Anh made in Jakarta, "Vietnam is making practical preparations in order to join ASEAN at an early date as a full-fledged member."[7] The Government's "Review of Foreign Affairs of the First Half of 1994" submitted to the Fifth Session of the Ninth National Assembly stated, "We are making preparations to join ASEAN as a full member."[8]

Subsequently, developments quickened. At the Twenty-Seventh ASEAN AMM, on 21 July 1994, ASEAN reached a consensus to accept Vietnam as a member, which triggered a Politburo meeting on 22 July. Within two hours, the Politburo had reached a final decision and instructed Foreign Minister Nguyen Manh Cam, who was already in Bangkok taking part in the AMM, to officially state that Vietnam was ready to join ASEAN in 1995.[9] The next day, Nguyen Manh Cam cabled from Bangkok, "the Politburo instruction has been fully executed."[10] On 17 October Nguyen Manh Cam sent a letter to his Brunei counterpart, who was the Chairman of the ASEAN Standing Committee (ASC) officially stating Hanoi's decision to join the organization. The ASEAN Senior Officials' Meeting (SOM) held in Brunei in November 1994 agreed that Vietnam would be accepted as a full member of ASEAN at the Twenty-Eighth ASEAN AMM in July 1995. The SEA/SPA Department therefore stressed, "Developments in 1994 show that the Vietnam-ASEAN relationship has entered a qualitatively new phase."[11]

In short, Hanoi considered the accession to the Bali Treaty as the first step to joining ASEAN and believed that its full membership would be a matter of time. Yet, this does not mean that the decision to join ASEAN came automatically. Indeed, from roughly the end of 1991 to April 1994, developments and policy statements related to the ASEAN membership question were the subject of continued internal discussions and debates in Hanoi. When the outcome has finally become clear, Hanoi proceeded towards full ASEAN membership, discarding the option of a prolonged observer status and associate membership. It is important to document and analyse the discussions and debates in some detail if we are to understand the factors that influenced Hanoi's decision to join ASEAN in 1995 and to promote Vietnam-ASEAN cooperation.

ASEAN IN THE OVERALL FOREIGN POLICY UNDER RENOVATION (*DOI MOI*)

Officially, the CPV National Congress held in December 1986 has been considered as the starting point of the process of political and economic reforms (known as *Doi Moi*) in Vietnam including changes in foreign policy. Yet, specific and comprehensive changes in Hanoi's foreign policy were worked out at a later date. The Thirteenth CPV Politburo Resolution (dated 20 May 1988) represented a "comprehensive change in the overall foreign policy", and "a fundamental change in foreign policy thinking relating to matters of security and development, national interests and international obligations, as well as alliances and the alignment of international forces".[12] The Resolution stressed, "economic weaknesses, political isolation, and the economic blockade are major threats to our country's security and independence; to preserve peace and to develop the economy are the highest strategic objectives and interests of the whole Party and the people of Vietnam."[13]

Many now believe that the Resolution was based on a new perception of security, that is comprehensive security. Previously, Hanoi saw security as strictly military. From 1986, it adopted a comprehensive security approach according to which the "security of any country should be based on the realities of its scientific and economic developments and at the same time should be mutually dependent on the security of other countries."[14] On the basis of this perception, a combination of the following factors—listed in order of importance, according to the Resolution—should be achieved to ensure the country's security, namely "a strong economy, a sufficiently strong national defence, and expanded international cooperative relations".[15] Thus, greater importance was given to the expansion of foreign relations as the necessary condition for overcoming political isolation and economic blockade and for building "a strong economy", which is associated with the international (read, capitalist) division of labour.[16] In other words, this was a new concept of comprehensive security that no longer gave priority to purely military aspect. Instead, the implementation of a new foreign policy was to play a bigger role while the value of military measures in ensuring national security and supporting the economic development of Vietnam would be diminished.[17] To this end, an international agreement on Cambodia must be achieved, and efforts made to broaden relations with all countries, particularly neighbouring countries and major powers. Against the background of this new thinking, which was made easier to accept by the general easing of international tensions and the tendency towards enhanced regional cooperation in various parts of the world following the end of the Cold War, Hanoi increasingly felt that the threats to its security were being reduced. Moreover, the diversification (*đa dạng hóa*) and multilateralization (*đa phương hóa*) of Hanoi's foreign relations further contributed to enhance Vietnam's sense of security after the collapse of the Soviet Union. William quotes a Vietnamese diplomat as saying "For the first time, we are relying on diplomacy to safeguard security. In the past, it was only used as a crown to military victory."[18]

What did the Resolution say about Vietnam-ASEAN relations? Hanoi no longer saw ASEAN as an opponent, and instead indirectly acknowledged the important role of the organization in the construction of a new regional order, and planned to improve relations with ASEAN countries. The Resolution stated:

> For the last ten years, we have consolidated the solidarity among the three Indochinese countries and considered this as a counterweight to ASEAN and a decisive factor for peace and stability in Southeast Asia. In the new context, we consider the establishment of a framework for Indochinese-ASEAN peaceful coexistence as the condition for maintaining peace, promoting economic development, and consolidating the relationship of cooperation and solidarity among the three countries. There is no question of a socialist bloc (consisting Vietnam, Laos and Cambodia) versus a capitalist bloc (that is, ASEAN). Along these strategic lines, we will work out a comprehensive Southeast Asia policy, which will focus first and foremost on enhancing multi-sided relations with Indonesia, breaking the stalemate in Vietnamese-Thai relations, expanding economic, cultural, and scientific-technical relations with other countries in the region, solving existing disputes and problems with these countries through negotiations, and promoting the construction of peace, stability, friendship, and cooperation in the region.[19]

The question of Vietnam's membership in ASEAN, however, was not raised in the Resolution.

As the socialist camp began to disintegrate, the CPV convened the Eighth Central Committee Plenum on 27 March 1990 to assess the situation and readjust its foreign policy objectives. The Resolution of the Conference wrote in part,

> Many important lessons could be learned from the ongoing crisis in many socialist countries: the relations between the Soviet Union and other socialist countries are different from our foreign relations, and the experiences of the socialist countries [in Europe] are different from ours. The new conditions force our people to make great efforts to independently solve our problems with a high sense of self-reliance and creativeness. We should be more proactive in conducting our foreign relations with a view to expanding and diversifying cooperative relations and actively taking part in the international division of labour.... [We should,] therefore, expand our external relations under the motto of "making more friends and having fewer enemies" to maintain peace for national construction and defence.[20]

The Resolution, however, did not mention specific objectives for and adjustments in Hanoi's relations with ASEAN countries.[21]

While the Seventh CPV National Congress held in July 1991 was noted for its announcement that "Vietnam wants to be a friend of all members of the world community which strive for peace, national independence, and development", the CPV CC Plenum held in June 1992 stressed relations with ASEAN. The Third CPV CC Plenum Resolution gave instructions on how to conduct Vietnam-ASEAN relations, "We should, as an immediate step, accede to the Bali Treaty, take part in ASEAN consultative forums, and actively conduct research on how to expand our relations with ASEAN in the future."[22]

The Third CPV CC Plenum was of great importance to the making of foreign policy in general and to the improvement of Vietnam-ASEAN relations in particular. In the first place, it officially acknowledged that national interests had become the compass for Vietnam's relations with regional countries. In a press article designed to explain the Resolution, Foreign Minister Nguyen Manh Cam wrote, "we hold peace and development as pervasive objectives for all activities, including foreign affairs. These objectives must serve the highest and long-term national interests."[23] The Plenum stressed that geographical proximity was the main consideration in the development of relations with ASEAN countries. Nguyen Manh Cam wrote in the same article, "Our foreign policy towards the region should enjoy special attention because of its geopolitical significance."[24]

Moreover, improvement of Vietnam-ASEAN relations was considered to be instrumental to the implementation of Hanoi's diversified and multilateralized foreign policy. In an opening speech at the Third Plenum, General Secretary Do Muoi said, "We attach great importance to the achievement of fundamental changes in our relations with major countries of the world. At the same time, we strive to develop rapidly our relations with the countries in the region."[25] Nguyen Manh Cam then explained how better relations with ASEAN would serve to improve relations with other countries. He pointed out that membership in ASEAN would help to achieve a "breakthrough" in the implementation of a diversified and multilateralized foreign policy. If this breakthrough was achieved, it would be easier for Hanoi to normalize relations with the US, to improve relations with other major powers, and overcome political isolation and economic blockade. In the same spirit, Nguyen Manh Cam also stressed,

"The implementation of the new regional foreign policy should enjoy a special attention because this will help to build a bridge for us to enter the wider world."[26]

We can now see that after 1988, there was a rather new approach to foreign policy approach in Hanoi, with close association with ASEAN as an increasingly important component. While this new foreign policy involved the concept of comprehensive security and diversification and multilateralization of international relations for the purpose of promoting national economic development, Vietnam's membership in ASEAN was seen as the cornerstone and prerequisite for its successful implementation. That is to say, after 1986, when peace and development became the highest national objectives for Hanoi, foreign policy as a whole and policy towards ASEAN in particular came to be were clearly influenced by realist thinking, with its emphasis on national interests and geopolitics. This constituted a setback for the ideological approach.

This interpretation is given additional plausibility in documents on the internal debates about the question of ASEAN membership, which reveal cost-benefit thinking was always high on the agenda. On 18 October 1991, in an interview with the *Bangkok Post*, Prime Minister Vo Van Kiet said,

> If the cooperative relations in ASEAN are of a friendly and peaceful nature and serve the end of maintaining regional peace and security, if individual members build good relations among themselves for the sake of developing their countries the way they see fit and on the basis of equality, mutual benefit, and independence, we are ready to join ASEAN.[27]

The statement did not set forth the conditions for Vietnam's membership of ASEAN. It simply revealed that Hanoi leaders were thinking about the advantages and disadvantages of ASEAN membership.

Following the decision to accede to the Bali Treaty (June 1991), national leaders began to ask MOFA and other institutions concerned to study the advantages and disadvantages of joining ASEAN more carefully. The CPV Secretariat Document No. 153 dated 25 February 1992 sent to MOFA and CERC wrote, "The CPV Secretariat has agreed that we accede to the Bali Treaty. On the ASEAN membership matter, the Secretariat instructs MOFA and CERC to systematically collect all the ASEAN and Vietnamese documents on the matter, hold elaborate discussions on the costs and benefits of membership, then submit their findings to the Politburo."[28] A series of memos, entitled "On the Relations between Vietnam and ASEAN," prepared separately by MOFA, are extremely suggestive in this regard. Because of their importance, these memos will be quoted at length. The first MOFA Memo, dated 8 July 1992, argued,

> ASEAN has been transformed into a regional politico-economic organization. We should consider ASEAN membership for the following reasons:
>
> - Multilateral cooperation in the region, even among countries of different political and social systems, is the general trend in the world where markets and production have been to a great extent internationalized. Even Laos and Cambodia have started to take part in regional cooperation. We therefore cannot stand outside this process. Our membership in ASEAN is in accordance with this process.
> - ASEAN membership will create an advantageous posture for us to conduct relations with major powers as well as other countries outside the region.
> - ASEAN consists of countries enjoying high rates of economic growth; with a population of more than several hundred million people, ASEAN is an important market for us. At the same time, ASEAN countries have strong potentials and resources to act as economic partners and investors in Vietnam.
> - Within ten to fifteen years, ASEAN will become a Free Trade Area. By then, the tariff barriers among them will be very low or will no longer exist. The competitiveness of their products will therefore be quite high. If Vietnam is not a member of ASEAN, we will not be entitled to enjoy trade preferences offered by AFTA, nor have access to ASEAN markets. In addition, we will have to face more obstacles in our trade with them.
> - We also need to cooperate with ASEAN in the effective exploitation and consumption of natural resources and in seeking solution of common problems such as protecting the environment, tackling piracy, drug-trafficking, etc. We can also take advantage of ASEAN's scientific and technological achievements as well as their expertise in management and marketing, etc.

The Memo then concluded,

> Southeast Asia is a region which is directly related to us in political, economic, and security terms. Promoting relations with individual ASEAN member countries and ASEAN as an organization is in accordance with our foreign policy of diversification and multilateralization, which is designed to create favourable international and regional conditions for reforms, national construction and defense in the new context. *For the sake of our political, security, and economic interests, we should consider becoming an ASEAN member in the future.*[29]

On 1 November 1992, another MOFA Memo, similar in contents, was sent to the Politburo to serve as a background document for discussions at its meeting on 7 November. The Politburo adopted the suggestions made in the MOFA Memo. The transcript of the 7 November meeting stated,

> The Politburo in principle agrees with the MOFA assessments and suggestions that stress the necessity to vigorously implement our regional policy, to promote friendly and cooperative relations with ASEAN countries and to create favourable conditions for becoming an official ASEAN member when appropriate.

Yet, there were two questions that the Politburo raised and required MOFA to further clarify before it could make a final decision. They were:

> (1) is there any possibility for the creation of an alternative arrangement, such as the region of peace, stability, friendship, cooperation, and development in Southeast Asia? and (2) are there any points in the ASEAN documents which indicate that ASEAN is an anti-communist, anti-socialist, and anti-Vietnamese? We need to find out this in order to avoid future complications.[30]

These two questions reflected caution rather than reluctance on the part of the Politburo. Addressing these two questions, MOFA sent two additional Memos to the Politburo. The 16 January 1993 Memo said,

> ASEAN's basic documents, including the ASEAN Declaration of 8 August 1967, the Kuala Lumpur Declaration of 27 November 1971, the Declaration on ASEAN Concord of 24 February 1976, the Treaty of Amity and Cooperation in Southeast Asia (TAC), the Manila Declaration of 15 December 1987, and the Singapore Declaration of 28 January 1992 *do not contain any point that are openly or tacitly suggestive that*

the organization is anti-communist, anti-socialist, and anti-Vietnamese in nature. ASEAN is not aimed at opposing any other country. These documents only state general and broad principles that lay the basis for cooperation among the members. The guidelines, objectives, and principles that regulate ASEAN cooperation are in harmony with those of the Bandung Declaration, the five principles of peaceful coexistence, and are *in principle in accordance with the principles in our Party's and State's foreign policy.*[31]

The other Memo, dated 16 February stressed, "there have been opinions that we should explore the possibility for a new regional organization and invite ASEAN to join it. We are of the view that this is unfeasible and impractical in the present context. Further, this will cause a new round of confrontation, which is not beneficial to us at all."[32]

Although the explanations given in the Memos were less than adequate, it seems that these two MOFA memos did succeed in convincing the Politburo, which on 19 February 1993 stated, "We agree that if asked, one can answer that: "Vietnam is ready to join ASEAN at an appropriate time." It also instructed, "a limited number of ASEAN cooperative programmes and projects should be selected for Vietnam to participate in and prepare for the eventual membership in ASEAN."[33] While it can be seen that MOFA worked hard to convince the leadership about the necessity of close relations with ASEAN—even going so far as to deliberately gloss over the fact that the organization was indeed anti-communist but not anti-Vietnamese—it is also interesting to note that during these internal debates no ideological arguments were voiced. In the same vain, Deputy Foreign Minister Vu Khoan wrote, "ASEAN membership meets the needs of our country, i.e., to enjoy a peaceful, stable, and cooperative environment conducive to development."[34]

The cost-benefit approach can also be found in the way Hanoi assessed the situation after it had joined ASEAN. Both public and internal documents stressed the benefits that the membership had brought. A MOFA Review issued on the fifth anniversary of Vietnam's ASEAN membership stated,

> In fact, Vietnam joined ASEAN in order to construct an increasingly favourable environment for us to actively expand our international relations for the sake of regime survival and development. In the main, we can see the benefits gained as follows:

- Consolidation of the trend towards peace and cooperation in the region, thus creating favourable conditions for reforms, economic construction and national defence in Vietnam,
- Promotion of economic relations,
- Enhancement of our international standing and further promotion of our relations with non-ASEAN countries,
- Contribution to and creation of favourable conditions for the integration of the Vietnamese economy into the rest of the region and the world as well as participation in the wider arrangements of WTO and APEC,
- Learning developmental lessons, gaining access to modern technologies, readjustments of bureaucratic procedures to make them more compatible with the practices and standards adopted in the region and in the world.

Because of these benefits, the report concluded, *"the decision to join ASEAN was a timely and correct one."*[35]

In short, Vietnam's aims in joining ASEAN can be summarized as follows. In the first place, for Hanoi, to join ASEAN and to develop friendship and cooperation with its members, was instrumental in facilitating the implementation of the overall objective to "have more friends and fewer enemies", the task that was laid down in the Thirteenth CPV Politburo Resolution and subsequently in the foreign policy of "being a friend of all countries", adopted by the Seventh CPV National Congress in June 1991. Further, since ASEAN enjoyed friendly relations and cooperation with all the major powers including the US, Japan, the EU, and other countries, ASEAN membership would facilitate Hanoi's efforts to promote amicable and cooperative ties with these countries. As a direct result, by acceding to the TAC and joining ASEAN, Hanoi would be able to reduce defence spending, strengthen security on its western and southern borders, and focus on its defence efforts on other areas. This would also create a favourable environment for Vietnam to concentrate on economic construction. In addition, as the founding ASEAN countries were economically more developed than Vietnam, by joining intra-ASEAN cooperation, Vietnam would be able to benefit and to learn from ASEAN's experience in nation-building, which would help enhance its own strength. More importantly, as ASEAN cooperation was based on the free will of all its members, and all decisions were taken on a consensus basis, such an alignment and association would in no way negatively affect Vietnam's independence and sovereignty, but would help to strengthen it. Finally, this was the first time that Vietnam joined a non-ideological alliance, an act which in itself demonstrated the weakening of ideological considerations. Many hoped that the benefits of ASEAN membership would, in the years to come, strengthen the tendency to de-ideologize Hanoi's foreign policy design and conduct.

A NEW BASIS FOR SINO-VIETNAMESE RELATIONS AND THE IMPLICATIONS FOR VIETNAM-ASEAN COOPERATION

One of the major causes of the initial hesitation in Hanoi (as well as in some ASEAN capitals) regarding ASEAN membership was the possibility that Vietnam might enter an alliance-type relationship with China following the collapse of the Soviet bloc in the early 1990s. In a seminar attended by ASEAN and Vietnamese scholars held in August 1991 in Hanoi, several ASEAN delegates expressed their concern that "Vietnam might associate with China and become a satellite state in the Chinese sphere of influence."[36] This concern was not totally groundless, for around that time, Hanoi leaders held debates about new directions for the nation's foreign policy and even initiated efforts at building a new Sino-Vietnamese relationship on the basis of socialism.

It is noteworthy that Beijing itself was not responsive to these efforts. From 1980 to 1987 Hanoi made eighteen official and secret attempts to resume negotiations on normalization of Sino-Vietnamese relations, but Beijing was not receptive. Further, in March 1988, China forcefully occupied features in the Spratly under Vietnamese jurisdiction. Hanoi, however, continued its efforts at normalization. Following the 1986 CPV National Congress and the adoption of the Thirteenth Politburo Resolution in May 1988, Hanoi revised the Preamble of the 1986 Constitution, dropping the phrase describing China as the "most dangerous and direct enemy", and proposed a mutual cessation of hostile propaganda and a relaxation of tensions along the land borders. China, however, remained silent. After 1988, Hanoi's initial withdrawal of its troops from Cambodia and initiatives taken by Vietnam and ASEAN countries for a possible solution to the Cambodia problem influenced the Chinese decision to accept the proposal for talks put forward by Foreign Minister Nguyen Co Thach on 15 December 1988. This led to the first two rounds of talks held in Beijing in January and May 1989.

When Beijing was internationally isolated in the aftermath of the Tiananmen Square incident, Hanoi put forward new proposals for talks. Another two rounds of negotiations took place in Hanoi and Beijing in May and June 1990 respectively, but there were no concrete outcomes. On 18 July 1990, when the US Secretary of State James Baker stated that the US would resume talks with Hanoi on normalization of US-Vietnamese relations, Beijing suddenly proposed that a Sino-Vietnamese summit should be held in Chengdu on 3 September 1990. Reviewing the above-mentioned developments in Sino-Vietnamese relations, a MOFA report concluded that Beijing was reluctant to normalize Sino-Vietnamese relations because it attached little importance to Hanoi's proposals. The report went on,

> For the last ten years, although we have been persistently in initiating negotiations and taking specific actions to promote the normalization of bilateral relations, China has not been responsive. It only agreed to sit down for talks when it met with difficulties in relations with other actors. Besides, it always attaches price tags, which are too high for us to accept. [37]

And when Beijing finally agreed to normalize the Sino-Vietnamese relations, it refused to consider the communist ideology as a basis for bilateral ties. When Hanoi proposed that the two sides should build solidarity to oppose imperialism and defend socialism, Beijing flatly rejected the idea. During the Chengdu Summit, CCP General Secretary Jiang Zemin explained the Chinese position in the following terms,

> Western countries are paying great attention to our relations. That is why we have not let any country, including Cambodia, know that you, our Vietnamese comrades, have come here. We are very cautious about this. We also know what the Western countries think. Vietnam is a socialist country under the leadership of the Communist Party. So is China. The Western countries therefore may be suspicious of this Summit and our negotiations. That is why we keep the Summit a secret. In this present international situation, it would not be wise and beneficial for our two communist parties to shake hands and promote cooperation.[38]

Hanoi later understood that Beijing's overall position was consistent as the CCP also rejected similar appeals by other remaining communist states including Cuba and North Korea. Beijing had cut ties with communist parties in Southeast Asia, which was the main reason for the 1990 decision by the Malayan Communist Party (MCP) to dissolve itself and for the MCP General Secretary Chin Peng to surrender to the Malaysian authorities. During his visit to four ASEAN countries in December 1990, Chinese Prime Minister Li Peng stated that the CCP no longer had contacts with any Communist parties in ASEAN countries and that ideology would not influence the promotion of China-ASEAN relations. To Hanoi's disappointment, Beijing even informed Washington of the details of the Sino-Vietnamese Summit. On 5 October 1990, Secretary of State James Baker told his Vietnamese interlocutors that Beijing had informed Washington of its rejection of the proposal put forward by the highest Vietnamese leaders for Sino-Vietnamese solidarity to defend socialism against US schemes to destroy it."[39]

Baker also told Hanoi that he had been informed by Beijing of its rejection of Vietnam's proposal for a "red solution" to the Cambodia problem.[40] During the Summit, Vietnamese leaders had suggested that cooperation between the two communist forces in Cambodia, namely the Hun Sen and Pol Pot factions, would not only help to prevent the non-communist factions from sharing power in a possible political solution there but also lay the groundwork for a new coalition of the remaining communist countries at a time when the Soviet bloc was disintegrating. Beijing, however, did not welcome this idea, first, because it was reluctant to offend the West, with which China's relations had sunk to a nadir as a result of the Tiananmen Square incident; second, because such a policy would harm Beijing's preference for a greater role by King Sihanouk in Cambodia; and third, because investment would be deterred. Chinese Ambassador to Vietnam Zhang Dewei said in Hanoi, "The red solution is not realistic, because if we implement it, we will draw attacks from all directions, thus isolating ourselves. At present, China defends socialism within its borders and does not raise the socialist flag in foreign policy."[41] During the Chengdu Summit, Li Peng also said,

> You Vietnamese comrades say that the two Cambodian communist parties should cooperate with one another to become a stronger force. I both

agree and disagree. Among the four factions in Cambodia, the communists are stronger in terms of military strength and organizational structures. Therefore, they should enjoy better positions. Yet, the reason I disagree is that the Cambodian communists are not the only force involved in the search for a political solution. We have to take into account the Sihanouk and Son San factions. These forces are not big but they enjoy international support. If we ostracize them, the Supreme National Council will be isolated, thus Cambodia cannot have peace and reconciliation. We must let the other two forces play their role.[42]

The negotiations on normalization therefore indicated that Beijing was unwilling to meet Hanoi's hopes for the restoration of a Sino-Vietnamese alliance based on communist ideology even one under the Chinese leadership. By the end of 1990, Hanoi was even more aware of Beijing's position. A MOFA document stated, "China has been rhetorical about the defence of socialism. Yet, China has never stated that it will defend socialism at the international level. That means China is only defending Chinese socialism and hegemonism."[43] Due to Beijing's unwillingness to forge new alliances with socialist countries, during the official visit to China by Do Muoi and Vo Van Kiet in November 1991, which was regarded as a landmark in the normalization of Sino-Vietnamese relations, both sides agreed that their relations would "not be abnormal as they had been for the last ten years, but would also not resemble those of the 1950s and 1960s." The two sides also agreed that their relations "would be based on the five principles of peaceful coexistence and would not harm any third parties as well as the foreign relations of either country."[44] A Sino-Vietnamese alliance based on communist ideology was, therefore, out of the question. Reviewing developments in Sino-Vietnamese relations during this particular period, a senior Vietnamese diplomat told Carl Thayer that between 1990 and 1991, Hanoi spent a whole year trying "to forge new relations with Beijing" but ultimately failed as Beijing considered Hanoi "comrades, not allies".[45]

When Hanoi no longer had any illusions about an alliance with China on the basis of communist ideology, the impetus for better relations with ASEAN became stronger. In this connection, the Central Committee Plenum in June 1992 stated that Vietnam should develop relations with ASEAN countries by first acceding to the TAC and then expanding cooperation with the organization. Although it was an unintended consequence of Hanoi's failure to build closer relations with Beijing, the promotion of Vietnam-ASEAN relations proved that Hanoi finally had to abandon the tradition of determining foreign policy on ideological grounds. Peace and development, among other things, now became the principal objectives of post-Cold War Vietnamese foreign policy, a shift which helped eliminate many of the differences between Vietnam and ASEAN countries and made ASEAN membership more receptive to leaders in Hanoi.

Hanoi's changed attitude towards ASEAN had far-reaching implications at all levels. There was first of all a reassertion that Vietnam belonged to Southeast Asia. In the 1976 Four-Point Position, Hanoi had claimed that Vietnam was a Southeast Asian state.[46] But when Hanoi repeated this claim in the late 1990s the substance had changed: it attached a greater importance to geographical proximity in promoting relations with ASEAN countries. Citing the Bangkok Declaration, which stated that ASEAN was open for participation by all countries in the Southeast Asian region, scholars and officials in Hanoi insisted that Vietnam had met the first necessary condition for a future membership in ASEAN. Moreover, as discussions on the formation of ASEAN have shown, the definition of a specific geographical region and the resultant practice of including certain countries into, or excluding them from, specific regional arrangements and organizations, have been suggestive of highly politicized choices.[47] In other words, regions and regional organizations are the subjective construction of the states concerned. Therefore, when Vietnam invoked geographical circumstances to categorize the ASEAN members as "regional and neighbouring countries" and to justify the promotion of relations with them on these grounds, it became clear that Hanoi's commitment to the region had been qualitatively consolidated. The MOFA SEA/SPA Department Report of 1992 wrote, "Southeast Asia is the region of first importance to us due to geographical proximity and strategic economic, political, and security interests."[48] New efforts by Hanoi to improve relations with ASEAN countries, therefore, were based on a new understanding of geopolitics rather than ideology.

Academic studies also sought to reinforce the political trend. That Vietnam belonged to Southeast Asia soon became the principal theme of major research in the fields of archaeology, anthropology, and history.[49]

In the 20 November 1994 proposal on the establishment of the Vietnam Association for Southeast Asian Studies, Pham Duc Duong claimed, "Southeast Asia is a geographical reality, a historical and cultural area in which Vietnam has its roots and age-old relations with other regional countries."[50] In addition, a number major historical accounts were introduced to suggest that Ho Chi Minh, together with other leading regional figures, had shared the dream of constructing relations among Southeast Asian countries on the basis of commonalities in historical experiences in the anti-colonial struggle for national independence in the post-World War II era.[51] Kim Ninh thus observed, "Vietnam increasingly wishes to demonstrate its historical, cultural, ethnic, and religious connections with the rest of Southeast Asia."[52]

The series of MOFA memos on promoting Vietnam-ASEAN relations, therefore, should be also seen in the context of the impossibility of returning to a Sino-Vietnamese alliance based on communist ideology. But this new reality provided impetus for Hanoi to appreciate the merits of a foreign policy genuinely based on geopolitical and nationalist grounds and the enhanced awareness of Vietnam's Southeast Asian connections. The CPV CC Plenum held on 18 June 1992 in Hanoi settled the discussions on future foreign policy orientations by attaching primary importance to a region-oriented policy which had "geopolitical value" and served as "bridges" for improving relations with major powers of the world.[53]

REDUCED COMMITMENTS TO WORLD REVOLUTION

In both word and deed, Hanoi was no longer committed to the socialist bloc and to world revolution. Foreign Minister Nguyen Manh Cam said in an interview, "Vietnam will contribute to revolutionary movement throughout the world in ways and to an extent that will be determined in accordance with the specific conditions of Vietnam and international practices."[54] This, in fact, represented a denial of commitments to support world revolution. As one of the poorest countries in the world Vietnam was not in a position to provide material support for revolutions anywhere. Further, revolutionary movements could not develop in conditions regulated by normal international practices. Against this background, phrases such as "the two camps", "the three revolutionary waterfalls", or Vietnam as "the outpost of the socialist bloc in Southeast Asia", etc., were gradually removed from the political vocabulary in Hanoi. In their stead, such words as integration, internationalization, regionalization, an equitable international order, etc., began to appear more regularly in the texts of public and internal documents.

Nguyen Manh Cam's statement, in fact, reflected a new consensus reached among leaders in Hanoi during the Eighth Central Committee Plenary Conference on 27 March 1990. The Plenary Conference Resolution stated in part, "We will actively contribute to the common struggle for peace, national independence, democracy, and socialism based on our specific conditions and capabilities." And, "We are fully aware that the best and most practical way to contribute to the cause of world revolution is to successfully implement the reforms initiated by our Party with a view to making Vietnam more politically stable, economically developed, and strong in term of national defence and security." Hanoi, therefore, wanted to defend socialism within the national borders.[55]

Changes in Vietnam-Laos and Vietnam-Cambodia relations were also suggestive of the break from old commitments. The Thirteenth CPV Politburo Resolution said,

> We must recognize that the situations in Vietnam, Laos, and Cambodia have been transformed ... While the struggle for national independence was going on, Vietnam was the main pillar for Indochinese security and national defense. At present, all three countries are independent, sovereign, and equal states, their Parties must hold responsibility before their respective nations, while being attentive to their international obligations with regard to the other fraternal Indochinese countries. Vietnam can no longer be the main source of economic support for Laos and Cambodia. That Laos and Cambodia are expanding their relations with Western and ASEAN countries is a matter of objective reality. Whether Laos and Cambodia will go along the socialist or nationalist paths will depend on the decisions taken by the parties and peoples of these countries in accordance with actual conditions and the aspirations of the peoples in these two countries.

The Resolution then concluded,

> Relations between Vietnam and Laos and Cambodia must be placed in this new perspective. The Indochinese countries will maintain their

traditional solidarity and enhance the effectiveness of mutual cooperation while respecting each other's legitimate national interests. Yet, to continue doing things by the old methods will not be suitable to the changed reality and will not serve to strengthen the friendly relations between Vietnam and Laos and those with Cambodia.[56]

To implement the Resolution, in December 1987, the CPV Politburo issued Decisions No. 35 and 36 on the reform of relations with the Lao People's Revolutionary Party (LPRP) and the Cambodian People's Party (CPP), according to which the Directorate for Vietnamese Experts in Cambodia, the Board of Vietnamese Senior Experts attached to the LPRP, and the Directorate for Vietnamese Experts in Laos were dissolved. By the end of 1988, Vietnamese experts had been withdrawn from Laos and Cambodia. Relations between the CPV and the LPRP and CPP began to be conducted via direct links between the Politburos of the respective parties and interstate relations were conducted through diplomatic channels.[57] Vietnam now began to observe more strictly the principles of respect for national independence, sovereignty and non-interference into domestic affairs in its relations with Laos and Cambodia. After Laos and Cambodia acceded to the Bali Treaty, interstate relations among the Indochinese countries were regulated in accordance with the principles of this document. Laos and Cambodia now enjoyed the status of "regional and neighbouring states", the same way as other ASEAN countries. According to Thayer, while Vietnam still stressed that a special type of relationship among the Indochinese countries continued to exist, the general belief in Hanoi was that the accession of Laos, Cambodia, and Vietnam to ASEAN had, in effect, terminated the concept of the Indochinese grouping.[58] Although the rhetoric of a "special relationship" lingered, what Hanoi really wanted was that "Laos and Cambodia will remain independent from and friendly with Vietnam."[59]

IMPROVED VIETNAM-ASEAN RELATIONS AND IMPLICATIONS FOR HANOI'S RELATIONS WITH MAJOR POWERS

Having recognized the impact of improved Vietnam-ASEAN ties on its relations with major powers, Hanoi became more willing to associate itself with the organization. To put it in a different way, Hanoi now understood that the earlier Vietnam became associated with ASEAN, the more beneficial its new ASEAN membership would prove to be in relations between Vietnam and the major world powers. The first MOFA Memo, dated July 1992 argued that ASEAN membership "will create an advantageous posture for us to conduct relations with major powers as well as countries outside the region."[60]

A. US-Vietnamese Relations

The linkages between ASEAN membership and improved US-Vietnamese relations have been documented. For example, the Government Report covering the first half of 1994 concluded that Hanoi's "foreign policy achievements" were one of the important factors behind Washington's 3 February announcement that it would halt its fifteen-year economic embargo against Vietnam.[61] A Memo prepared by the MOFA North America Department gave the following account of US-Vietnamese relations following the lifting of the economic embargo.

> The relationship is developing towards normalization. The US has been supportive of our ASEAN membership, as seen in the statement by Secretary of State Warren Christopher on 23 February. In addition to this, during the visit by the presidential representatives from 1 to 4 July 1994, Washington for the first time discussed in an open way broad issues related to regional situations. Washington holds that the two countries have great potentials for economic and security cooperation and asserts that one of the US foreign policy objectives is to build US-Vietnamese relations in accordance with US strategy and interests in the Asia-Pacific region in the post-Cold War era.[62]

On 11 July 1995 Washington normalized diplomatic relations with Vietnam, shortly before the ceremony to admit Vietnam into ASEAN, which took place in Brunei on 28 July 1995.[63] It was obvious that besides the internal dynamics of the bilateral relationship, improvements in Vietnam-ASEAN ties also contributed to the normalization of US-Vietnam relations.

B. Sino-Vietnamese Relations

Vietnam's ASEAN membership served to stabilize Sino-Vietnamese relations. During his visit to China, on 19 May 1995 Foreign Minister

Nguyen Manh Cam reported to Hanoi the opinion of his Chinese counterpart Qian Qichen, who said: "We know that Vietnam will soon join ASEAN. I do believe that after Vietnam joins ASEAN, peace and stability in Southeast Asia will be further promoted. China is pleased with the present development in Sino-Vietnamese relations. And with Vietnam's membership in ASEAN, our relations will be further developed."[64] In November 1995, during the visit by the CCP General Secretary Jiang Zemin to Hanoi, a joint declaration was released, which among other things, stated that:

> The two sides will promote relations in many fields. At the same time disputes between the two countries, including territorial ones, will be settled in accordance with the guiding principle that takes into consideration the broader bilateral relationship, mutual respect and sympathy, friendly consultations, international law and practices. The two sides pledge that existing disputes between the two countries should not harm the normalized bilateral relations.[65]

In February 1999 Hanoi and Beijing agreed on a formula for promoting the bilateral relationship according to which Sino-Vietnam relations would be based on "friendly neighbourliness, all-sided cooperation, long-term stability, and future-orientedness". A MOFA official thus commented, "Developments of Hanoi's multilateral relations, i.e., Vietnam's membership in ASEAN, paved the way for developments in its bilateral, i.e., Sino-Vietnamese, relations."[66]

C. Japan-Vietnamese Relations

Japan-Vietnam relations were perhaps most closely affected by improvements in Vietnam-ASEAN ties. The Ministry of Public Security provided its assessment on the ASEAN tour by Japanese Prime Minister in January 1993,

> According to our sources, Japan welcomes the rapprochement between Vietnam and ASEAN countries. Japan proposes to convene a Forum on the Comprehensive Development of Indochina for broad discussions on the socio-economic situation, economic reforms, developmental needs in agricultural, energy, transportation and communications, social and cultural sectors, and the role to be played by the international community in meeting these needs.[67]

Other ministries, including MOFA also agreed with this assessment. In 1994, an IIR study concluded that ASEAN played an important role in Japan-Vietnam relations. According to the study, for economic, political, and security reasons, Tokyo had wanted to develop relations with Hanoi in the early 1970s. Yet, the deterioration in Vietnam-ASEAN relations, among other things, had prevented the relationship from developing. Therefore, when "Vietnam began the course of reform, improving relations with ASEAN countries and normalizing relations with the US, there was no reason for Japan not to develop all-sided relations with Vietnam and promote them on a par with, and possibly at a higher level than those between Japan and ASEAN countries.[68] In April 1995, Do Muoi officially visited Japan and came firmly to the conclusion that Vietnam's ASEAN membership had greatly contributed to the improvement of Japan-Vietnam relations in the economic, political, and security fields. Foreign Minister Nguyen Manh Cam and CERC Director Hong Ha, who were accompanying Do Muoi, jointly sent a cable from Tokyo, saying,

> All the persons that the General Secretary has met, from the Emperor to Cabinet members, representatives of political parties, mass organizations and business communities, have expressed their respect to and enthusiasm towards Vietnam. They want to promote an all-sided, friendly, and stable relationship with Vietnam. They are eager and ready to expand bilateral relations. This visit has shown that our international standing is on the rise.[69]

It was, therefore, no accident that the normalization of US-Vietnam relations, the signing of the Framework Agreement on EU-Vietnam cooperation, and the admission of Vietnam to ASEAN took place in July 1995. Improved international standing was the main theme of many important documents during that time. For example, the MOFA report on the Twenty-Eighth AMM, which was held in Brunei from 28 July to 3 August 1995, wrote, "When attending the AMM for the first time in the capacity of a full-fledged ASEAN member, we found that more opportunities had been opened up for us to expand relations with other countries, thus enhancing the international and regional standing of Vietnam."[70] The report also stressed that during the meeting with Nguyen Manh Cam, his American counterpart stated that Washington would begin talks on a trade agreement with Hanoi to promote economic relations.[71]

In short, the ASEAN member status has helped Hanoi to improve its "standing vis-à-vis and relations with major powers."[72] Five years after joining ASEAN, the MOFA ASEAN Department gave the following evaluation, "the membership created more conditions for us to enhance our international standing, further improve our relations with non-ASEAN countries."[73] Ambassador Le Van Bang expressed a similar view in his 29 March 1999 cable from Washington, DC:

> Our foreign policy and its implementation have shown their correctness and effectiveness. We should improve relations with all states. And when major powers, especially the US and China are trying to win ASEAN to their side, we should sufficiently invest in the enhancement of our standing in ASEAN in order to consolidate our posture vis-à-vis the US and China, thus further improving relations with these countries.[74]

The MOFA ASEAN Department Review completed five years after Vietnam joined ASEAN considered membership a "breakthrough", a "spearhead", and a "strategic solution" for the country to break away from international isolation and encirclement.[75] In other words, had Vietnam not improved first ties with ASEAN and then joined the organization, relations with major powers could not have developed as they actually did.

CHINA FACTOR IN VIETNAM'S DECISION TO JOIN ASEAN

With an international solution to the Cambodian problem in hand, Hanoi was able to normalize relations with China in 1991. Yet, in spite of repeated professions of friendship from the Hanoi leadership, most Vietnamese, while positively responding to China's traditional concern about the safety of its southern borders, consider they have solid reasons to regard China as Vietnam's traditional and most dangerous enemy, citing the repeated wars launched by almost all Chinese feudal dynasties against Vietnam, China's seizure of the Paracels and its perceived intention to occupy the Spratly, the border war against Vietnam in 1979, the refusal to build bilateral relations on ideological grounds, and above all, China's continued policy to treat Vietnam as its satellite. Therefore, it is widely argued that while promoting friendly relations with China, Vietnam must remain vigilant and endeavour to enhance its own strength in all respects. It was frequently argued, during these years, that if Vietnam became an ASEAN member, China would be dealing not with Vietnam alone, but with the combined forces of ASEAN.[76] It is, therefore, logical to surmise that Hanoi did have China in mind while promoting its relations of friendship and cooperation with ASEAN, which may give weight to the general thesis about the "China threat" in the aftermath of the Cold War.[77]

China as the Perceived Threat

Between 1979 and 1986, China was viewed unequivocally as the main threat to Vietnam.[78] Subsequently, however, the perception of China as a threat was increasingly nuanced. The 1981 Constitution had declared that China was the "direct and dangerous" enemy of Vietnam. Yet at the same time, considering that it had won the 1979 border war with China and observing that China was now busy with the Four Modernizations Programme, Hanoi judged that although tensions on Sino-Vietnamese borders remained, a second border war with China was unlikely. That is to say, the Vietnamese leadership thought that the military threat from China had been minimized and that condition of relative peace already existed. A document entitled "On the Situation in Southeast Asia and Guidelines for Our Diplomatic Struggle" in October 1981 said,

> China is large, but it is not strong. Internally, it is not stable; externally, it has contradictions with most of the countries in the world, especially in Asia and Southeast Asia. Therefore, China's scope of actions, especially in the military field, will be limited in nature and will take place only in very specific conditions.[79]

The MOFA Annual Report of 1981 wrote, "The possibility that China would teach a second lesson is increasingly limited."[80] When signs of a Sino-Soviet rapprochement appeared in 1982, MOFA claimed, "Relatively peaceful and stable conditions in Southeast Asia already exist."[81] From 1980, in fact, partly due to improvements in Sino-Soviet relations, Hanoi had made efforts to mend the fence with China. According to a MOFA document, between 1980 and 1987, Hanoi made eighteen attempts to resume talks on normalization of relations with Beijing.[82] In October 1988, Hanoi sent a message of congratulations on the Thirty-Ninth National Day of the PRC, officially recognizing that the PRC was still a socialist country. In December 1988, it removed the phrase of "dangerous and direct enemy" from the Constitution. Following the secret Sino-Vietnamese Summit meeting held in Chengdu in September 1990, relations between Vietnam and China were normalized in 1991, as mentioned above.

In a broader context, after 1986, the perception of China as a threat changed further due to the easing of global tensions, especially among the great powers, and also because of the radical changes in Vietnam's overall perception about threats and security. The Thirteenth Politburo Resolution in May 1988 identified "economic backwardness and political isolation" as "the biggest threat to Vietnam's security and independence". During the Mid-term CPV National Congress in January 1994, the Vietnamese leadership introduced a list of four threats that included poverty and lagging behind other states in economic terms, corruption and inefficient bureaucracy, peaceful evolution (i.e., non-military efforts at destroying the legitimacy of the communist regime in Vietnam), and the complicated external environment. The threat perception—put in the contexts of the post-Cold War era and the ongoing reforms in Vietnam—had thus changed: they seemed to reflect Hanoi's concerns over regime survival, rather than survival of the state.[83] Moreover, in the Third Central Committee Resolution in 1992, China, Laos, Kampuchea and the ASEAN states were for the first time put in the same category of close neighbours with whom friendship must be cultivated.[84] Therefore, at the time when Hanoi began to contemplate joining ASEAN, China had ceased to be a threat in the conventional sense. In this regard, the need to rely on ASEAN to balance China was not the main reason for Hanoi's desire to improve relations with ASEAN. This interpretation is given greater plausibility because of the fact that Beijing was not against Vietnam's membership of ASEAN. Commenting on the ASEAN decision to admit Vietnam made at the Twenty-Seventh ASEAN AMM, Chinese Foreign Minister Qian Qichen told his Vietnamese counterpart in Bangkok, "China welcomes Vietnam's membership in ASEAN because this will contribute to peace and stability in the region."[85]

While Beijing may have had some reservations about Vietnam's ASEAN membership, possibly viewing it as an attempted balancing act on the part of Vietnam, Hanoi had by now realized that efforts to forge ASEAN into some sort of counterweight to China had serious limitations. Quite simply, ASEAN countries did not want to confront China. Following the normalization of relations between Indonesia and China in 1990, all ASEAN countries started to improve their relations with Beijing in many fields. Further, China became increasingly important for ASEAN countries. As the Vietnamese Ambassador to Singapore Nguyen Manh Hung wrote in 1994, "Recent statements by Lee Kuan Yew and other high-ranking officials have shown that China is becoming more important to Singapore economically, politically, and strategically."[86] As a result, ASEAN did not want to let tensions in Sino-Vietnamese relations to negatively affect ASEAN-China relations. In 1994, attending the Twenty-Seventh AMM as an observer and learning that Vietnam would be able to join ASEAN in the following year, Foreign Minister Nguyen Manh Cam also observed,

> While accelerating the process of admitting Vietnam into ASEAN, the organization also upgraded its relations with China, granting the later consultative partner status and establishing the ASEAN-China joint cooperative commission. Related to the East Sea (South China) problems, ASEAN tried to avoid confrontation with China and dismissed the impression that ASEAN was critical of China.[87]

In addition, Hanoi became increasingly aware that ASEAN was not a military organization. A MOFA Memo submitted to the Politburo on 1 November 1992 stated: "Military cooperation between ASEAN countries is of a bilateral nature; among ASEAN countries, there are no mechanisms for multilateral military cooperation."[88] Deputy Foreign Minister Vu Khoan, who led a fact-finding mission to visit ASEAN member countries and the ASEAN Secretariat from 3 to 14 October 1994 in order to "study in depth the ASEAN modes of cooperation, cooperative mechanisms within ASEAN, and possibilities for Vietnam to take part in ASEAN cooperation," wrote,

> First and foremost, ASEAN is not a military organization. Officials in all the countries that the delegation visited stressed the political and economic nature of ASEAN cooperation, and confirmed that ASEAN did not have collective military cooperation. *ASEAN is not a military organization* and *has never intervened into disputes that involved member states*; security cooperation in ASEAN is bilateral and trilateral only.[89]

The new understanding helped leaders in Hanoi to realize that there was no chance for Vietnam to develop military cooperation with ASEAN or to rely on military cooperation within the ASEAN frameworks to strengthen its posture with regard to any third party. One member of the mission told the author that the ASEAN emphasis on the non-military nature of ASEAN cooperation seemed intended to convey to Hanoi the message that ASEAN did not expect Vietnam to seek military support from the organization. The same official also commented that if Hanoi had previously misunderstood ASEAN, considering that the organization was an alliance of the collective-defence type, it had to pay dearly for this misperception. There was no way Hanoi could turn ASEAN into a military bloc to defend Vietnam. The decision to join ASEAN, therefore, was not based on the hope that ASEAN could strengthen Vietnam's posture in a military sense.[90] Further, even if ASEAN might agree on building united armed forces of its own, which was highly unlikely, the organization's military synergy could not match China's capability. The Vietnamese Ambassador to the Philippines Vu Quang Diem wrote in a cable sent to Hanoi: "Even if all the Southeast Asia countries could stand together, their forces could not compete with those of China. Moreover, at the present and in the future, there is no such desire by the Southeast Asian countries to stand together, due to their different interests."[91]

It is clear, therefore, that Hanoi's decision to join ASEAN was not based on the wish to take advantage of membership to balance against China.

ASEAN AND THE US AS HELPERS: THE SOUTH CHINA SEA DISPUTES CONNECTION

Against the background of improved Sino-Vietnamese political and economic ties following normalization of relations, solutions to territorial disputes were negotiated. In 2000, the two countries signed an Agreement of Land Borders. The two sides were also engaged in negotiations on the demarcation of maritime boundaries and fishing in the Tonkin Gulf. Yet, disputes about jurisdiction over the Paracels and Spratly islands remained unsolved. Both Hanoi and Beijing showed no signs of compromise on these thorny issues. In 1974, China seized entirety of the Paracels from the Saigon regime. In 1988, China troops seized seven features in the Spratly under Vietnam's jurisdiction. Subsequently, developments related to the Spratly became one of the most salient problems in the Sino-Vietnam relationship. Other ASEAN countries including Malaysia, the Philippines and Brunei are also claimants over parts of the Spratly. After Vietnam joined ASEAN, it became likely that ASEAN countries would strictly follow the principle of solving disputes among themselves through peaceful means. It therefore seemed that the dispute over the Spratly would become the one between China and ASEAN.

However, if Hanoi believed that it could take advantage of its ASEAN membership to consolidate its position vis-à-vis China on the Spratly issue, and that the ASEAN member states would rally their forces to collectively cope with Chinese expansionism, its hopes would be proved unfounded.

A. Sino-Vietnamese Military Clashes, 1988

In mid-March 1988, China sent warships to the Spratly. Following a brief but fierce naval conflict at the Johnson South Reef that claimed sixty-four Vietnamese lives, China seized three of the features from Vietnam. By mid-April, China had occupied seven features, and for the first time set its foot on the Spratly.

On 17 March 1988, Hanoi sent diplomatic notes to ASEAN countries and asked its ambassadors posted in the region to assess reactions of the ASEAN member states to the incident and garner their support for Vietnam. Hanoi soon found out that although ASEAN countries were concerned over the new Chinese move, they in general remained aloof, wishing to distance themselves from the Sino-Vietnamese dispute and refraining from openly supporting Hanoi and criticizing Beijing. On 18 March, Director General of the Malaysian ASEAN Department told the Vietnamese Ambassador Tran Le Duc, "We sympathize and agree with Vietnam's position. We closely follow the developments and hold that Vietnam's proposal to solve the dispute through negotiations is in accordance with our position."[92] On 17 March, the Philippines State Department issues a statement expressing the country's concerns over the Sino-Vietnamese conflict. However, as Hanoi concluded, as a matter of self-interest, Manila did not want to worsen its ties with Beijing. According to a report by the Asia-3 Department,

> Being one of the claimants and currently occupying eight features, the Philippines is concerned over the clashes and therefore agrees with the measures [of peaceful solutions] that we have proposed. But in general, the Philippines is very much afraid of China. And in particular, as preparations for the coming visit to China by President Aquino are underway, Manila cannot openly voice its support to us.[93]

Indonesia also remained silent for a host of reasons. According to a report, "although Indonesia dislikes China, it shows no support to us. If Jakarta supports us, it will be in trouble with Malaysia and the Philippines, the two ASEAN claimants over the Spratly. In addition to this, Jakarta's relations with Beijing will be affected. Last but not least, Indonesia may be busier with its domestic politics." As a result, the report concluded, Indonesia "turned a deaf ear to the incident and showed no public statement in order not to displease any party concerned."[94]

Nor was Thailand supportive of Vietnam. On 21 March, Ambassador Le Mai met the Thai Foreign Ministry's Director General in charge of Political Affairs to inform the latter of Hanoi's 17 March diplomatic note. The Thai interlocutor said: "We wish that there would be some solution to this matter. But we find it difficult to voice our opinion, because apart from China and Vietnam, there are other claimants over the Islands."[95] Hanoi then came to believe that Thailand wanted to take advantage of the Sino-Vietnamese clashes because Vietnam would have to face more pressures and subsequently would have to solve the Kampuchean problem in a way that benefited Thailand.[96]

Singapore also kept silent over the incident. According to Hanoi, it was because Singapore "has no relationship with the Islands. In addition, this is a sensitive and complicated issue on which Singapore finds difficult to publicly voice its opinion. Therefore, Singapore remained silent and adopted a wait-and-see approach, thus avoiding getting involved and displeasing any party concerned."[97]

In short, during the 1988 Sino-Vietnamese conflict in the Spratly, ASEAN countries, including the claimants over Spratly themselves, did not openly criticize Beijing and support Hanoi. The failure of ASEAN countries to form a united front and back up the principle of peaceful solution to the disputes, their unwillingness to complicate relations with China, together with tensions between Vietnam and ASEAN due to the existing Kampuchea problem, and the non-intervention attitude by Moscow during the incident had all helped China to achieve its goal of setting its foot on the Spratly.

B. Crestone and Tu Chinh (Vanguard Bank), 1992

On 22 July 1992 after acceding to the Bali Treaty and becoming an ASEAN observer, Vietnam and the ASEAN countries signed the ASEAN Declaration on the South China Sea, which called on the parties concerned to exercise restraint and resolve all sovereignty and jurisdictional issues pertaining to the sea by peaceful means; to explore the possibility of cooperation there on safety of maritime navigation and communication, etc.; to apply the principles of the Bali Treaty as the basis for establishing a code of international conduct of the South China Sea; and to subscribe to the Declaration.

Hanoi welcomed this Declaration. In term of timing, the Declaration followed China's February 1992 passage of a Law on Territorial Sea and Contiguous Zone in asserting its sovereignty over offshore islands and thus over the Tu Chinh (Vanguard Bank) and the May 1992 agreement between China's National Offshore Oil Corporation and the Crestone Energy Corporation under which the latter was allowed to explore for oil in the Vanguard Bank, the area within Vietnam's exclusive economic zone and continental shelf. In addition, the Chinese government even promised to provide military protection for Crestone's exploration activities in the disputed area.[98] Policy planners in Hanoi therefore considered that the Declaration represented a positive joint effort by ASEAN to stop China from using force to further occupy the Islands. One MOFA document even surmised that the ASEAN decision to grant Vietnam and Laos observer status in July 1992 might have been influenced by the need for more regional cooperation. But "the immediate impulse", according to the document, "was the Chinese actions in the South China Sea".[99] Hanoi also believed that because ASEAN had succeeded in forging such a collective position, Beijing would feel obliged to show its support to the Declaration.[100] If this were the case, Hanoi might not now find itself standing alone to face Chinese pressure as it had done in 1988. The benefits of joining ASEAN would thus be vindicated.

However, there have also been different explanations of the ASEAN Declaration. Some researchers have argued that when the ASEAN countries stated that they attached importance to the principle of peaceful solution to territorial disputes over the Spratly, they in fact were merely urging Hanoi not to use force to back its claims with regard to Malaysia and the Philippines. A MOFA report stressed that Hanoi was not one of the authors of the Declaration and that ASEAN was anxious to know if Hanoi accepted it.[101] One researcher even argued that the accession to the Bali Treaty and the Declaration had ushered in a new and difficult period in Vietnam's foreign relations, in which Hanoi had to learn to live according to the ASEAN Way, that is to stop thinking of using force and start learning to rely on negotiations to solve the disputes it had with the ASEAN states.[102] Therefore, ASEAN's stress on peaceful solutions to disputes was believed to have put constraints on Hanoi's future actions in the Islands. More importantly, the ASEAN 1992 Declaration on South China Sea did not lay any strong groundwork for concerted action by ASEAN to cope with China. ASEAN, instead, adopted a non-confrontational approach towards China and the parties concerned showed their preference to begin talks with Beijing to seek solutions on a bilateral basis. As one observer concluded, although Hanoi had shared with ASEAN countries "mutual interests in countering Chinese advances in the South China Sea", the ASEAN "non-provocative stance towards China" was a positive factor for Hanoi in improving relations with Beijing.[103] In addition, the Chinese actions in the South China Sea in 1992 did not have any direct link with Hanoi's accession to the Bali Treaty, as already in June 1991 Hanoi had decided to accede to the Treaty with the final goal being to join ASEAN. Chinese actions, however, might have provided greater impetus for the arguments in Hanoi in favour of ASEAN membership, as in June 1992, the CPV Third Plenum for the first time mentioned, Vietnam's membership in ASEAN and MOFA in July the same year began to produce a series of Memos arguing for ASEAN membership, although the consensus in Hanoi at that time was that this would not be immediately realized.

C. Crestone and Tu Chinh, 1994

The incident involved the late April 1994 oil exploration project by Benton (previously Crestone) in the Tu Chinh area. Hanoi was successful in preventing the project from being conducted. Yet, in retaliation, Beijing sent warships to the bloc access to a rig in the area, where drilling activities by a Vietsopetro (a joint venture between Vietnam and Russia) were taking place.[104]

By that time, Vietnam's membership in ASEAN had become a matter of simple procedures. As mentioned above, in April 1994, Vietnamese President Le Duc Anh announced that Vietnam was making preparations to join ASEAN at an early date. But although Hanoi had tried to enlist ASEAN support over the incident, its efforts were to no avail. A cable by Vietnamese Ambassador in Beijing Dang Nghiem Hoanh stated,

> Following the Ministry's instructions, on 26 April, I went to see the Malaysian Ambassador who had just returned to Beijing from Kuala Lumpur. The Ambassador told me the following: "(i) Malaysia is very much concerned because this affects not only Sino-Vietnamese relations, but the region as well. (ii) But Malaysia supports negotiated solutions, which should require great patience because there is no other alternative."[105]

Dang Nghiem Hoanh also met the Indonesian Ambassador in Beijing, who said: "The situation involving Tu Chinh is very sensitive. The two sides should find common points to start negotiations. Indonesia supports the prevention of conflicts in the South China Sea and the promotion of regional cooperation."[106] The reactions by other ASEAN countries were similar. Vietnamese Ambassador to the Philippines Vu Quang Diem sent a cable from Manila, saying: "On 3 May, Filipino Deputy Foreign Minister Severino told me, "We [the Philippines] are concerned over the latest dispute, but hope that Vietnam and China could solve it in an amicable way. Only after this, could all the parties concerned proceed to the negotiations on a multilateral basis to solve the problem."[107] On 18 May 1994, Ambassador Dang Nghiem Hoanh cabled Hanoi the contents of the talks in Beijing between Malaysian Prime Minister Mahathir and his Chinese counterpart Li Peng

> The Malaysian Ambassador in Beijing informed me about the talks, stressing that Mahathir and Li Peng had agreed that the two sides had a common need for the improvement of friendship and cooperation. As far as the Spratly are concerned, Mahathir "expressed his entire support for the Chinese position to peacefully solve the disputes, showed his

opposition to the internationalization of the disputes, and stressed that parties concerned should first and foremost make efforts through conducting bilateral negotiations and improving bilateral relations to find solutions to the disputes."

When Dang Nghiem Hoanh asked whether the two Prime Ministers discussed the Chinese proposal to "shelve the disputes and promote joint exploitation" the Malaysian Ambassador replied: "Mr Mahathir did not mention this proposal. But in principle, Malaysia thinks that this proposal can be discussed."[108]

Cables sent from Kuala Lumpur also helped Hanoi to better understand ASEAN's position. For example, on May 28 Vietnamese Ambassador Ngo Tat To met the Director of the Southeast Asian Affairs Department of the Malaysia Foreign Ministry to find out Malaysia's position towards the dispute. Reporting his meeting to the MOFA, he said,

Because Malaysia is afraid of China, the country's policies are, (i) to consider China as a friend, not an enemy, because if China is approached otherwise, a self-fulfilling prophecy will be materialized; (ii) with regard to the South China Sea, Malaysia supports negotiated settlements and joint exploitation. Malaysia referred to the Thai-Malaysian agreement to shelve disputes over sovereignty and promote joint exploration and exploitation as an "exemplary" one that others should follow.[109]

In short, individual ASEAN countries did not support Hanoi. And by suggesting bilateral solutions, they also implied that ASEAN countries would not forge a collective position to support Vietnam on this matter.

Hanoi, however, continued its efforts to obtain ASEAN's support. On 20 May 1994, Vietnamese Foreign Minister Nguyen Manh Cam sent a letter to his ASEAN counterparts to explain Vietnam's position and explore whether ASEAN could support it. The MOFA records showed that it took a month for the ASEAN countries to reply to this letter. Moreover, the replies revealed that ASEAN countries did not take sides in the dispute. The Malaysian Foreign Minister's letter dated 21 June wrote:

Disputes involving questions of sovereignty and jurisdiction are sensitive and complex. I would like to assure your Excellency that Malaysia remains firmly committed to the settlement of all disputes peacefully, through negotiations. Malaysia notes that all parties involved in the territorial disputes in the South China Sea have expressed similar commitments. I would also like you to know that Malaysia, in cooperation with all parties concerned, will work to promote adherence to this principle. Indeed, all parties have a particular responsibility to ensure that peace and stability of the area remain undisturbed.[110]

The reply by Brunei's Foreign Minister was similar. It said,

> Brunei Darussalam is guided by the principles contained in the ASEAN Declaration on the South China Sea of 1992 which emphasize the need to resolve all sovereignty and jurisdictional issues by peaceful means without resort to force. We are of the view that all parties should refrain from undertaking any activity in the disputed areas as it may complicate matters further.[111]

The Singaporean Foreign Minister officially replied: "It is important for all countries which are parties to the disputes or have an interest in the South China Sea to exercise restraint and to work constructively to seek the peaceful resolution of the disputes."[112] Finally, the letter dated 29 June 1994 by Filipino Foreign Minister wrote: "The Philippine government puts an emphasis on the necessity to resolve all sovereignty and jurisdictional issues pertaining to the South China Sea be peaceful means and urges all member nations concerned to exercise restraint with the view to creating a positive climate for the eventual solution of all disputes."[113]

From the timing of these replies and their similar contents, it is possible to surmise that the ASEAN countries consulted among themselves before reaching a consensus to stay away from the Sino-Vietnamese dispute. ASEAN—as an organization—did not want to get involved in the dispute between China and Vietnam over the islands; as a result, Hanoi found it very difficult to take advantage of better relations with ASEAN to improve its position vis-à-vis China with regard to territorial disputes. ASEAN even failed to mention the Sino-Vietnamese dispute over Tu Chinh. The Vietnamese Ambassador to Thailand Le Cong Phung reported the outcomes of the ARF SOM on 25 and 26 May: "Although there were discussions about Chinese actions in the South China Sea in general and Tu Chinh in particular, SOM reached a consensus not to include the South China Sea item in the ARF agenda although countries might raise the issue on an individual basis."[114]

Hanoi also lobbied ASEAN to support Vietnam in international fora. In a memo to Vietnamese Prime Minister Vo Van Kiet, MOFA suggested he raise the following points when he met the Malaysian counterpart in late May in Kuala Lumpur:

> (i) Vietnam proposes that Malaysia, as one of the claimants, should use its very important international role and prestige to support Vietnam in the disputes with China over the Spratly Islands; (ii) Vietnam also hopes that the Malaysian and Vietnamese delegations to the Eleventh NAM Foreign Ministers' Meeting in Cairo from 31 May to 3 June 1994 could cooperate with each other in order to introduce the issue of the Spratly Islands into the final declaration of the meeting in a manner to benefit Vietnam.[115]

Records of the Eleventh NAM Foreign Ministers Meeting, however, suggested that this lobbying effort gained very limited success. Foreign Minister Nguyen Manh Cam sent a cable to the CPV Politburo outlining the result of the meeting: "This is the first time that the ten Southeast Asian countries could agree on the text of the NAM Ministerial meeting's Final Communiqué."[116] The Final Communiqué, however, only mentioned in brief positive developments towards peace and stability in Southeast Asia and failed to address the region's territorial disputes, including the Spratly. It seemed that Hanoi was not happy with that outcome, which was evidenced in *Nhan Dan's* coverage of the meeting. On 30 May, the newspaper carried a short piece of news, stating that Foreign Minister Nguyen Manh Cam would head the Vietnamese delegation to the meeting. That was the only time the newspaper mentioned the meeting. In the issues that followed, no commentary and reportage of the meeting could be detected.

There is little evidence, therefore, to suggest a connection between Vietnam's membership in ASEAN and regional solidarity against China in the territorial disputes over the South China Sea. Moreover, the timing was suggestive of the Chinese strategy: Crestone showed that Beijing could take initiative to create tension with Hanoi at the very time the latter was about to join ASEAN. While foreign observers might still believe that the Crestone incident would force Vietnam to further rely on ASEAN,[117] Hanoi was already aware of the lukewarm attitude of ASEAN countries and had few expectations about obtaining the organization's support. In the memo for the delegation to attend the Twenty-Seventh ASEAN AMM and the First ARF Meeting in Bangkok, MOFA proposed that

> Issues related to the East Sea (the Vietnamese expression for the South China Sea), which are extremely important to us and attract international public opinion, will not be put on the agenda, because of the strong Chinese lobby in many of the parties concerned. ASEAN countries, having taken their bilateral relations with China into consideration, have suggested that the South China Sea not be put for discussion. Against that background, our approach should be like this: in the plenary sessions, we will not take initiative to raise this particular issue. In other sessions, we may raise it, but in a constructive and non-confrontational manner.[118]

In a report after the ASEAN AMM and ARF Meeting, MOFA said, "On several occasions, issues related to the South China Sea were raised. Yet, all the countries tried to address them indirectly and make the impressions that they did not criticize China by name."[119] A report covering the third quarter of 1994 by the Southeast Asian and South Pacific Affairs Department said: "on the one hand, ASEAN countries agreed to accept Vietnam's full membership in 1995 and reiterated the principles spelled out in the ASEAN Declaration on South China Sea. Yet, on the other hand, there have been signs that some countries including Malaysia and the Philippines wanted to avoid confrontation and seek bilateral agreements with China."[120] In short, by this time, Hanoi might have been aware that for a host of reasons ASEAN was not eager to side with Hanoi in the dispute with China and that the ASEAN claimants of the Spratly preferred to deal with China on a bilateral basis.

D. Mischief Reef, 1995

In February 1995, the Philippines discovered that China had occupied Mischief Reef, a structure in the Philippines' jurisdiction, and had started to construct durable facilities there. The Philippines released a strong statement against China and, before long, tensions mounted in the relationship between Manila and Beijing.[121] This was the first time Beijing entered into a territorial dispute with a member state of ASEAN, of which Vietnam was due to be a member in five months' time. Therefore, Hanoi was curious to observe how Manila and ASEAN would react to the Chinese action.

Although belatedly, ASEAN showed collective support for the Philippines. Nguyen Trung Thanh, Deputy Director of the MOFA ASEAN Department cabled from Jakarta, informing what he had been told about the contents and the mood of the ASEAN-China Senior Officials Meeting (SOM) in Hangzhou in April 1995. He wrote,

> ASEAN Secretary General Ajit Singh, who has just returned from the meeting, informed me as follows:
>
> - China made it clear in the unofficial meeting held from 9:30 p.m. to 11:00 p.m. the previous evening, that it did not support the inclusion of the South China Sea in the meeting's agenda. ASEAN, however, asked to have a session on the South China Sea.
> - ASEAN stressed that there were in fact disputes over sovereignty in South China Sea and asked that China should show a certain level of transparency about its policy on this issue, especially about the base line according to which China's jurisdiction in the South China Sea was defined. The Chinese Foreign Minister, however, refused to do so.
> - ASEAN made it clear that ASEAN was not against the ideas of joint exploitation and development in the South China Sea. Yet, this should be implemented within the ASEAN-China frameworks, and not on any bilateral basis.
> - ASEAN proposed that China utilize the ASEAN-China SOM frameworks for continued discussions on the South China Sea.[122]

Nguyen Trung Thanh also highlighted comments by Singh: "This is the first time since the 1992 Manila Declaration that ASEAN has undertaken *a concerted action* vis-à-vis China on the South China Sea. This has succeeded in forcing China to recognize that its actions in the area caused real concerns for ASEAN."[123]

However, before the Hangzhou meeting, Hanoi had learned that tensions between Manila and Beijing had been reduced, mainly due to bilateral efforts, and partly because of ASEAN's failure to provide Manila with strong support. On 25 February, Ambassador Vu Quang Diem sent a cable to MOFA, which read in part:

> "the Philippines is in a weak position because it gets very little regional and international support. As a result, although unwillingly, Manila has had to enter into negotiations with Beijing and will be pushed around

because of its weak position. Manila is alone in this fight, and there is a real danger that Manila will be obliged to compromise, especially when Beijing offers joint exploration and exploitation."

In the same cable, he informed Hanoi, "The Philippines has agreed to enter bilateral talks with China in March 1995 in Bangkok."[124] Therefore, in light of these developments, MOFA officials thought that while ASEAN would appreciate Vietnam's membership of the organization, Hanoi would not be able to take advantage of ASEAN to improve its position in any future disputes with China because the ASEAN support for the Philippines—already an ASEAN member state—was inconsiderable. The Vietnamese Ambassador to the US Le Van Bang believed that Chinese actions in Mischief "might force ASEAN countries to quickly admit Vietnam as a full-fledged member". Yet, on the other hand, he asserted, "China warns us that even when Vietnam has joined ASEAN, China could attack Vietnam because Mischief has shown that ASEAN cannot deter China from attacking the Philippines."[125]

By the year-end, Hanoi had become more aware that the Philippines preferred to solve disputes with China bilaterally. When Vietnamese President Le Duc Anh visited the Philippines in December 1995 to explore, among other things, the possibility of the two sides joining hands to improve their stance vis-à-vis China in South China Sea, Manila made clear that only bilateralism would work. According to a MOFA report about the visit, the Philippines informed the President, "The Philippines has reached an eight-point agreement with China with regard to the islands. In addition, a joint legal team and a mechanism for regular bilateral consultations between the Philippines and China were set up. As a result, the situation in South China Sea has improved." Manila then suggested, "Vietnam should do likewise", and according to the report, "Manila showed its willingness to serve as a bridge between Hanoi and Beijing."[126]

MOFA officials, therefore, were not eager to advocate a policy based on the belief that ASEAN would come to Hanoi's support in its disputes with China over the islands. They sought instead to design a policy that would have elements of accommodation with Beijing. Vu Quang Diem, for example, wrote: "We should not have illusions about China. Yet, we should not be hostile towards China. We should have a proper policy and a flexible strategy which could allow us to enjoy friendship with China and at the same time protect our independence and sovereignty."¹²⁷ They also suggest that Hanoi should take advantage of improved Sino-Vietnamese relations to hold bilateral talks with Beijing to ease tensions related to, and hopefully to solve territorial disputes. Ambassador to Beijing Dang Nghiem Hoanh suggested:

> When China continues to diversify its foreign relations and seems to adopt a policy that favours negotiated settlements to disputes, we should seize the opportunity to make important decisions so that by the year 2000 we will have designed a policy that would on the one hand further improve our relations with China and limit uncertainties in the Sino-Vietnamese relationship, thus ensuring stable conditions for industrialization and modernization as well as protection of our territorial integrity.¹²⁸

In the similar vein, in the talking points prepared for the national leaders, MOFA suggest the following lines: "After Vietnam has joined ASEAN, we will continue to expand friendly and cooperative relations with other countries. Vietnam's membership in ASEAN serves peace, cooperation, friendship, and development in South East Asia and does not aim to oppose any third party."¹²⁹ In July 1994, when the CPV Politburo held a meeting to make the final decision to join ASEAN, the highest leaders in Hanoi agreed, "Our purpose in joining ASEAN is not to side with one party to oppose another. We will not harm any third party." The Politburo also instructed, according to the transcripts of the meeting,

> As we join ASEAN, we should improve relations with other countries, especially the neighbouring countries; we should accelerate the implementation of the cooperative projects that we have signed with China; and we should openly and directly inform China about our decision to join ASEAN so that they understand our position with regard to our membership in ASEAN.¹³⁰

To reiterate, Hanoi did not think of rallying forces to balance China when it was considering membership in ASEAN.

THE AMERICAN CONNECTION

Some observers may have wondered whether Hanoi would use its membership of ASEAN to improve relations with the US, for the purpose of constructing indirect deterrence against Beijing. A 1992 report by the MOFA American Affairs Department seemed to provide evidence of this calculation. After stressing the predominant role of the US in the Asia-Pacific region in the aftermath of the Cold War and concluding that the "containment elements" had become more visible than the "engagement elements" in US China policy, the report stated: "to serve its interest in Southeast Asia, the US wants to maintain peace and stability in Southeast Asia as well as improve the region's economic and political postures with a view to preventing any single superpower from dominating the region. Therefore, the US wants to accelerate the integration of the Indochinese countries into Southeast Asia and check Chinese expansion in the region, encourage improvements in the Vietnam-ASEAN relations and improve its own relations with Vietnam, Laos and Kampuchea."[131] The report then suggested:

> Against this background, we have strategic interests in normalizing relations with the US. In the growing complicity of the situation due to China's violation of our territorial integrity and expansionism in the East Sea, diversification of our foreign relations and normalization of relations between Vietnam and the US have become more urgent in order to rally force to check the Chinese expansionist schemes. Maintaining peace and stability and checking Chinese expansionism in Southeast Asia have become a matter of common interest between the US and Vietnam. The US therefore supports Vietnam to join ASEAN and integrate itself into the regional and international communities.[132]

Ambassador to the US Le Van Bang also said, "We should 'make friends' with all the superpowers, including the US and China, and welcome the US to contribute to peace, stability, and development in the region."[133] Le Van Bang even supported the exchange of military attachés as well as an increase in "military and security relations" between Hanoi and Washington following normalization of relations.[134]

Yet, Hanoi soon realized that a policy of seeking to rely on the US to help check China might not be feasible for a variety of reasons. In the first place, Washington attached a greater importance to improvements of Sino-US relations. A MOFA report on the November 1994 Seattle meeting between Clinton and Jiang Zemin in the framework of the APEC Summit (the first Sino-US Summit held after the Tiananmen Square incident) noted that both China and the US were readjusting their strategies and reducing tensions in the bilateral relationship. The US, according to the report, had encouraged Beijing to engage in the multilateral frameworks in the Asia-Pacific, which would serve as a means to accelerate China's reforms and integration into the rest of the world, thus raising the costs of Chinese actions that would destabilize the region.[135] The report also took note of the fact that during the meeting, Clinton and Jiang did not mention developments related to South China Sea and Vietnam and stated that, "President Clinton told the Press following the APEC Summit that the US wanted Vietnam to integrate itself into the region after solving to the fullest extent the MIA issues." The implication was, according to the MOFA report, that the Spratly disputes "do not play an important role in the dynamics of the US-Vietnamese relations".[136] In other words, Hanoi had become more aware that US was unwilling to become involved in the territorial disputes in the South China Sea. Specifically with regard to the Spratly, Hanoi observed, "The US tried to avoid taking sides with the claimants and only urged the parties concerned to refrain from using force."[137] In a broader context, the US did not want to confront China. According to a MOFA report, the Sino-US relations had been further stabilized after the Cold War. Washington's China policy combined both containment and engagement elements, while the debates on the China threat continued in the US. China, for its part, wished to further cooperate with the US to obtain greater access to the US market, technologies, and funds. As a result, despite ups and downs, both sides tried to avoid direct confrontation.[138] On 26 April 1994, during the Crestone incident, Ambassador Dang Nghiem Hoanh sent a cable from Beijing quoting the American Ambassador there as telling him, "Crestone is a private company and the US Government does not control it," and the Malaysian Ambassador as remarking, "I do not think that the was a Sino-US policy coordination in the South China Sea. Yet, the US will do nothing unless Sino-US relations worsen."[139]

The US position towards Mischief Reef also helped Hanoi understand that if Washington did not intend to take sides in the Sino-Philippines dispute, there would be even less hope for Hanoi to get US support. When Mischief occurred, the US adopted a neutral position even though it still honored the security treaty with the Philippines after Manila had terminated the lease of bases to the US. Ambassador Le Van Bang sent a cable from Washington, informing Hanoi, "On 10 February, the US Embassy in Manila made a statement that the US-Philippines security treaty did not include the Spratly; the US did not want to create tensions in the relationship with China; it did not want to take sides in the disputes over the Spratly in general and over Mischief in particular."[140] Ambassador Vu Quang Diem also cabled from Manila, "According to a confidential document of the JICPAC, which kept the Philippines informed of the situation in South China Sea, the US has made it clear that if Washington takes part in any discussions about the situation in the South China Sea, this does not imply that Washington supports any country in the territorial disputes there."[141]

Contacts with American officials confirmed even more strongly Hanoi's belief that it could not hope to rely on the US in any disputes with China. In August 1995, after a meeting with Stanley Roth, director of the Asian Affairs Bureau in the National Security Council, the Vietnamese Ambassador to the UN Ngo Quang Xuan informed Hanoi,

> Mr Roth reiterated the US neutral position on the Spratly disputes and said that the parties concerned should not waste more time in seeking opportunities for negotiated settlements. With regard to Vietnam, he asserted that the idea to use Hanoi to counterbalance Beijing is shortsighted, and Senator McCain's proposal to normalize relations with Vietnam on the basis that Hanoi could help the US cope with China by military means is an overstatement.[142]

Therefore, in light of the Sino-American relationship and Washington's unwillingness to take sides in territorial disputes in Southeast Asia,[143] Vietnam did not seriously consider the possibility of association with the US to check the Chinese expansion in the South China Sea, although some in Hanoi seemed to favour better relations with Washington in the military and security fields.

Hanoi's unwillingness to enter close relations with Washington was also influenced by other factors. First and foremost, the legacies of the Vietnam War created obstacles to forging a consensus in Hanoi's policy towards the US. The 1992 report by the American Affairs Department acknowledged, "At present, there are different views in Vietnam about the

US. Therefore, the improvement of Vietnam-US relations is facing many difficulties and obstacles." The report then suggested,

> It is urgent that we should build a consensus among different offices and organizations, at both national and provincial levels, on the ways we view the US, so that we can recognize and take advantage of the commonalities between Vietnam and the US to improve this bilateral relationship.[144]

To state in other words, by this time Hanoi was ready to join ASEAN but was not equally eager to forge a close relationship with the US.

Hanoi was also on its guard about "Washington's short- and long-term schemes [to oppose Vietnam]," according to the same report, which said among other things,

> The US still advocates the policy of peaceful evolution towards Vietnam and encourages Vietnam to adopt a market economy and conduct political reforms to create a multi-party system, which will benefit the US in the long run. In the foreseeable future, following normalization of relations, the US will resort to human right issues as well as use economic relations and technological transfer as policy tools, thus causing difficulties for us, although it will be less likely to use force and support its lackeys to conduct subversive activities in Vietnam.[145]

Human rights would be an especially thorny issue in the bilateral relationship because many in Hanoi thought that "human rights will be one of the main points in the post-Cold War political and ideological struggle," with the US using human rights as a pretext to "interfere in Vietnam's domestic politics."[146] Therefore, lingering suspicions about US intentions towards Vietnam also prevented Hanoi from bettering relations with Washington. As a result, while ideologists still considered the US as "an enemy", pragmatists, who recognized "strategic interests" in Vietnam-US relations, failed to forcefully argue for continued improvement of ties and to propose specific formulas for bilateral security cooperation to consolidate these perceived strategic interests. The official compromise position, therefore, was: "in the Vietnam-US relations, we should be flexible in order to maintain and enhance the relationship that has now been normalized; at the same time, we should be resolute in the struggle [with the US] to protect our security, our interests, and national sovereignty, as well as oppose the US scheme to promote long-term peaceful evolution."[147]

Overall events in 1994 and 1995 in the South China Sea and the normalization of US-Vietnamese relations in 1995 seemed not to greatly influence Hanoi to change its reserved approach to the US. For example, commenting on the prospects for Vietnam's relations with Washington, one standard policy announcement in 1997 wrote,

> Vietnam is ready to develop cooperative relations with the US in many aspects, especially in the economic, trade, and scientific and technological fields, in accordance with interests of the peoples of the two countries as well as in harmony with peace, cooperation and development in Southeast Asia. We will consider security and military relations provided they remain within the contexts of two countries enjoying normal diplomatic ties.[148]

Hanoi, therefore, did not envisage that the US would play an important role in the search for possible solutions to disputes in South China Sea. This was evidenced in a policy announcement on impacts of the normalization of US-Vietnamese relations on the South China Sea problem that said in part: "We will not permit the US-Vietnamese relationship to harm the interests of any third party. On issues related to the Spratly, our consistent policy is to patiently solve the disputes through peaceful means and through negotiations with the parties concerned and in accordance with international law and the 1982 UN Convention on the Law of the Sea."[149] When asked by the author if this wording might in any way tacitly justify Hanoi's acceptance of a future role by the US in the solutions to territorial disputes in South China Sea, a senior diplomat said,

> The US is not a claimant to the Islands, therefore will not play any role in the negotiations on sovereignty in the area. Besides, the principle of peaceful solutions to the disputes excludes the possibility of a US military intervention. Lastly, the protection of freedom of navigation through the area will require the involvement of other actors, including the EU and Japan. Therefore, at best, the US will play a political role in a multilateral mechanism for the South China Sea, if such a mechanism is established at all."[150]

CONCLUSION

The evidence that Vietnam and ASEAN formulated policies to balance China is weak. In fact, it is clear that Hanoi did not want to use its membership of ASEAN to rally a coalition of forces against China. ASEAN countries had no inclination to participate in any such coalition. Similarly, there has been little evidence to show that the US wanted to take advantage of its improved relations with Hanoi to balance Beijing. Evidence for an anti-Chinese association between ASEAN and the US is even weaker. As ASEAN countries and China seemed to prefer bilateral approaches to solving the disputes in the South China Sea, efforts at establishing multilateral mechanisms to at least stabilize the situation in the area met with many difficulties. Facts on the ground suggest that Hanoi's membership of ASEAN and its improved relations with the US were not aimed at balancing China and checking its territorial ambitions in the area. ASEAN was not instrumental for Vietnam in traditional terms of security.

Hanoi's approach was, basically, a classical realist one. The Vietnamese leadership in the post-Cold War era, was shifting to a foreign policy free from ideological considerations and designed to serve national economic and security interests, the overall objective being to have more friends and fewer enemies, to build a strong country, and to enjoy greater freedom to cope with future uncertainties while reducing military spending. Any thought of balancing in the decision to join ASEAN was far more subtle than neo-realists might imagine.

In addition, the actual achievements along the realist cost-benefit approach to Vietnam's membership of ASEAN can be overstated. In the first place, many projected benefits from ASEAN membership had been gained through the process of improving relations with individual ASEAN countries since the late 1980s and the early 1990s. Hanoi's withdrawal of troops from Cambodia in 1989, the UN-sponsored political solution to the Cambodia problem in 1991, and the accession of Vietnam and Laos to the Bali Treaty in the same year had removed the obstacles to the improvements of Vietnam-ASEAN relations. In fact, relations between Vietnam and individual ASEAN members, especially Thailand, had been normalized and were developing in every field. In addition, from 1991, the year the Soviet Union collapsed, to 1995, the year Vietnam joined ASEAN, Hanoi had managed to seek new resources from ASEAN and other countries to replace Soviet aid, trade and investments, and was thus able to live comfortably without the Soviet Union. Therefore, even in the absence of ASEAN membership, by 1995, Vietnam-ASEAN relations had been greatly improved and Hanoi was no longer isolated. In November 1994, Deputy Foreign Minister Vu Khoan wrote, "With the October 1991 Paris Agreement on the overall political solution to the Cambodia problem, the key obstacles to Vietnam-ASEAN relations over the last ten years was removed. Relations between Vietnam and ASEAN members could thus rapidly develop bilaterally and multilaterally."[151] In other words, membership in ASEAN did not radically change the dynamics of Vietnam-ASEAN cooperation.

Second, the actual benefits of ASEAN membership were less than might have been expected. In relative economic terms, in 1994, both trade with and investments from ASEAN countries reached 30 per cent of Vietnam's total foreign trade and FDI and remained at this level thereafter.[152] The percentage of trade, however, subsequently tended to shrink. In 2003, for example, trade with ASEAN countries accounted for some 20 per cent of Vietnam's total trade.[153] The next chapter will show in detail the economic difficulties that accompanied ASEAN membership. The trade deficit is a case in point: in absolute terms, the volume of Vietnam-ASEAN trade increased. But the growth of trade from US$2.583 billion in 1994 to US$3,490 billion and US$4.152 billion in 1995 and 1996 respectively, according to a MOFA source,[154] was accompanied by huge trade deficits. Besides, the AFTA scheme had created more challenges for Vietnam's economy. Hanoi believed in fact, that the ASEAN membership had brought about "new difficulties and challenges in the course of economic development".[155] Even in traditional security terms, as this chapter has shown, ASEAN could not, and would not, serve the purpose of balancing China. At the same time, even before 1995, improved Vietnam-ASEAN relations had eliminated ASEAN itself as a security concern for Hanoi.

Third, some in Hanoi had argued that Vietnam's membership of ASEAN would make it easier to solve disputes, especially those related to territorial issues, between Vietnam and some ASEAN states.[156] ASEAN was well known, however, for its ability to shelve disputes among member states rather than to solve them. At the time Vietnam was considering membership most intra-ASEAN disputes remained unsolved. From the early 1990s, Hanoi started negotiations with Thailand, Malaysia and

Indonesia on overlapping sea zones, but with varying results. For example, Vietnam and Thailand reached an agreement on the overlapping sea zone in the Gulf of Thailand in 1994 but it was not until June 2003 that it was able to reach a similar agreement with Indonesia. According to the MOFA Borders Committee, "many things remained to be done" with regard to the demarcation of sea borders between Vietnam and Thailand, Malaysia, and Indonesia.[157] Negotiations on border demarcation between Vietnam and Cambodia faced many obstacles even after both countries had joined ASEAN.[158] Therefore, the impact of ASEAN membership on the solution of territorial disputes was limited.

Finally, some people in Hanoi were still concerned about differences in political and social systems between ASEAN and Vietnam. This gave rise to the fear of "peaceful evolution," which, it was thought, entry into ASEAN might help promote in the context of the collapse of the Soviet bloc.

Therefore, in terms of cost-benefit, some in Hanoi thought that continued observer status would be more beneficial and that there was no pressing need to hastily join ASEAN. Taking into account this view, the MOFA Memos stressed that the process of joining ASEAN would be long and complicated due to the differences in levels of economic development and socio-political systems. For example, the 8 July 1992 Memo of MOFA said, "Because of differences in the socio-political systems, disparities in economic development, and incompatibility in mechanisms between Vietnam and ASEAN countries, we cannot become an ASEAN member at an early date." The memo suggested the following steps:

- Step One: signing the Bali Treaty and becoming an ASEAN observer
- Step Two: taking part in a limited number of Cooperative Committees and Projects in order to take advantage of ASEAN technologies, knowledge, and experiences, thus preparing for full membership in the future. We should, however, try to avoid the political strings attached to membership
- Step Three: becoming a full-fledged ASEAN member. This will be a long process. At present, both Vietnam and ASEAN are not ready. Prior to ASEAN membership, we should promote bilateral relations with individual ASEAN members and multilateral relations with ASEAN

in order to study the ASEAN mechanisms; and we should also create conditions in Vietnam for ASEAN membership in the future.[159]

Therefore, while considering that Vietnam's full membership of ASEAN would be eventfully achieved, high-ranking policymakers in Hanoi initially thought it would take a long time. But in the end, it took three years for Vietnam to join ASEAN. The next chapters will provide further research on factors that had influenced Hanoi's decision on the ASEAN membership.

Notes

1. Nguyen Manh Cam, "On the Implementation of the New Foreign Policy", *Communist Review*, August 1992, p. 12.
2. MOFA ASEAN Department Report, "On Vietnam-ASEAN Relations" (Về quan hệ Việt nam–ASEAN), prepared for the Twentieth Diplomatic Conference, November 1995, p. 2.
3. SEA/SPA Department Report on Vietnam-ASEAN relations in 1992 (Báo cáo của Vụ Đông nam Á và Nam Thái bình dương về quan hệ Việt nam–ASEAN trong năm 1992), p. 15.
4. MOFA ASEAN Department November 1995 Report, "On Vietnam-ASEAN Relations", p. 3.
5. The Memo on Vietnam's Membership of ASEAN, prepared by the CERC dated 15 September 1993. The Memo (p. 5) also revealed that during the meeting, there was a suggestion that in official policy statements, Hanoi should use the phrase "all-sided cooperation" with regard to cooperation with ASEAN countries. The majority opinion, however, held that this phrase was less appropriate than the phrase "multifaceted cooperation", which was actually used.
6. For the text of the New 4-Point Policy, see *People's Army*, 17 October 1993; see also MOFA ASEAN Department Study, *5 Years after Vietnam Joined ASEAN: Achievements, Challenges, and Prospects* (Năm năm sau khi Việt Nam gia nhập ASEAN: Thành tựu, Thách thức, và Triển vọng), October 2001, p. 41.
7. MOFA ASEAN Department November 1995 Report, "On Vietnam-ASEAN Relations", p. 3.
8. Ibid., pp. 5 and 11.
9. Transcripts of the Politburo Meeting on the question of Vietnam's membership of ASEAN, (8:00–10:30 a.m., 22 July 1994) coded 229/BBK/BCT.

10. Nguyen Manh Cam's 23 July 1994 cable from Bangkok stated in part, "The Politburo's instruction has been implemented in full."
11. MOFA SEA/SPA Department Annual Report "On the Situation in Southeast Asia and Our Foreign Policy with Regard to the Region in 1994" (Về tình hình Đông nam Á và chính sách đối ngoại của chúng ta đối với khu vực trong năm 1994), p. 7.
12. Text of the Thirteenth Politburo Resolution, May 1988, p. 17.
13. Ibid., pp. 3–4.
14. Ibid., p. 4. Ogawasara and others have suggested that Hanoi's new perception of security is closer to the concepts of "comprehensive security" and "mutual security" adopted by many other countries in East and Southeast Asia. See Ogasawara Takauki, "Vietnam's Security Policy in the Post-Cambodia Period: Diplomatic Dimension", in *Asia-Pacific and Vietnam-Japan Relations*, edited by Dao Huy Ngoc and Matsunaga Nobuo (Hanoi: Institute for International Relations, 1994), pp. 107–8. See also Nguyen Vu Tung, "Vietnam's New Concept of Security", in *Comprehensive Security in Asia: Views from Asia and the West on a Changing Security Environment*, edited by Kurt Radtke and Raymond Feddema (Boston: Brill, 2000), pp. 409–10.
15. Text of the Thirteenth Politburo Resolution, May 1988, p. 4.
16. Vietnam's participation in the international division of labour has been discussed in Hanoi since the early 1980s. High-ranking officials including Nguyen Co Thach and Phan Van Khai argued in favour of increased economic interdependence on the global scale and a new type of labor division outside the socialist bloc. See Gareth Porter, "The Transformation of Vietnam's Worldview: From Two Camps to Interdependence", *Contemporary Southeast Asia* 19, no. 1 (June 1997): 1–19. A new foreign policy slogan calling for "economic diplomacy" emerged, highlighting the importance of economic and diplomatic means, rather than military, in the search for security and development.
17. Nguyen Vu Tung, "Vietnam's New Concept of Security", pp. 409–10.
18. Michael C. William, *Vietnam at the Crossroad* (London: The Royal Institute of International Affairs, 1992), p. 60.
19. Text of the Thirteenth Politburo Resolution, pp. 11–12.
20. MOFA Policy Planning Department, "On Vietnam's Foreign Policy after 1986" (Về chính sách đối ngoại của Việt nam sau năm 1986), p. 11.
21. Even scholars in Hanoi could not agree among themselves on the question of ASEAN membership. The IIR study, *ASEAN: Establishment, Development, and Prospects* (December 1990) concluded (p. 18b), "In case Vietnam wishes to become an ASEAN member, the joining process will be a relatively long

one, for it involves the concept of a 'security alliance'. ASEAN members are debating among themselves about Vietnam's membership. Therefore, there may be two possibilities: (i) early joining ASEAN, and (ii) joining a broader forum or organization in Southeast Asia, participating in some specific ASEAN cooperative projects, and then ultimately joining ASEAN."

22. MOFA ASEAN Department November 1995 Report "On Vietnam-ASEAN Relations", p. 2.
23. Nguyen Manh Cam, "On the Implementation of the New Foreign Policy", *Communist Review*, August 1992, p. 12.
24. Ibid., p. 12.
25. Ibid.
26. Ibid.
27. SEA/SPA Department, Transcripts of the Interview by Prime Minister Vo Van Kiet given to the *Bangkok Post*, 18 October 1991.
28. The CPV Central Committee Document, coded 153-CV/VPTW, dated 25 February 1992.
29. The MOFA Memo of 8 July 1992 submitted to the Politburo, pp. 1 and 3–4. Emphasis as in the original.
30. Transcripts of the Politburo Meeting on 7 November 1992.
31. MOFA Additional Memo dated 16 January 1993 entitled "On Relations between Vietnam and ASEAN" (Về quan hệ giữa Việt nam và ASEAN), p. 2. Emphasis as in the original.
32. MOFA Additional Memo dated 16 February 1993 entitled "On Relations between Vietnam and ASEAN", p. 2.
33. Transcripts of the Politburo Meeting on 19 February 1993.
34. Vu Khoan, "Vietnam and ASEAN", *Communist Review*, November 1994, p. 31.
35. MOFA ASEAN Department Report, "On Vietnam-ASEAN Relations", prepared for the 22nd Diplomatic Conference, November 1999, pp. 10–11. Emphasis as in the original.
36. Pham Nguyen Long (The Institute for Southeast Asian Studies), Proposal for a ministerial-level study on "Regional Integration in Southeast Asia", 1993, p. 14.
37. MOFA 21 December 1990 Report, "On Some Strategic and Tactical Issues in Our Struggle for a Solution to the Cambodia Problem and Improvement of International Relations" (Về một số vấn đề chiến lược và chiến thuật trong cuộc đấu tranh vì một giải pháp cho vấn đề Campuchia và đẩy cải thiện quan hệ quốc tế), p. 15.
38. Ibid., p. 17.

39. Ibid., pp. 16–17.
40. Ibid., p. 17.
41. MOFA 21 December 1990 Report, "On Some Strategic and Tactical Issues in Our Struggle for a Solution to the Cambodia Problem and Improvement of International Relations", p. 16.
42. Ibid., p. 16.
43. Ibid., p. 18. Former Deputy Foreign Minister Tran Quang Co's Memoir also gives a fuller account of Sino-Vietnamese negotiations during this period.
44. Interview by Foreign Minister Nguyen Manh Cam to *Greater Solidarity* (*Đại đoàn kết*) newspaper, December 1991.
45. Luu Doan Huynh's Personal Note. See also Carlyle A. Thayer, "Comrade Plus Brother: The New Sino-Vietnamese Relations", *Pacific Review* 5, no. 4 (September 1992): 402–6.
46. Nguyen Duy Trinh, *Taking Advantages of Favorable International Conditions and Contributing to the Construction of Socialism and Fulfillment of International Obligations* (Hanoi: Truth Publishing House, 1978), p. 40.
47. Benedict Anderson, *Imagined Community: Reflections on the Origin and Spread of Nationalism* (London: Vecto, 1991); Donald G. McCloud, *System and Process in Southeast Asia: The Evolution of a Region* (Boulder, CO: Westview Press, 1986); Milton Osborne, *Southeast Asia: An Illustrated Introductory History* (Boston: Allen & Unwin, 1985; Donald K. Emmerson, "Southeast Asia: What's in a Name?", *Journal of Southeast Asian Studies* XV, no. 1 (March 1984); Tim Huxley, "Southeast Asia in the Study of International Relations", *Pacific Review* 9, no. 2 (1996); D.G.E. Hall, *History of South East Asia*, 4th ed. (New York: Red Globe Press, 1981).
48. SEA/SPA Department Annual Report of 1992 (Báo cáo tổng kết năm 1992), p. 1.
49. Ha Van Tan, *Ethnological Roots of the Ancient Viet Race* (Hanoi: Truth Publishing House, 1992); Le Van Lan and Pham Van Kinh, *Cultural Exchanges with Southeast Asia: Vietnam and the Region* (Hanoi: National Politics Publishing House, 1986); Cao Xuan Pho, *Cultural Similarity: Vietnam and Other Countries in South East Asia* (Hanoi: National Politics Publishing House, 1990). Kim Ninh also observed that since early 1990s, the Institute for Southeast Asian Studies has been conducting a series of research projects and publications on these themes. Kim Ninh, "Vietnam: Struggle and Cooperation", p. 734, fn. 9. Luu Doan Huynh suggested to the author that since the early 1960s, there were intellectual debates in Hanoi on the original roots of the Vietnamese nation. Some researchers then had presented

their arguments, based on archeological, cultural, and historical evidence, to show that Vietnam was a part of Southeast Asia.
50. The 20 November 1994 proposal for the establishment of Vietnam Association for Southeast Asian Studies, p. 1.
51. The National Center Social Sciences and Humanities, The State-Level Research Program (coded KX.02) on Ho Chi Minh Thoughts and the Branch-Study on Ho Chi Minh Thoughts about Regional Solidarity and Cooperation in Southeast Asia (coded KX. 02.09), Hanoi, 1994. MOFA, *President Ho Chi Minh and Foreign Relations* (Hanoi: National Politics Publishing House, 1994). See also Zakaria Haji Ahmad, "Question for Greater Communality in Southeast Asia: A Political and Security Perspective", Paper presented at the Third International Symposium on Interaction for Progress: ASEAN-Vietnam All-Round Cooperation, Manila, 4–9 December 1993, p. 1.
52. Kim Ninh, "Vietnam: Struggle and Cooperation", p. 454.
53. Nguyen Manh Cam, "On the Implementation of the New Foreign Policy", *Communist Review*, August 1992, p. 3.
54. Nguyen Manh Cam, *Foreign Affairs Weekly*, October 1991, p. 2.
55. MOFA Policy Planning Department, "On Our Foreign Relations after 1986", p. 11.
56. Text of the Resolution, pp. 9–10.
57. MOFA Policy Planning Department, "On Our Foreign Relations after 1986", p. 9.
58. See Carl Thayer's lecture on reforms in Vietnam at the Australian National University, 12 October 1994.
59. The Thirteenth Politburo Resolution, p. 10.
60. MOFA 8 July 1992 Memo, pp. 1 and 3–4.
61. The Government Report covering the first half of 1994 submitted to the Fifth Session of the IXth National Assembly, p. 6.
62. MOFA North America Department Report on "US-Vietnamese Relations after the US Lifting of the Economic Embargo against Vietnam on 3 February 1994" (Về quan hệ Mỹ – Việt sau khi Mỹ dỡ bỏ cấm vận kinh tế chống Việt nam), to prepare for the Nguyen Manh Cam–Warren Christopher meeting in Bangkok.
63. Exchanges between Carlyle Thayer and IIR scholars in Hanoi, 10 July 1995.
64. 19 May 1995 cable by Foreign Minister Nguyen Manh Cam from Beijing.
65. Text of the Sino-Vietnamese Joint Declaration in November 1995.
66. Bui Thanh Son, "50 Years of Sino-Vietnamese Relations", *The IIR Proceedings*

of the Seminar on 50 Years of Sino-Vietnamese Relations (Hanoi, January 2000), p. 20.
67. 4 February 1993 Report by Minister of Internal Affairs Le Minh Huong submitted to the CPV Central Committee Secretariat and the Government.
68. The IIR Study, *Vietnam-Japan Relations: Past, Present, and Prospects* (Hanoi April 1994) p. 83.
69. Hong Ha and Nguyen Manh Cam, cable sent on 20 April 1995 to the CPV Politburo, Advisors, Government, MOFA and CERC leaders.
70. MOFA Report "On the 28th AMM, 28 July–3 August 1995", p. 11.
71. Ibid., p. 9.
72. The Government Report "On the World Situation and Vietnam's Foreign Policy in 1996" (Báo cáo về tình hình thế giới và chính sách đối ngoại của Việt nam năm 1996), submitted to the National Assembly November 1996 Session, p. 12.
73. MOFA ASEAN Department November 1999 Report "On Vietnam-ASEAN Relations", pp. 10–11.
74. Le Van Bang 29 March 1999 cable from Washington, DC.
75. MOFA ASEAN Department Study, *5 Years after Vietnam Joined ASEAN: Achievements, Challenges, and Prospects,* October 2001, p. 43.
76. Hoang Anh Tuan, "Vietnam's Membership in ASEAN: Economic, Political, and Security Implications", *Contemporary Southeast Asia* 16, no. 3 (December 1994). Others share similar view. For example, Johnston writes that Canadian diplomats have noted that privately PRC Ministry of Foreign Affairs specialists in regional security have acknowledged that the existence of the ASEAN Regional Forum (ARF) and other multilateral relationships with states in the region have reduced the probability that China could use force to resolve its claims. Johnson's interview with Canadian diplomats involved in regional security dialogues, October 1998, in Alastair Iain Johnston, "Is China a Status Quo Power?", *International Security* 27, no. 4 (Spring 2003), p. 28, fn 48.
77. Richard Betts and Thomas Christensen, "China: Getting the Question Right", *National Interests*, no. 62 (Winter 2000/2001), pp. 17–29.
78. This section was adapted from the chapter entitled "Vietnam's Decision to Join ASEAN: The South China Sea Disputes Connection", co-authored with Dang Cam Tu, in *Vietnam's Foreign Policy under Doi Moi*, edited by Le Hong Hiep and Anton Tsvetov (Singapore: ISEAS – Yusof Ishak Institute, 2018), pp. 186–207. Reproduced with permission.
79. MOFA 31 October 1981 Report, "On the Situation in Southeast Asia and the Guidelines for Our Diplomatic Offensives", p. 4.

80. MOFA Annual Report of 1981, "On the World Situation and Our Foreign Policy", p. 16. MOFA Report, "Reviewing Our Foreign Policy since 1978", for the Sixteenth Diplomatic Conference in 1983 (p. 11) wrote: "The chance for China to carry out major military operation is less likely."
81. MOFA 10 June 1982 Memo to Le Duc Tho, "On the Diplomatic Activities for the Coming Period", p. 3.
82. MOFA 21 December 1990 Report, "On Some Strategic and Tactical Issues in Our Struggle to Solve the Kampuchea Problem and Improve International Relations", p. 14.
83. For a comprehensive analysis of Hanoi's threat perception, see Nguyen Vu Tung, "Vietnam's New Concept of Security", in *Comprehensive Security in Asia: Views from Asia and the West on a Changing Security Environment*, edited by Kurt Radtke and Raymond Feddema (The Netherlands: Brill, 2000), pp. 405–24.
84. Nguyen Vu Tung, "Vietnam-ASEAN Cooperation in Southeast Asia", *Security Dialogue* 24, no. 1 (March 1993): 88–90.
85. MOFA Report on the Twenty-Seventh AMM and the First ARF Meeting (Báo cáo về hội nghị ngoại trưởng ASEAN lần thứ 27 và cuộc họp lần thứ nhất của ARF), p. 10.
86. Ambassador Nguyen Manh Hung's 18 April 1994 cable from Singapore.
87. MOFA Report on the Twenty-Seventh AMM and the First ARF Meeting, p. 10.
88. MOFA 1 November 1992 Memo. Deputy Foreign Minister Vu Khoan also reiterated this statement in his article entitled "Vietnam-ASEAN Relations", in *The Communist Review* (November 1994).
89. MOFA 18 October 1994 Report "On the Results of the Visit to ASEAN countries and the ASEAN Secretariat", (Về kết quả chuyến thăm tới các nước ASEAN và Ban thư ký ASEAN), p. 2. Emphasis as in the original.
90. Interviews by the author (Hanoi, November 2002).
91. Ambassador Vu Quang Diem's 30 December 1995 cable from Manila.
92. Ambassador Tran Le Duc's 18 March 1988 cable from Kuala Lumpur.
93. Asia-3 Department Report, "On the Regional Countries' Reactions to the MOFA 17 March 1988 Diplomatic Note on the Spratly" (Về phản ứng của các nước trong khu vực đối với công hàm của Bộ Ngoại giao ngày 17/3/1988 về vấn đề Trường Sa), pp. 1–2.
94. Ibid., p. 2.
95. Ambassador Le Mai's 22 March 1988 cable from Thailand.
96. Asia-3 Department Report, "On the Regional Countries' Reactions to the MOFA 17 March 1988 Diplomatic Note on the Spratly", p. 2.

97. Ibid., p. 3.
98. See also Liselotte Odgaard, *Maritime Security between China and Southeast Asia: Conflict and Cooperation in the Making of Regional Order* (Burlington, VT: Ashgate Publishing Company, 2002), pp. 3 and 85. Beijing was said to have aroused anger among leaders in Hanoi when the CPV General Secretary Nguyen Van Linh visited Beijing in May and was received in the same room where the agreement with Crestone had been signed a few days earlier. My exchange with Hanoi researchers, June 2003.
99. MOFA 4 August 1992 Report, "On the 25th ASEAN AMM" (Về hội nghị ngoại trưởng ASEAN lần thứ 25), p. 5.
100. MOFA Report "On the 27th ASEAN AMM and the First ARF Meeting" (July 1994). It also would be helpful to mention here efforts initiated by Indonesia in 1992 to organize a series of conferences to have academic discussions on issues related to the Islands, in which Vietnam has been a regular participant. Hanoi saw these conferences as an additional forum to keep the matter alive, test some hypothetical solutions, and in a best scenario, shape some form of collective action by ASEAN with regard to China.
101. MOFA 4 August 1992 Report, "On the 25th ASEAN AMM", p. 5.
102. Hoang Anh Tuan, "Vietnam's Membership in ASEAN: Economic, Political, and Security Implications", *Contemporary Southeast Asia* 16, no. 3 (December 1994).
103. Ramses Amer quoted in Liselotte Odgaard, *Maritime Security between China and Southeast Asia*, p. 127.
104. Ibid., p. 85.
105. Ambassador Dang Nghiem Hoanh 26 April 1994.
106. Ambassador Dang Nghiem Hoanh's 17 May 1994 cable from Beijing.
107. Ambassador Vu Quang Diem's 6 May 1994 cable from Manila.
108. Ambassador Dang Nghiem Hoanh's 18 May 1994 cable from Beijing.
109. Ambassador Ngo Tat To's 28 May 1994 cable from Kuala Lumpur.
110. Malaysian Foreign Minister's 21 June Letter to Foreign Minister Nguyen Manh Cam.
111. Brunei Foreign Minister's 25 June Letter to Foreign Minister Nguyen Manh Cam.
112. Singaporean Foreign Minister's 13 June Letter Foreign Minister Nguyen Manh Cam. Commenting on Lee Kuan Yew's statement in an interview with the *Wall Street Journal* late May that "The Chinese decision to support Crestone would lead to small-scaled conflicts. The best way to check the China threat is to integrate China into the world economy". Ambassador Nguyen Manh Hung said: "Mr Lee's statement is to show Singapore's

neighbouring countries that Singapore is independent from China and not to harm its relations with China." Nguyen Manh Hung's 3 June 1994 cable from Singapore.
113. Filipino Foreign Minister's Letter to Foreign Minister Nguyen Manh Cam.
114. Ambassador Le Cong Phung's 30 May 1994 cable from Bangkok.
115. Southeast Asian and South Pacific Affairs Department's Talking Points prepared for the Prime Minister Vo Van Kiet's meeting with his Malaysian counterpart Mahathir Mohamad on the occasion of the former's participation in the Twenty-Seventh Pacific Basin Economic Conference (PBEC), in Kuala Lumpur (22–25 May 1994), p. 2.
116. Foreign Minister Nguyen Manh Cam's 5 June 1994 cable from Cairo.
117. For example, Jacques Pomonty's comment on *Le Monde Diplomatique* on 22 April 1994 held that Crestone might make Hanoi "more resolute in joining ASEAN and normalizing relations with the US". MOFA Press Department, 26 April Report "Some Comments in the Foreign Press with regard to Crestone-related developments", p. 8.
118. MOFA ASEAN Department Memo for Foreign Minister Nguyen Manh Cam, "Vietnam's Participation in the 27th ASEAN AMM and the First ARF Meeting, 22–25 July 1994, Kuala Lumpur", p. 4.
119. MOFA Report on the Twenty-Seventh ASEAN AMM and the First ARF Meeting, p. 7.
120. MOFA Southeast Asian and South Pacific Affairs Department Report covering the third quarter of 1994, p. 8.
121. Liselotte Odgaard, *Maritime Security between China and Southeast Asia*, pp. 4 and 83–84.
122. MOFA ASEAN Department Deputy Director Nguyen Trung Thanh's 5 April 1995 cable from Indonesia.
123. Ibid. Emphasis as in the original.
124. Ambassador Vu Quang Diem 25 February 1995 cable from Manila.
125. Ambassador Le Van Bang 18 February 1995 cable from Washington, DC.
126. MOFA 5 December 1995 Report, "On the Outcomes of President Le Duc Anh's official visit to the Philippines" (Về kết quả chuyến thăm chính thức của chủ tịch nước Lê Đức Anh tại Phi lip pin), p. 4. Deputy Foreign Minister Vu Khoan on 21 May stressed the tendency in Manila to find solutions with China bilaterally, saying: "In private talks, the Philippines did not mention the recent intrusions into the country's territorial water by Chinese vessels. The reasons for Manila's failure to mention these intrusions include the coming bilateral talks between the Philippines and China on 26 May." Vu

Khoan's 21 May cable from Manila to report on the outcomes of the ARF Meeting at the Deputy-Minister Level.
127. Ambassador Vu Quang Diem's 30 December 1995 cable from Manila.
128. Ambassador Dang Nghiem Hoanh 19 May 1997 cable from Beijing.
129. MOFA, Talking Points on Policy Announcements by national leaders.
130. Concluding note of the Politburo Discussions on Vietnam's membership in ASEAN, 22 July 1994.
131. MOFA 15 September 1992 Report, "On the US Foreign Policy and Vietnam-US Relations", prepared for the Nineteenth Diplomatic Conference, pp. 7–8.
132. Ibid., p. 11.
133. Ambassador Vu Quang Diem's 30 December 1995 cable from Manila.
134. Ambassador Le Van Bang's 18 February 1995 cable from Washington, DC.
135. 30 November 1993 MOFA Report signed by Deputy Foreign Minister Le Mai's, pp. 3–4.
136. Ibid., p. 5.
137. Ibid.
138. MOFA American Affairs Department, 15 September 1992 Report "On the US Foreign Policy and Vietnam-US Relations" (Về chính sách đối ngoại của Mỹ và quan hệ Việt – Mỹ), presented at the Nineteenth Diplomatic Conference (Hanoi, 1992).
139. Ambassador Dang Nghiem Hoanh, 26 April 1994.
140. Ambassador Le Van Bang's 18 February 1995 cable from Washington, DC.
141. Ambassador Vu Quang Diem's 5 May 1994 cable from Manila.
142. Ambassador Ngo Quang Xuan's 15 August 1995 cable from New York.
143. According to Vu Khoan, the US confirmed that its traditional policy was not get involved in the territorial disputes in the South China Sea, and that China had pledged to ensure freedom of navigation in the area (Deputy Foreign Minister Vu Khoan's report on 21 May 1997 ARF Meeting).
144. MOFA American Affairs Department, 15 September 1992 Report "On US Foreign Policy and Vietnam-US Relations" presented at the Nineteenth Diplomatic Conference (Hanoi, 1992), p. 11.
145. Ibid., p. 10.
146. Deputy Foreign Minister Le Mai's 27 June 1973 Report "On the Developments and Outcomes of the UN Human Rights Conference, Geneva, 14–25 June 1993".
147. MOFA American Affairs Department, 15 September 1992 Report "On the US Foreign Policy and Vietnam-US Relations", presented at the Nineteenth Diplomatic Conference, p. 11.

148. MOFA, "Talking Points for National Leaders Policy Announcements in 1996".
149. Ibid.
150. Interview by the author with a MOFA senior official, November 2002.
151. Vu Khoan, "Vietnam and ASEAN", p. 31.
152. MOFA ASEAN Department Study, *5 Years after Vietnam Joined ASEAN: Achievements, Challenges, and Prospects,* p. 51.
153. Tran Uyen, "On Vietnam-ASEAN Relations," *Hanoi Moi,* 27 August 2003.
154. MOFA ASEAN Department Study, *5 Years after Vietnam Joined ASEAN: Achievements, Challenges, and Prospects,* p. 51.
155. Document coded 3917/QHQT signed by Deputy Prime Minister Phan Van Khai on 17 July 1995.
156. Nguyen Vu Tung, "Vietnam-ASEAN Cooperation in Southeast Asia", *Security Dialogue* 4, no. 1 (March 1993), p. 90.
157. MOFA Borders Committee Draft Report, "On Existing Problems Related to Vietnam's Borders with the Neighboring Countries" (Về các vấn đề tồn tại trên biên giới của Việt nam với các nước láng giềng), submitted to the Twenty-Fourth Diplomatic Conference, Hanoi, August 2003, p. 1.
158. Ibid,. p. 1.
159. MOFA 8 July 1992 Memo on Vietnam's ASEAN membership.

5

JUMPING ON A MOVING TRAIN: Vietnam Joins ASEAN

When Hanoi considered joining ASEAN, the organization had been seen as one of the "most successful experiments in regionalism in the developing world."[1] But from the mainstream liberal institutionalist point of view, even now, ASEAN is not an exemplary international organization with strong institutional frameworks. ASEAN is a loose organization and its decisions, which are made by consensus, are not legally binding.[2] In addition, ASEAN cooperation is not about collective defence or collective security. Moreover, ASEAN was not instrumental in supporting the economic development of Vietnam, and as the 1997 financial crisis unfolded, ASEAN itself experienced serious economic problems.

These facts would lead one to the following question: What had Hanoi known about the organizational structures and institutional arrangements

---

* An earlier version of this chapter has been published under the title "Testing the Neoliberal Institutionalist Argument: Cooperation between Vietnam and ASEAN", in *Vietnam's New Order: International Perspectives on the State and Reform in Vietnam*, edited by Mark Sidel and Stephanie Balme (New York: Palgrave Macmillan, 2007), pp. 51–70. Reproduced with permission of SpringerNature.

of ASEAN, about its principles and norms, its cooperative projects, and especially its limitations before it decided to join the organization? The answer to this question may help clarify several points. For example, if Hanoi had believed that ASEAN had serious economic and security limitations, it would have surely been more unwilling to consider membership; or if ASEAN were supranational in nature, Hanoi would have been more reluctant to join the organization; and if it had not been easy to understand the organizational structure of ASEAN and its working procedures, and if membership had entailed major political and economic changes, the process of joining ASEAN and adjusting to the new cooperative environment would have been longer. In short, this chapter will examine whether Hanoi had a good understanding of ASEAN before it decided to join the organization, and to what extent this understanding contributed to the decision in favour of, and the subsequent preparations for, Vietnam's membership of ASEAN.

THE CHRONOLOGY OF JOINING ASEAN

According to a MOFA Southeast Asian and South Pacific Affairs Department report, by mid-June 1991, the decision to join the Bali Treaty had been made, and Hanoi officially stated that it was ready to accede to the Treaty.[3] The department's activities, listed in weekly working schedules, showed that the accession was one of the main focuses during this time.

1. The week from 24 and 30 June 1991: to prepare for the Bali Treaty accession
2. The week from 1 to 6 July 1991: to continue research on Vietnam's accession to the Bali Treaty.
3. The week from 15 to 20 July 1991: to review and conduct research on Vietnam's relations with regional countries over the last ten years.
4. The week from 12 to 17 August 1991: to review Vietnam-ASEAN relations since 1975 and to prepare a memo on further improvement of these relations.
5. The week from 19 to 24 August 1991: to complete the detailed outline for the "Overview of Vietnam-ASEAN Relations: 1975–1991", and to continue research on Vietnam's accession to the Bali Treaty.

6. The week from 9 to 16 September 1991: to hold discussions on Vietnam-ASEAN relations since 1975, and to draft the letter of accession.

Having been certain of ASEAN's positive response, on 16 September 1991, Foreign Minister Nguyen Manh Cam sent an official letter to his ASEAN counterparts expressing Vietnam's readiness to accede to the Bali Treaty and confirming that this was one of the first steps towards the eventual membership in ASEAN.[4] On 15 October, giving an interview to a Thai daily, *The Nation*, Nguyen Manh Cam said, "If invited, Vietnam is ready to take part in the AMM Meetings." On 21 October, Prime Minister Vo Van Kiet told the *Bangkok Post*, "Vietnam wants to join ASEAN." On 31 October, Deputy Foreign Minister Vu Khoan stated in Singapore, "Vietnam wishes to be an ASEAN member."[5]

Following the Fourth ASEAN Summit in January 1992 which officially welcomed Vietnam's accession to the Bali Treaty, the CPV Politburo on 25 February sent a note to MOFA and the CERC giving the green light to the accession,[6] and Hanoi began to focus on the preparations for the signing ceremony.[7] For example, the working schedules of the Southeast Asian and South Pacific Affairs Department revealed that in the week from 9 to 14 March the Department was tasked with finding out the procedures and steps necessary for accession. On 20 May, Nguyen Manh Cam sent a letter to his ASEAN counterparts expressing the hope that Vietnam could become an ASEAN observer following its accession to the Bali Treaty. In June, MOFA had to coordinate with other ministries to work out plans for further cooperation with ASEAN in the capacity of an ASEAN observer. In the second week of July, before the AMM, MOFA finalized the documents for the Vietnamese delegation to the meeting.[8] On 22 July 1992, at the Twenty-Fifth AMM in Manila, Vietnam and Laos became parties to the Bali Treaty and observers to ASEAN.

It was clear that Vietnam and ASEAN did not want the observer status to last interminably. Hanoi studied the case of Papua New Guinea, which had remained an observer since 1979, and tried not to follow its example. On 16 December 1991, Kausikan, Director of the Southeast Asian Affairs Department of Singapore told the Vietnamese Chargé d'Affaires, "If Vietnam wants to associate with ASEAN, it should study Papua New Guinea's observer status."[9] On 24 May 1993, at Hanoi's request, the Singaporean Chargé d'Affaires met the Deputy Director of the Southeast Asian and South Pacific Affairs Department Nguyen Duy Hung to present information related to Papua New Guinea. He said, according to the transcripts of the meeting, "Papua New Guinea is not eligible to join ASEAN although ASEAN cannot strip PNG of its observer status. Geographically, PNG does not belong to Southeast Asia. Besides, it is not active and lacks initiative in taking part in ASEAN cooperation." He concluded, "Vietnam should not follow the PNG example."[10]

Hanoi also received advice from other ASEAN countries. Following a meeting with the Thai Ambassador in Hanoi on 31 January 1992, Le Cong Phung, Director of the Southeast Asian and South Pacific Affairs Department, submitted a report which said, "The Thai Ambassador suggested that Vietnam should send delegations to various ASEAN countries to study ASEAN mechanisms and individual ASEAN member countries' experiences in participating in ASEAN cooperation." The Ambassador also stressed that Vietnam should study the experiences of Brunei, the newest member of ASEAN. Le Cong Phung then suggested,

> Because the Fourth ASEAN Summit has welcomed Vietnam's accession to the Bali Treaty and further association with ASEAN, the study of ASEAN's organizational and institutional frameworks and mechanisms, as well as its modes of activities has now become timely and even urgent. We should send a departmental-level mission to the ASEAN Secretariat, and to Indonesia, Thailand, and Malaysia for this purpose.[11]

In short, the observer status was the first step to the eventual full membership in ASEAN. According to a MOFA document, the most important question of membership was not "whether", but "when and how".[12]

To become ASEAN member, however, was not an immediate step. There was a common understanding in Hanoi that it would take time before Vietnam could become a full-fledged member of ASEAN. On 18 October 1991, Vo Van Kiet told the *Bangkok Post* that Vietnam should improve bilateral relations with individual ASEAN members while Hanoi studied the "suitable forms and scopes of relations with ASEAN". On 31 October, Vu Khoan said in Singapore, "Vietnam wishes to become an ASEAN member. Following the accession to the Bali Treaty, Vietnam hopes to take part in the annual ASEAN AMM. However, it will take a long time before Vietnam becomes an official member of ASEAN."[13] While agreeing with the accession to the Bali Treaty, the Politburo also instructed MOFA and the CERC to "undertake further study and prepare policy suggestions for the Politburo on the question of membership".[14] In June 1992, the CPV Third Central Committee Plenum adopted a resolution that said in part, "For the time being, we will accede to the Bali Treaty and take part in dialogues with ASEAN. We should at the same time actively seek ways to further expand relations with ASEAN in the future."[15] According to a Southeast Asian and South Pacific Department Affairs document, at the end of October 1992, when MOFA sought the Politburo's opinion on the membership issue, it was instructed to "continue to do more research".[16]

During 1993, work continued on the question of ASEAN membership. On 19 February 1993 the Politburo instructed MOFA,

> As an observer, we should select some cooperative projects in ASEAN and actively take part in them to gain knowledge and experience in national construction and development and for full participation in ASEAN in the future. When ASEAN reaches a consensus on Vietnam's membership, we should be ready to join ASEAN as a fully-fledged member.[17]

Also in February, Hanoi stated that it would join ASEAN at an appropriate time.[18] During his October 1993 visit to Malaysia, Singapore, and Thailand, General Secretary Do Muoi stated Vietnam's four-point ASEAN policy and officially said: "Vietnam plans to improve multisided relations with all individual ASEAN member states and with ASEAN as a regional organization. Vietnam is ready to join ASEAN at the appropriate time."[19]

These statements revealed that Hanoi was still uncertain as to whether ASEAN was ready to accept it as a member and also showed a general understanding in Vietnam that it would take between five to ten years to learn the ASEAN principles, rules, and decision-making procedures as well as to become more aware of the members' rights and obligations before joining the organization. Between 1991 and 1992, the IIR Southeast Asian Studies Division conducted an independent research on ASEAN. The authors reviewed major changes in the international and regional strategic environment following the end of the Cold War and argued for an overall improvement in Vietnam-ASEAN relations. The research, however, proposed that in the immediate future Vietnam should not join ASEAN. The authors cited differences in the political systems and levels of economic developments between Vietnam and ASEAN countries in order to support their views on a gradual approach to ASEAN membership. They argued that the developmental gap between Vietnam and ASEAN as well as the backwardness of the country's economy and bureaucracy in the early stage of reforms would prevent Hanoi from reaping the benefits of integration into ASEAN. Moreover, Hanoi had a very limited knowledge of ASEAN's organization and activities. The general idea, therefore, was that more research on ASEAN should be conducted before making the final decision on membership and that Hanoi should consider its observer status as "an active apprenticeship" to get better acquainted with the ASEAN processes before becoming a full-fledged ASEAN member.[20]

Thus, at that time, the general mood in Hanoi was that Vietnam should adopt a gradual approach with regard to the membership issue. Many believed that the ASEAN Way was new, and Hanoi had little experience with it. One researcher wrote,

> It took thirty years for ASEAN to develop the habit of building consensus among its members, thus forming "an ASEAN spirit" or "a state of mind" which helped turn ASEAN into a forum for enhanced cooperation and confidence building. Yet, consensus building is time-consuming and involves compromises. Therefore, the ASEAN spirit requires, among other things, sophistication, diplomatic skills, and great patience to handle difficulties and disputes and promote cooperation.[21]

Another researcher even went further and put forward the argument that the ASEAN Way was in fact a challenge for Hanoi. According to him, Hanoi was more familiar with the "quick fix approach" to problems and therefore tended to resort to force in solving disputes. This approach to regional issues ran counter to the ASEAN Way that preferred gradualism and to the ASEAN principle that upholds non-use of force in international relations. Therefore, it would be a long time before Hanoi could learn and act in accordance with ASEAN principles and norms. He then suggested that Vietnam's membership in ASEAN should not be immediate and that its success or failure would greatly depend on the learning process upon which Hanoi was about to embark.[22]

By 1994, however, Hanoi had come to desire early admission to ASEAN. In April 1994, during an official visit to Indonesia, Vietnamese President Le Duc Anh stated, "Vietnam is taking concrete steps to gain an early membership of ASEAN."[23] On 27 June 1994, the Cabinet Office, replying to MOFA's 16 April memo concerning the composition of the Vietnamese delegation to the Twenty-Seventh AMM to be headed by Foreign Minister Nguyen Manh Cam, instructed, "on this occasion, Comrade Nguyen Manh Cam should explore the possibility of Vietnam's full membership of ASEAN."[24] A MOFA July 1994 memo said, "We should reiterate the following position: together with ASEAN's active support, Vietnam is taking concrete measures to prepare for an early full membership in ASEAN."[25] In fact, Hanoi was trying to find out whether ASEAN had reached a consensus on the exact timing of its membership. The talking points for Nguyen Manh Cam suggested that the Foreign Minister would pose this specific question in the private meetings with his ASEAN counterparts: "What is the ASEAN proposal for a possible time-frame or a road map for Vietnam to join ASEAN?"[26]

At the Twenty-Seventh AMM, ASEAN countries stated that ASEAN would welcome Vietnam to be the seventh member and that the timing would be ideally before the ASEAN Summit to be held by the end of 1995. Upon receiving this information, on 22 July 1994, the Politburo held a meeting and concluded that Vietnam would join ASEAN in 1995.[27] In an interview to *Nhan Dan* on 29 July, Nguyen Manh Cam said, "the common understanding that was reached during the AMM meeting was that Vietnam will become a full member of ASEAN in 1995."[28] On 17 October 1994, Nguyen Manh Cam sent a letter to the Brunei's Foreign Minister, the then Chairman of the ASEAN Standing Committee to officially request ASEAN to admit Vietnam as a member in the Twenty-Eighth AMM to be held in Brunei in July 1995. Hanoi became a new member of ASEAN on 22 July 1995, three years after it gained the observer status and one year after the CPV Politburo's decision to join ASEAN was made.

HASTY PREPARATIONS

Even though Hanoi wanted an early admission, by July 1994, it seemed that it was not totally ready. The MOFA July 1994 memo for the delegation to the Twenty-Seventh AMM in 1994 said, "There has been a high consensus among ASEAN countries on Vietnam's membership in ASEAN. Yet, they have not reached an agreement on the timing. For our part, we are not ready, having not acquired all the necessary conditions."[29]

Therefore, when Hanoi actually began its preparations to become an ASEAN member after the July 1994 decision, the admission was just one year away. As a result, little could be done. In terms of institutional preparations, on 14 September 1994 the ASEAN Department was set up in MOFA. Initially, its staff included only ten persons. Afterward, other ministries also set up ASEAN units or divisions. Vu Duc Dam, a senior official in the Cabinet Office in charge of ASEAN-related issues between 1994 and 1996, told the author that by the end of 1994, the Prime Minister had ordered the formation of an ASEAN Unit in the Cabinet Office to keep him informed about ASEAN-related issues and assist him in directing these activities.[30] In terms of capacity building, one of the most important activities was to train Vietnamese officials with English language and other skills to work in the multilateral context. About 300 officials were given short intensive English courses, out of which number, 100 were trained abroad. According to Dam, the most important criteria for selecting the staff of the ASEAN Unit was fluency in English.[31] In addition, the MOFA ASEAN Department published the first ASEAN guidebook to introduce ASEAN to the public at large. Several months before the admission, the national television and radio networks started to propagate ASEAN among the public. Although Hanoi boasted that despite time constraints it could set up "basic and important infrastructure" for taking part in ASEAN cooperation,[32] one must say that the institutional preparations were made in a "hectic and hasty" manner and the results were modest.[33] And according to a document prepared by the ASEAN Department, after the admission, Hanoi still faced personnel problems. This document stressed, "for the sake of effective cooperation in ASEAN, Vietnam needs a contingent of officials who are fluent in English and possess a profound knowledge to work within ASEAN institutions. To train such a contingent is an urgent task for us."[34]

Vu Duc Dam also told the author that other institutions, including the ASEAN Unit in the Cabinet Office, were dependent on MOFA's knowledge about ASEAN.[35] It seemed, however, that even MOFA was not ready to provide sufficient knowledge on ASEAN. As mentioned above, in February 1992, the Politburo instructed MOFA and the CERC to undertake further studies and prepare policy suggestions for the Politburo on the question of membership and insisted in October 1992 that more research should be done before the membership question could be addressed. By that time, however, MOFA had still not produced any comprehensive studies on ASEAN. In fact, serious efforts to conduct such studies were made only after the question of membership became pressing. For example, in February 1993, Hanoi stated that it would join ASEAN at an appropriate time; but it was not until March that Deputy Foreign Minister Tran Quang Co signed the MOFA 1993 Research Programme that instructed the Departments and Units concerned to identify issues related to ASEAN cooperation, such as modes of association with ASEAN including the associate member and full-member statuses. This programme listed the following specific objectives:

- to find out about the organizational and institutional structures of ASEAN, the modes of ASEAN operation, and the interests and obligations connected with the full-fledged membership;
- to clarify the advantages and disadvantages in Vietnam-ASEAN relations with a view to identifying potentialities and limitations in Vietnam-ASEAN interaction;
- to list the ASEAN existing cooperative projects and those in which Vietnam would be able to participate as an observer; and
- to find out advantages and disadvantages for Vietnam to cooperate in ASEAN as an associate member and as a full-fledged member.[36]

The programme revealed that even MOFA, which functioned as Hanoi's ASEAN watcher, was not quite clear about the basic facts of the organization and the suitable modes of association with it. In other words, research on ASEAN seemed to have lagged behind political decisions.

Yet, even according to MOFA, the outcomes of these studies were not satisfactory. A MOFA 1993 annual report stated that in 1993 the findings of a research project on ASEAN were submitted to the Ministry. The report, however, stressed, "More should be done in 1994 to improve the Ministry's general knowledge and research capability so that MOFA will be in a better position to provide proper and timely policy suggestions, thus contributing to building a proactive posture for Vietnam's international relations."[37] Perhaps, as a result of poor research, ASEAN remained something "very new" to many policymakers when the ASEAN Department was established in October 1994, according to the Department's first Director Nguyen Ngoc Son.[38] In 1995, the ASEAN Department and the IIR conducted a joint research project on ASEAN. This project stated that to join ASEAN had been a correct decision and warned that Vietnam should expect to host the Sixth ASEAN Summit in 1998, a most difficult task for a full member.[39]

At the national level, efforts to establish the Vietnamese Association for Southeast Asian Studies (ASEAR) were launched in July 1994 with a view to, among other things, "coordinating the studies on political, economic, and cultural development in Southeast Asia, modes of Vietnam-ASEAN relations and providing State and Party offices with professional and academic consultations, reviews, and appraisals on all matters related to the region and Vietnam's policies towards the region."[40] On 7 July 1994, Nguyen Duy Quy, Director of the National Center for Social Sciences and Humanities, signed the official document to sponsor the association. On 20 November 1994, the proposal for ASEAR was sent to the Government Office to obtain the Prime Minister's approval. ASEAR was officially established in 1996.

As mentioned above, in January 1992, there were suggestions that Hanoi should dispatch fact-finding missions to ASEAN countries to obtain a better understanding of the grouping. The first high-ranking delegation, consisted of departmental-level officials from the Cabinet Office, MOFA, Ministry of Trade (MOT), Ministry of Finance (MOF), and the State Planning Commission and headed by Deputy Foreign Minister Vu Khoan, visited all ASEAN countries and the ASEAN Secretariat from 3 to 14 October 1994. It was the task of the delegation to "study in depth the ASEAN modes of cooperation, mechanisms for intra-ASEAN cooperation, and possibilities for Vietnam to take part in ASEAN cooperation."[41] In addition to the confirming that ASEAN was not a military organization (see the previous chapter) the other important first-hand information and findings of the delegation involved the ASEAN Way, especially consensus and gradualism, which might allow Hanoi to join the organization in an "on-the-job training" process. A report of the delegation said, "We have clearly understood the principle of consensus building in the decision-making process: all the decisions have to be made on consensus. If the ASEAN members cannot agree on one thing, they have to consult among themselves and wait until all can come to an agreement." The delegation learned further that even when ASEAN agreed to launch a cooperative project, the participation of all members was not mandatory. The report said, "we also learnt the ASEAN 6-X formula: it is not necessary for all the 6 members to take part in a specific cooperative project. With five or even two countries agreeing to participate, the project could be implemented." In some cases participation also served the purpose of showing solidarity, the delegation was told. For example, "for the sake of showing solidarity with other members, Brunei and Singapore have participated in several cooperative projects although they do not expect to gain direct benefits from them."[42]

The report also said that the delegation gained "a deeper understanding" about specific matters including "the institutional arrangements and operating system of ASEAN at both regional and national levels, annual membership dues, the number of meetings and the costs of organizing them." According to the report, the delegation tried to find out about "the costs and benefit of ASEAN membership," and was reassured that "while it is very difficult to quantify the costs and direct benefits of membership, the indirect benefits are great. Thai officials, for example, told us that Thailand could link the reduction of military expenditures to its membership in ASEAN." The report, therefore, said that

> The study tour has been of practical significance while we are preparing to join ASEAN. With what we have learnt, we now better understand the nature of ASEAN cooperation, and this provides us with a clearer idea about the next steps [proceeding towards full-fledged membership of ASEAN].

The report also promised to provide the Prime Minister with a follow-up memo listing these steps.[43] Efforts to study ASEAN continued in earnest until just two weeks before Vietnam was officially admitted to the organization. On 8 July 1995 two Study Groups were set up. The first group, consisted of officials from MOFA, MOT, the Cabinet Office, General Department of Customs and the State Planning Commission, was to conduct studies on AFTA and Vietnam's participation in AFTA projects.

The second group, consisted of officials from MOFA, the Ministry of Public Order (MOPO) and the Cabinet Office, was to conduct studies on visa-related issues for ASEAN citizens. The tasks assigned to these two groups included "organization of in-depth study and research with a view to showing the advantages and disadvantages for Vietnam as a member of ASEAN and submitting policy suggestions".[44] In addition, in January 1996, the ASEAN National Committee (ANC) Office placed an order with the National Center for Social Sciences and Humanities to conduct research on ASEAN and AFTA with a view to providing the ANC with more information, analyses and policy suggestions regarding a host of issues the ANC had to deal with.[45]

Thus, Hanoi began to study about ASEAN, its institutional arrangements and working procedures and to set up institutions in Vietnam to manage Vietnam-ASEAN cooperation, only after a decision had been taken by the leadership to join the organization. That is to say, Hanoi's understanding of ASEAN institutions and operating systems may have facilitated the steps taken to participate in ASEAN cooperation, but was not instrumental in bringing about Hanoi's decision to join the organization. And how detailed Hanoi's understanding of ASEAN was prior to the eventual accession is still open to doubt.

POST-ADMISSION AWARENESS AND ADJUSTMENTS OF DOMESTIC INSTITUTIONS

Developments that led to the eventual membership in July 1995 indicated that the decision to join ASEAN was made in the absence of a detailed understanding of ASEAN mechanisms and processes, especially those related to economic cooperation. The post-admission period also showed that the adjustment of existing domestic institutional arrangements, the establishment of new institutions in Vietnam to promote cooperation with ASEAN, and Vietnam's actual participation in cooperative undertakings were of a reactive and ad-hoc nature.

Personnel

Hanoi still knew little about ASEAN's systems and procedures even after it had joined the grouping. A report of the ANC's second meeting on

20 January 1996 said: "Ministries and other institutions in Vietnam do not have sufficient information on the way the ASEAN system works and performs its activities, both in general and in specific fields." Even the ANC Office "lacks information", according to the report.[46] After joining ASEAN, Hanoi sent two departmental ranking officials to work in the ASEAN Secretariat in Jakarta to "further study the ASEAN systems and report to the ANC and MOFA."[47] Yet, Nguyen Hoang An, the Deputy Director of MOFA ASEAN Department, one of the two officials, complained that they were assigned by the ASEAN Secretariat to work on "issues of low politics, including drug trafficking and prostitution".[48] Hanoi was informed of only one quarter of the approximately 300 ASEAN meetings held in 1996. Due to short notice and financial constraints, in 1996, Hanoi could only attend about thirty meetings.[49] The opportunities to learn first-hand about ASEAN systems and procedures were, therefore, quite limited.

The learning through participation process in ASEAN functional cooperation did not go well either. Following the February 1993 Politburo instruction, in 1994 Hanoi participated in six ASEAN functional cooperation projects. In its biennial review of participation in ASEAN functional cooperation, the ASEAN National Secretariat said,

> Our participation in this type of cooperation remained passive and reactive. When attending ASEAN conferences and meetings, our officials for most of the time sat quietly and failed to participate in the discussions. We failed to put forth new ideas and projects for the promotion of cooperation. The reasons for this include our limited knowledge and understanding of ASEAN and its approach cooperation, our officials' lack of knowledge and skills to work in multilateral settings, as well as institutional and financial constraints. In addition, we sometimes failed to assign the proper officials to attend ASEAN meetings and did not have a specialized staff to supervise the implementation of projects. Above all, however, fluency in English still remains a major problem.[50]

In a November 1999 report, MOFA suggested, "Regular courses should be conducted to improve the knowledge and skills of the officials who work on ASEAN-related issues. Knowledge about ASEAN decision-making procedures, capacity to propose and implement cooperative projects, and English skills are most needed in order to ensure our effective and beneficial participation in ASEAN."⁵¹ In short, it seemed that at least in terms of personnel, Hanoi was not properly prepared to take a more active and substantial part in ASEAN cooperation.

Institutional Arrangements

All the institutional arrangements to coordinate ASEAN-related activities in Vietnam were made after Hanoi had decided to join ASEAN and the process of institutional adjustments was also reactive. On 6 October 1995, the Vietnamese Prime Minister issued a directive "On the Effective Participation in ASEAN Cooperation", which instructed officials

(1) to set up within ministries and ministerial-level government agencies ASEAN Units and/or Departments, which consist of skilled and English-fluent officials, to implement ASEAN-related activities in the specific fields,
(2) to set up the ANC within the Cabinet Office to coordinate Vietnam's cooperation in ASEAN at the national level,
(3) to assign to the MOFA ASEAN Department the task to serve as the ASEAN National Secretariat (ANS) to report on ASEAN-related activities in Vietnam and to give adequate information about ASEAN activities, programmes, and projects to the ANC through the ANC Office.⁵²

On 10 October 1995, the Vietnamese Prime Minister signed a decision to establish the ANC, which would be led by a Deputy Prime Minister and had the principal functions of "assisting the Prime Minister to direct Vietnam-ASEAN relations on security, political, economic, cultural, and scientific-technological fields and to coordinate ASEAN-related activities at the national level".⁵³ The ANC was headed by Deputy Prime Minister Tran Duc Luong.

Snags soon developed in the division of labour among the newly established institutions. For example, the second ANC report dated 20 January 1996 revealed that MOT, MOF and to a lesser extent, the General Department of Customs had disagreements concerning their responsibilities over AFTA-related activities.⁵⁴ This was due to the ambiguity of a November

1995 decision by the Prime Minister according to which MOF would be in charge of AFTA and MOT in charge of economic and trade relations with ASEAN.[55] As a result, the ANC report suggested,

> Individual ministries and ministerial-level agencies should be allowed to take the initiative in working out plans of action with regard to specific ASEAN-related activities. At the same time, more coordinating work should be done to avoid overlapping responsibilities between and among government agencies and to encourage officials to take an active approach in their work.[56]

These disputes reflect a greater confusion that pervaded the institutional arrangements and bureaucratic mechanisms in Vietnam, and in this case the principal victim, ironically, was the ANC. Vu Duc Dam explained why the ANC was established: the Prime Minister, among others, was aware that ASEAN cooperation, especially in trade and investment, did not involve empty promises but concrete commitments and strict implementation, and this required a well-coordinated performance by the bureaucracy. He was also aware of the state of compartmentalization among government units. Therefore, the setting up of the ANC (headed by a Deputy Prime Minister and with staff members from the Cabinet Office) would be ideal to overcome poor coordination and institutional inertia.[57] The initial outcomes, according to Dam, were encouraging. For example, the ANC could "force" the General Department for Customs and the General Department of Statistics to complete the work of converting the existing six-digit coding system for taxation into an eight-digit one in accordance with the ASEAN system. Between 1993 and 1995, the two Departments had worked on this project but had completed only 50 per cent of the job. Yet, the ANC, invoking Vietnam's AFTA commitments and making use of the Deputy Prime Minister's power, exerted its influence on them and the rest of the job was completed within four months.[58]

Yet, after three years of existence, the ANC "died without a death certificate", according to Dam. On 10 February 1998, the new Prime Minister Phan Van Khai issued Decision No. 31/1998/QD-TTg to establish the National Committee for International Economic Cooperation (NCIEC) whose principal tasks were to assist the Prime Minister in coordinating and directing activities by ministries, ministerial-level agencies, and provincial authorities with regard to ASEAN, ASEM, APEC, WTO, as well as other international and regional economic and trade organizations.[59] According to Dam, "the ANC turf" now overlapped with that of the NCIEC, which had a greater power. Therefore, following the birth of the NCIEC, "the ANC gradually became powerless, and just existed on paper."[60]

There have been several explanations for this institutional confusion. According to Dam, the establishment of NCIEC was due to the need to streamline the Cabinet Office. As a result, the actual division of labour with regard to ASEAN-related activities was redefined. Because the MOT Multilateral Trade Department now was functioned as a support unit of the NCIEC, issues related to economic relations with ASEAN were within the responsibility of the MOT. MOFA, and MOPO to a lesser extent, could be responsible for political and security cooperation with ASEAN and directly report to the CPV Politburo and the CPV Standing Secretariat. In addition, as Hanoi intensified its negotiations with the WTO and its activities in APEC, ASEAN and AFTA became a lesser focus even in the NCIEC. Dam concluded that the departmentalization of ASEAN-related activities became even greater.

Nguyen Thanh Huy, an official of the MOFA ASEAN Department, seemed to agree with the compartmentalization thesis of Dam. According to him, the MOFA ASEAN Department also ceased to serve as the de facto ANS, because other ministries and government agencies stopped reporting to the ANS "after they had established direct contacts with their ASEAN counterparts and thus felt that they did not need instructions."[61] Reacting to this, an ANC report said, "the Government should make it clear that cooperation with ASEAN is the undertaking of the whole society, not just of those specific ministries or units within ministries."[62] Dam, however, insisted that "the ANC's death" and the growing compartmentalization of the bureaucracy harmed Vietnam-ASEAN cooperation in the absence of the lack of a coordinating body at the national level that could ensure the provision of "public goods" for ASEAN-related activities.[63]

By the end of 1999, concerns over the lack of efficient personnel and institutional arrangements for ASEAN-related activities remained as they had been before July 1995. A report of the MOFA ASEAN Department to the Twenty-Second Diplomatic Conference in November 1999 said, "We are still in need of skilled officials, funds, and coordinating institutions for the promotion of cooperation in ASEAN."[64] By the end of 2002, the Government also acknowledged "the state of unpreparedness in terms of personnel, legal and institutional frameworks, and coordination at both central and provincial levels has obstructed the promotion of Vietnam's international relations in general and with ASEAN in particular."[65]

In short, it became clear that Hanoi had not been fully aware of the ASEAN structures as well as its procedures before joining it. The knowledge was not improved much thereafter. Vietnam's actual performance in ASEAN, including the initiation, appraisal, and implementation of cooperative projects, was further hindered by the lack of efficient personnel, funds, and the confusion in institutional arrangements.

Vietnam and AFTA

Vietnam's participation in the AFTA scheme clearly illustrated the above-mentioned unpreparedness. By January 2003, when AFTA began to take effect partially in Vietnam, Hanoi was not fully aware of the opportunities and challenges for the economy in general and for businesses in particular.

Joining ASEAN, Vietnam had to participate in AFTA, which basically required that by 2003 ASEAN member countries should apply the Common Effective Preferences Tariffs (CEPT) by reducing the tariffs to between 0 per cent and 5 per cent for intra-ASEAN trade. Due to Vietnam's low level of economic development, the Twenty-Seventh ASEAN Economic Ministers' Meeting (AEM) agreed that Vietnam would begin to implement CEPT by 2006. These timetables were adjusted during the Sixth ASEAN Summit (Hanoi, 1998) at which the original ASEAN members agreed to fully apply CEPT in 2003. Hanoi also decided to partially implement CEPT in the same year.

The reduction of tariffs requires reforms of tax regimes, enhancement of competitiveness, and shifts in investment priorities. Hanoi seemed to be aware of the challenges posed by AFTA. A 1996 annual report by the Government said,

> From now on we have to do our best to enhance the efficiency, productivity, and products' quality with a view to improve the competitiveness of the economy, thus being able to take advantage of economic integration into the region.[66]

Such slogan-like proclamations, however, are not sufficient to move a whole system away from its inertia. Hanoi moved slowly on both research and implementation of AFTA. For example, AFTA-related research activities were not conducted even after Vietnam had joined ASEAN. According to a report by the ANC, the MOF established a Research Unit on AFTA (RUA) that had twelve members representing all the ministries concerned. Yet, by January 1996, when the second ANC meeting was convened, the RUA was still inactive.[67] In addition, the MOF failed to meet the deadline of January 2003 according to which Vietnam had to introduce a new tax regime for 755 types of goods whose import taxes would be cut, along the CEPT lines, to less than 20 per cent from 40–50 per cent. The new deadline now was July 2003. This lateness, according to Le Thi Bang Tam, the then MOF Deputy Minister, was due to the fact that MOF had failed to prepare legal and institutional frameworks for the tax cut and the conversion of existing tax regimes applied to about 10,800 tax lines to meet the ASEAN standards.[68]

At the same time, the government did not do enough to raise the awareness of enterprises about AFTA. One of the policy suggestions by the MOFA with regard to AFTA read: "We should provide our enterprises with more information about AFTA so that they will be more prepared for it."[69] Yet, Nguyen Minh Vu, an official of the MOFA Multilateral Economic Cooperation Department, cited the figures of a survey to show that only 25 per cent of Vietnamese enterprises knew of AFTA and that the understanding of AFTA by these enterprises was still very poor. Moreover, also according to Vu, the government had not worked out a reasonable investment strategy based on a comprehensive study of comparative advantages that Vietnamese enterprises enjoy and had failed to provide enterprises with sufficient information. As a result, many enterprises in Vietnam had invested in sectors whose products could not compete with goods produced in other ASEAN countries.[70]

These limited efforts by the government were further hampered by protectionist pressures from enterprises. According to the Report of the Second ANC Meeting, on 19 September 1995, the government promulgated Decree No. 91/CP that gave general guidelines for the implementation of CEPT in Vietnam. Based on this decree, the MOF created a list of 2,265 goods items subject to tariff cuts. After MOF circulated the list to other ministries and departments for review, it was suggested that only 1,622 of these items be subject to tariff cuts.[71] In July 2003 when a new tax regime along CEPT lines was introduced, only 755 types of goods were subject to tariffs cuts. The new tax level, which was less than 20 per cent, represented a big effort by Hanoi as compared with the previous level of between 40 and 50 per cent. However, it was still far from meeting the ASEAN demand of tariff reductions up to between 0 and 5 per cent.

Pham Chi Lan, the then Deputy Director of the Vietnam Chamber of Commerce and Industries, (VCCI) observed, "I have travelled widely to talk about the pressures of AFTA on Vietnam's economy. Yet, what I found is startling: enterprises still remain idle, blaming the government for the hasty process of joining AFTA and requesting government support."[72] Assessing the level of preparedness on the part of government, Nguyen Hoai Son—an MOT Multilateral Trade Policy Official—said, plans of actions that the government had worked out were too general and failed to hold departments and ministries concerned accountable for the implementation of AFTA. As a result, when the "moment of truth" arrived, no specific entity could be held responsible for the tasks that had been pledged but left undone.[73] Due to this low level of preparedness, Vietnam's economy was certain to face great difficulties when AFTA was finally implemented. According to a report of the MOF, when tariffs were reduced to less than 20 per cent, 62.5 per cent Vietnamese enterprises would become uncompetitive in the region. Moreover, if import taxes were reduced to 15 per cent by 2004 and 5 per cent in 2006, Vietnamese glass, automobile, steel and electronics producers would have to close down due to their failure to compete on a regionwide basis.[74]

In short, bureaucratic inertia and protectionist pressures from state enterprises have prevented the preparation for and implementation of AFTA in Vietnam, thus hampering the progress of the country's economy.

In November 1995, a MOFA report stated, "We have to take part in AFTA, the ASEAN's biggest economic cooperative project. This is a difficult matter that requires careful consideration. We have to reform the existing tax regimes, closely examine the tax reduction processes, and create the list of goods on which tariffs must be reduced and the timetables for tariffs reduction.[75] By mid-2003, it was clear that Hanoi still lagged behind in its commitments. Hanoi alone, however, cannot be blamed for being slow in AFTA-related matters. Justifying the postponement of the AFTA implementation for six months, Trade Minister Truong Dinh Tuyen said, "For AFTA, meeting deadlines in many cases is an act of willingness by individual member states."[76] In a broader context, what was lacking was the ASEAN's institutional and legal power to force member states to adhere to their commitments to the organization's cooperative projects. Even ASEAN scholars acknowledged that ASEAN lacked viable institutional and legal mechanisms and legality to foster regional cooperation, ironically at a time when proposing cooperative projects in various fields had increasingly become the habit of ASEAN leaders at their meetings in which initiatives mainly serve the purpose of gaining political scores.[77] The Singaporean scholar Chia Siow Yue even maintained that ASEAN had so far failed to work out specific steps to follow up political decisions. It had also failed to agree on specific timelines and yardsticks to measure successes and failures, which could help hold member states accountable for their part in regional cooperation. She stressed that institution building for better regional cooperation still remained a major task for ASEAN.[78] A Draft "Concept Paper on the ASEAN Economic Community" prepared by a group of scholars in the Singapore Institute of Southeast Asian Studies (ISEAS) wrote in February 2003,

> ASEAN still maintains a very loose institutional structure although there has been a strengthening of its institutions in recent years. ASEAN does not presently operate on the overriding principle of using a formal, detailed, and binding institutional structure to prepare, enact, and execute policies for economic integration. The "ASEAN Way" of dialogue is still very much entrenched with *Musyawarah* (discussion and consultation), *Mufakat* (unanimous decision) and Consensus being the *modus operandi* of the organization.[79]

As noted earlier, the case of Vietnam's membership in ASEAN seems to suggest that the decision to join ASEAN was made in the absence of a detailed understanding of the institutional arrangements of ASEAN and the lack of preparedness in terms of personnel and institutions in Vietnam for the new type of regional cooperation. Bureaucratic inertia was also part of the problem. Yet, the ASEAN Way also contributed to this. In fact, when Hanoi became more aware of the loose structures and the accommodating approach of ASEAN, it became more committed to go ahead with the membership issue. One senior official told the author that for many Vietnamese officials who gained first-hand experiences in ASEAN cooperation, "it is like jumping on a moving train, whose direction and pace can be negotiated and whose passengers can know more about each other as the train goes along." That explained why preparations for membership and for Vietnam-ASEAN cooperation could be minimal, according to the same official.[80]

VIETNAM'S MEMBERSHIP IN ASEAN: THE ECONOMIC GAINS

The previous chapter has shown the limitations of ASEAN in providing Vietnam support with regard to national security especially in the South China Sea. The following section seeks to see whether considerations about economic gains would justify Vietnam's membership in ASEAN. The increased trade turnovers between Vietnam and other ASEAN countries have often been cited to illustrate the "correctness of the decision to join ASEAN".[81] The MOFA Document "On Vietnam-ASEAN Relations" in November 1999 reported that in the period from 1990 to 1999, the growth rate in trade was on an average of 26.8 per cent per annum and that trade with ASEAN accounted for 32.4 per cent of Vietnam's total foreign trade. In addition, as compared with 1994, Vietnam-ASEAN trade increased by 1.3 times. The report, therefore, considered the growth in Vietnam-ASEAN trade relations as a benefit of ASEAN membership.[82]

A closer look, however, suggests that Vietnam's trade deficits with ASEAN also increased for the period from 1990 to 2000, as demonstrated in Table 5.1.

Other sources also indicated that after 1995, Vietnam's total trade deficit with ASEAN doubled. According to the Vietnam General Department of Statistics, total trade deficits in the period from 1995 to 1997 reached US$9.1 billion, equivalent to 41 per cent of the export values. The IMF, however, reported that Vietnam's actual total trade deficits were US$18.4 billion, twice the export volume for the same period.[83] Vietnam-ASEAN trade followed the same pattern. Dao Huy Giam reported that the volume of Vietnam's imports from ASEAN was always double the volume

TABLE 5.1
Trade Deficits between Vietnam and ASEAN, 1990–2000 (US$ million)

	1990	1991	1992	1993	1994	1995	1996	1997	1998	1999	2000
Exports	349	524	576	643	893	1,112	1,778	2,023	2,020	2,516	2,619.4
Imports	539.8	811.1	953	1,319	1,689.6	2,378	2,999.2	3,245.2	3,386.5	3,290.9	4,449.1
Balance	–191	–287	–377	–676	–797	–1,266	–1,215	–1,223	–1,366	–775	–1,830

Source: Vo Hung Dzung, "Vietnam's Foreign Trade from 1991 to 2000: Achievements and Problems", *Economic Studies*, no. 11 (294), November 2002, pp. 29–31.

of its exports to ASEAN.[84] The deficits were expected to rise when Vietnam reduced tariffs in accordance with the AFTA/CEPT schemes.

In general, trade deficits were not healthy for a developing economy like Vietnam at the time it joined the organization.[85] Yet, trade deficits with ASEAN were especially negative for Vietnam in several aspects. In the first place, the decision to join ASEAN and AFTA, especially the decision to adhere to the CEPT from 2003 (three years earlier than originally committed) created additional pressures on Vietnam's young industries, which were not yet able to compete in the regional market, or generate jobs for a growing labour force. The reduction of tariffs was expected to further reduce the competitiveness of Vietnamese goods even in the domestic market, as ASEAN-originated products were cheaper. Against this background, a report by Ministry of Trade argued that by 2006 when tariffs were reduced to the 0–5 per cent range, the serious imbalance in Vietnam-ASEAN trade would be fully exposed, forcing uncompetitive industries to close down if they failed to readjust their investment and production strategies. The report also saw few efforts by local industries and enterprises to cope with the challenges posed by AFTA: "Vietnamese enterprises have not been fully aware of the challenges of economic integration into ASEAN. They just lobby for more protectionist policies from the Government and fail to make initiatives to meet the challenges and take advantage of the opportunities that economic integration provides."[86] The possibility of lost jobs and related social and political problems, therefore, loomed large in the wake of economic association with ASEAN.

Secondly, it was anticipated that as Vietnam's trade deficit grew and AFTA became fully operative, the markets for Vietnamese exports would become more limited. With respect to the products which Vietnam and the other ASEAN countries export, and when tariffs were fully reduced, it was expected that Vietnamese goods, which were already less competitive than those produced in ASEAN countries such as Singapore, Malaysia, Thailand, Indonesia, and the Philippines, would become even more expensive. According to a 2001 MOT report, agricultural products, fertilizers, automobiles, motorcycles, bicycles, home appliances and electronics, cement, construction glass, ceramics, paper, sugar, toys, textile, and garments, were Vietnamese export items that would lose market shares to ASEAN competitors.[87] Even in ASEAN markets, the volume of Vietnam's exports would tend to shrink. Another 2001 MOT report predicted that revenues from crude oil exported to ASEAN markets would fall by 10 per cent of total revenues of exports to ASEAN countries from 36 per cent in 1997, 16 per cent in 1998, and 20 per cent in 2001. Moreover, if Indonesia and the Philippines were to become self-sufficient in rice while Myanmar became a rice exporter, the percentage of rice in the total revenues of exports to the region would be less than the present level of 20 per cent. Exports to ASEAN market would further decline, the report suggested.[88]

Lastly, it was predicted that pressures on the government budget would also rise. As imports from ASEAN countries accounted for about 30 per cent of Vietnam's total imports, the tariffs cuts along the AFTA line would lead to a major decline in government revenues.[89] It was suggested that this might not be the case for other ASEAN countries because their trade with Vietnam only accounted for 1 per cent of their total trade.[90] Moreover, while the percentage of import taxes accounted for nearly 20 per cent of Vietnam's government budget revenue, the figure for other ASEAN countries was at about 10 per cent.[91] In short, for Vietnam, in real terms, economic association and integration with ASEAN seemed likely to prove more costly than expected.

As discussed above, in terms of institutions, Vietnam was not ready for joining ASEAN. Moreover, after becoming an ASEAN member, its institutional arrangements for ASEAN cooperation still remained anemic. Table 5.2 suggests this weakness.

The weakness of Vietnamese institutions at the time was no surprise, in view of its state of underdevelopment. The point, however, is that after nearly a decade of ASEAN membership, little institutional improvements had been achieved and obstacles to economic cooperation had not been removed. This tends to prove the weakness in the argument by some people in Hanoi that the membership in ASEAN and adherence to ASEAN working procedures would force Vietnam to further reform its domestic institutions and make them more efficient. They optimistically maintained, "although membership in ASEAN has brought about more challenges for Vietnam, it has offered us a valuable opportunity to do our best to reform and to become more mature as we integrate ourselves into the region."[92]

TABLE 5.2
Comparison of Soft Infrastructure (Max 5 Points)

Country	Labour Quality	Technology	Financial System	Geographic Conditions	Tax Regime	Policy Transparency	Administrative Efficiency	Average
Singapore	4.1	3.6	4.6	4.1	4.5	4.3	4.2	4.2
Malaysia	2.9	3.0	3.0	3.3	3.0	3.0	3.2	3.0
Brunei	2.8	2.6	3.3	2.9	3.3	3.0	2.3	2.9
Thailand	2.7	2.6	3.3	2.9	3.3	3.0	2.3	2.9
Philippines	3.1	2.8	2.6	2.7	2.7	2.4	2.2	2.6
Indonesia	2.5	2.2	2.6	2.6	2.3	1.9	1.8	2.3
Vietnam	2.7	1.9	1.6	2.1	1.8	1.4	1.5	1.9

Source: Dao Huy Giam, "Swimming without Life Vest", *Foreign Affairs Weekly*, Special Issue, p. 29.

A MOFA report also stressed, "Membership of ASEAN will help us to readjust bureaucratic procedures and working styles so as to be more compatible with international and regional standards."[93] Others, however, had reservations about joining ASEAN at an early date. They argued that the decision to join ASEAN was not based on a careful study of the AFTA and other economic cooperation projects and the implementation of these projects in Vietnam had not been based on institutional and personnel preparedness. As a result, economic integration and association with ASEAN became more problematic as the legal, administrative, and institutional frameworks were still "incomplete and incompatible with regional standards and practices", while businesses were still inactive.[94] Partly reflecting the "revisionist" argument, a government report in late 1997 read, in part,

> Our country's integration into the regional and global economy is an urgent but a new and complicated task that requires adequate awareness, ceaseless efforts, and good coordination by the whole system. Regrettably, our knowledge and awareness of the principles, fields of cooperation, and working procedures of the regional organizations that we have to integrate ourselves in are still at the primitive level; in addition to this, interest and efforts by agencies and officials concerned have not been up to the mark.[95]

The IX CPV National Congress in 2001 also stressed in its resolution that the party should focus its efforts, among other things, on conducting research on foreign affairs, training a competent contingent of officials to work on international affairs, and completing the establishment of mechanisms and frameworks for managing foreign affairs.[96] According to Dang Dinh Quy, the then Deputy Director of the MOFA Foreign Policy Department, this was a tacit acknowledgement of the weak capacity of the Foreign Service and of the other institutional arrangements that support the country's international relations. These weaknesses represent major obstacles to Hanoi's efforts to enhance international and regional cooperation, according to Dang Dinh Quy.[97]

The revisionists further argued that ASEAN institutional power had not been sufficient in creating external pressures on Vietnam to carry out more radical legal and institutional reforms, for better economic performance in the domestic and regional contexts. They seemed to question the official argument that the membership in ASEAN would further contribute to the reform process in Vietnam and to the economic well-being of the country. In other words, one may detect a certain sense of regret at the "hasty decision to join ASEAN" and some level of disappointment at the modest economic and institutional gains that resulted from the membership. Some even suggested that the 1997 financial crisis, which hit the founding ASEAN members so devastatingly, had deflated the "developmental myth" of the Southeast Asian economic "tigers". To counter such arguments, in November 1999, a MOFA report said,

> [We should] find suitable ways and measures to help the party and governmental officials and the people at large to correctly understand the nature and forms of ASEAN cooperation, the advantages and disadvantages of this type of regional cooperation, as well as the limits of ASEAN so that we do not have illusions and high expectations about cooperation with ASEAN as was the case when Vietnam became the member of CMEA in the past. We, however, should not have a pessimistic view about ASEAN and underestimate the importance of our country's participation in the ASEAN's cooperative activities, especially at a time when ASEAN is facing difficulties and challenges.[98]

CONCLUSION

This chapter suggested that the decision to join ASEAN was made against the background that Hanoi had understood little about institutional arrangements and working procedures of the organization. But at the same time, it turned out that because ASEAN still had loose institutional framework, and moreover, its member states were still reluctant to institutionalize ASEAN to make it a supranational organization, it was relatively easier for Vietnam to decide to join ASEAN. For the same reason, Hanoi faced little pressures from ASEAN to readjust its domestic institutional arrangements and make them more compatible to those of other ASEAN members while it was more difficult for Hanoi to participate and reap benefits from ASEAN economic cooperation.

The fact remained that Hanoi decided to become an ASEAN member at an early date. While Vietnamese leaders, for reasons that will be discussed in the next chapter, quickly decided to join ASEAN, this happy and rapid change in their thinking obscured the necessity of having a good grasp of the modalities of intra-ASEAN cooperation and of the necessity to train a contingent of experts on ASEAN and to build efficient institutional arrangements before joining it. This failure was bound to create long-term difficulties in economic cooperation with ASEAN in the future. In other words, Hanoi decided to join and promote cooperation with ASEAN at a time when the institutional arrangements of both ASEAN and Vietnam were not sufficiently developed to support Vietnam-ASEAN cooperation in particular and ASEAN cooperation in general, and when the economic and strategic gains for Vietnam in associating and integrating with ASEAN could only be of limited significance. Therefore, the rationale for this decision should be sought in a logic that lies outside the realist and institutionalist frameworks.

Notes

1. See, for example, Amitav Acharya, "A New Regional Order in Southeast Asia: ASEAN in the Post-Cold War Era", *Adelphi Paper*, No. 279, August 1993, p. 3.
2. The Document that gave birth to AFTA is only nine-pages long and an annex of the Joint Declaration of the Sixth ASEAN Summit held in Singapore (January 1992) while the Treaty on the North American Free Trade Area (NAFTA) contains 22,000 pages and serves as a legally binding document. For the recent discussions on ASEAN institutional disadvantages, see Marty Natalegawa, *Does ASEAN Matter? A View from Within* (Singapore: ISEAS – Yusof Ishak Institute, 2018); Mari Elka Pangestu and Rastam Mohd Isa, eds., *ASEAN Future Forward: Anticipating the Next 50 Years* (Kuala Lumpur: ISIS Malaysia, 2017); Kishore Mahbubani and Jeffrey Sng, *The ASEAN Miracle: A Catalyst for Peace* (Singapore: Ridge Books, 2017).
3. MOFA Southeast Asian and South Pacific Affairs Department (SEA/SPA) report, "Several Points on the Contemporary Vietnam-ASEAN Relations" (Một vài điểm về quan hệ Việt nam – ASEAN hiện nay), dated 26 June 1991.
4. SEA/SPA Department Report, "Reaction by Regional Countries to the Visit to some Southeast Asian Countries by the Chairman of the Ministers' Council Vo Van Kiet, 24 October–1 November" (Phản ứng của các nước trong khu vực về chuyến thăm của chủ tịch hội đồng bộ trưởng Võ Văn Kiệt đến một

số nước Đôngg nam Á). Thai Prime Minister Anand held that the process of confidence building and regional harmony was taking place with the Vietnamese decision to join the TAC. Ibid., p. 2.

5. SEA/SPA Department Report covering October 1991.
6. The Office of the CPV Central Committee Document Coded 153-CV/VPTW dated 25 February 1992.
7. SEA/SPA Department Report covering the First Quarter of 1992, p. 8.
8. SEA/SPA Department Weekly Working Schedules from May to July 1992.
9. SEA/SPA Department Report covering the Third Quarter of 1991, p. 8.
10. Transcripts of the meeting by SEA/SPA Department Deputy Director Nguyen Duy Hung with the Singaporean Chargé d'Affaires dated 25 May 1993.
11. Memo by SEA/SPA Department Director Le Cong Phung, dated 31 January 1992.
12. Transcripts by the SEA/SPA Department of the meeting by Deputy Foreign Minister Vu Khoan with the Thai National Defense Academy Delegation. Vu Khoan said during the meeting: Vietnam wants to become an ASEAN member. See also ASEAN Department Report, "On Vietnam-ASEAN Relations" (Về quan hệ Việt nam – ASEAN), prepared for the Twentieth Diplomatic Conference, November 1995, p. 3.
13. SEA/SPA Department Report covering October 1991.
14. The Office of the CPV Central Committee Document Coded 153-CV/VPTW dated 25 February 1992.
15. ASEAN Department Report, "On Vietnam-ASEAN Relations", prepared for the Twentieth Diplomatic Conference, November 1995, p. 2.
16. SEA/SPA Department 1992 report, "On Vietnam-ASEAN Relations".
17. MOFA Report, "On the 27th ASEAN AMM and the 1st ARF Meeting" (Về hội nghị ngoại trưởng ASEAN lần thứ 27 và cuộc họp lần thứ nhất của ARF), dated 28 July 1994, p. 3.
18. ASEAN Department Report, "On Vietnam-ASEAN Relations", prepared for the Twentieth Diplomatic Conference, November 1995, p. 3.
19. *People's Army*, 17 October 1993. See also ASEAN Department Research Paper, "5 Years after Joining ASEAN: Achievements, Challenges, and Prospects" (October 2001), p. 41.
20. IIR Southeast Asian Session Research Project, "ASEAN: The Formation, Development, and Prospects" (1991). Nguyen Vu Tung also argued that joining ASEAN should not be an immediate step. Nguyen Vu Tung, "Vietnam-ASEAN Relations", *Security Dialogue*, March 1994.
21. Nguyen Vu Tung, "On ASEAN's Activities since Its Establishment", IIR *International Studies*, no. 3, July, 1994, pp. 35–36.

22. Hoang Anh Tuan, "ASEAN Dispute Management: Implications for Vietnam and an Expanded ASEAN", *Contemporary Southeast Asia* 18, no. 1 (June 1996).
23. ASEAN Department Report, "On Vietnam-ASEAN Relations", prepared for the Twentieth Diplomatic Conference, November 1995, p. 3.
24. The Document by the Government Office, coded 180/QHQT dated 27 June 1994.
25. MOFA Memo, "On Foreign Minister Nguyen Manh Cam's Participation in the 27th AMM and 1st ARF Meeting" (Báo cáo trình Bộ chính trị và Ban bí thư về sự tham gia của bộ trưởng ngoại giao Nguyễn Mạnh Cầm tại hội nghị ngoại trưởng ASEAN lần thứ 27 và cuộc họp lần thứ nhất của ARF), submitted to the CPV Politburo and Secretariat, dated 15 July 1994, p. 2.
26. ASEAN Department, Talking Points "On Issues Related to Vietnam-ASEAN Relations" (Về các vấn đề liên quan đến quan hệ Việt nam – ASEAN), prepared for the ASEAN-Vietnam Consultative Meeting during the Twenty-Seventh AMM, Bangkok, July 1994, p. 1.
27. Nguyen Manh Cam's 23 July 1994 cable to the Politburo stressed: The Politburo instruction has been realized to the fullest extent.
28. Nguyen Manh Cam's interview given to *Nhan Dan*, 29 July 1994.
29. MOFA Memo, "On Foreign Minister Nguyen Manh Cam's Participation to the 27th AMM and 1st ARF Meeting", submitted to the CPV Politburo and Secretariat, dated 15 July 1994, p. 2.
30. Interview by the author with Vu Duc Dam, who was also one of the secretaries for Prime Minister Vo Van Kiet. (Hanoi, 15 January 2003). Mr Dam became Deputy Prime Minister in 2013.
31 Interview by the author with Vu Duc Dam on 15 January 2003.
32. Nguyen Ngoc Son, "Those Unforgettable Days", *Foreign Affairs Weekly*, Special Issues for the Fifth Anniversary of Vietnam's Joining ASEAN. The same line can also be detected in a Talking Point the MOFA had prepared in 1995 for National Leaders.
33. Nguyen Ngoc Son, "Those Unforgettable Days".
34. ASEAN Department 1996 Report, "One Year after Joining ASEAN" (Một năm sau khi gia nhập ASEAN), p. 8.
35. Interview with Vu Duc Dam, 15 January 2003.
36. MOFA, The 1993 Research Programme, p. 2.
37. MOFA Policy Planning Department Report, "Review of the Situation and Foreign Policy for 1993" (Kiểm điểm tình hình và chính sách đối ngoại năm 1993), p. 8.
38. Nguyen Ngoc Son, "Those Unforgettable Days", p. 7. A talking point prepared

for President Le Duc Anh's visit to France and some Middle East and African countries in April 1995 said: "Vietnam lacks a contingent of officials who are knowledgeable about ASEAN and are fluent in English in order to actively participate in the ASEAN activities. To train these officials is an urgent task for Vietnam and we welcome and highly appreciate any assistance from foreign countries and international organizations in this regard."

39. MOFA ASEAN Department and IIR Southeast Asian Session Research Project, "ASEAN, Vietnam-ASEAN Relations, and Prospects", (1995).
40. The Draft Regulations of the Association of Southeast Asia Researchers (ASEAR), p. 2.
41. MOFA 18 October 1994 Report, "On the Results of the Working Visit by the Inter-ministerial Delegation to Some ASEAN Countries and the ASEAN Secretariat" (Về kết quả chuyến thăm làm việc của đoàn liên ngành tại một số nước ASEAN và Ban thư ký ASEAN), p. 1.
42. MOFA 18 October 1994 Report, "On the Results of the Working Visit by the Inter-ministerial Delegation to some ASEAN Countries and the ASEAN Secretariat", p. 6.
43. Ibid., p. 9.
44. The 8 July 1995 Government Office Decision coded 3750/QHQT Concerning the Formation of Study Groups on ASEAN Cooperation.
45. Report by the Secretary-General of the ASEAN National Committee (ANC) at the ANC Second Meeting (Hanoi, 20 January 1996), p. 4.
46. Ibid., pp. 10 and 14.
47. The Government Office, "Conclusions of the First ANC Meeting" (Hanoi, 20 November 1995), p. 5.
48. Interview by Nguyen Hoang An, ASEAN Department Deputy Director with the author, Hanoi, August 2002. It is difficult for the author to support the complaint of Nguyen Hoang An because it is always natural to start with easy issues and then gradually to move to more difficult ones. In view of the knowledge gap between Vietnam and ASEAN at that time, Vietnamese officials should have been more modest. Further, they should have taken advantage of every opportunity to learn as much about ASEAN as possible, in addition to the assignment given to them by the ASEAN Secretariat.
49. Report by the Secretary-General of the ASEAN National Committee (ANC) at the ANC Second Meeting (Hanoi, 20 January 1996,) p. 2.
50. ANC Review, "Two Years of Vietnam's Participation in ASEAN Functional Cooperation" (Hai năm Việt nam tham gia hợp tác chuyên ngành ASEAN), 2 October 1997, p. 7.

51. MOFA ASEAN Department Report, "On Vietnam-ASEAN Relations", prepared for the 22nd Diplomatic Conference, November 1999, p. 14.
52. Prime Minister's Decision No. 637.
53. Prime Minister's Decision No. 651.
54. Report by the Secretary-General of the ASEAN National Committee (ANC) at the ANC Second Meeting (Hanoi, 20 January 1996), pp. 11–12.
55. Government's Decisions on 6 November 1995, coded 6358/VPUB.
56. Report by the Secretary-General of the ASEAN National Committee (ANC) at the ANC Second Meeting (Hanoi, 20 January 1996), p. 15.
57. Interview with Vu Duc Dam by the author, Hanoi, on 15 January 2003.
58. Ibid. According to the Report by the ANC Secretary-General at the ANC Second Meeting (p. 3), the work of coding goods was completed in December 1995.
59. MOFA General Economical Department, *Globalization and Vietnam's Economic Integration* (Hanoi: National Politics Publishing House, 1999), p. 256.
60. Interview with Vu Duc Dam by the author, Hanoi, 15 January 2003.
61. Interview with Nguyen Thanh Huy, MOFA ASEAN Department Official by the author, Hanoi, 26 January 2003.
62. Report by the Secretary-General of the ASEAN National Committee (ANC) at the ANC Second Meeting (Hanoi, 20 January 1996), p. 13.
63. Interview with Vu Duc Dam by the author, Hanoi, 15 January 2003.
64. MOFA ASEAN Department Report, "On Vietnam-ASEAN Relations", November 1999, p. 12.
65. The Government Report, "On the World Situation and Our State's Foreign Affairs in 2002" (Về tình hình thế giới và quan hệ đối ngoại của nhà nước ta trong năm 2002), submitted to the Second Session of the XIth National Assembly, November 2002, pp. 9–10.
66. The Government Report, "On Our State's Foreign Affairs in 1996 and the Review of the 1991–1996 Period" (Về quan hệ đối ngoại của nhà nước ta trong năm 1996 và kiểm điểm giai đoạn 1991–1996), submitted to the Tenth Session, the VIII National Assembly, October 1996, p. 6.
67. Report by the Secretary-General of the ASEAN National Committee (ANC) at the ANC Second Meeting (Hanoi, 20 January 1996), p. 4.
68. *Trade Newspaper*, 14 January 2003.
69. MOFA ASEAN Department, "On the Vietnam-ASEAN relations", November 1999, p. 14.
70. *Lao Dong*, 7 August 2002. Another example to illustrate the absence of serious

research prior to participating ASEAN cooperative projects: After December 1999, Vietnamese national leaders declared their strong commitment to participation in the ASEAN East-West Corridor Project designed to construct a web of roads connecting ASEAN countries, starting from Singapore to Vietnam, via Laos and Cambodia. Hanoi attached a great economic and political importance to the project, which could "place Vietnam in a better position in international communications and transportation" (see Viet Chung, "The East-West Corridor Project", *Foreign Affairs Weekly*, Special Issue marking the Fifthth Anniversary of Vietnam's Joining ASEAN, p. 34.) The implementation of the project, however, faced major difficulties, not least in fact, that the original ASEAN members apply right-hand-side traffic rules while Vietnam applies left-hand ones. The difference has, in theory and practice, removed Vietnam from the integrated project to connect all ASEAN countries by the web of roads. Indeed, it had made the construction of such a web itself problematic. Interviews by the author with MOFA ASEAN Department officials in Hanoi, August 2002.
71. Report by the Secretary-General of the ASEAN National Committee (ANC) at the ANC Second Meeting (Hanoi, 20 January 1996,) p. 3.
72. Pham Chi Lan, *Trade Newspaper*, December 2002. The Report "Opportunities and Challenges Brought about by AFTA", by the MOT Multilateral Trade Policy, (p. 8) also stressed: "Vietnamese enterprises have not been aware of the opportunities and challenges that lie ahead in the process of economic integration. Many of the enterprises have not got rid of the dependent mentality, demanding the State to adopt protectionist policies, thus failing to readjust investment and production plans in order to take advantage of the opportunities offered as well as face the challenges posed by economic integration."
73. Interview by the author with Nguyen Hoai Son, MOT Multilateral Trade Policy Official, Hanoi, May 2003.
74. Hanh Phuong, "The AFTA Roadmap: Challenges to the Vietnamese Economy", *Lao Dong*, 4 January 2003.
75. MOFA ASEAN Department Report, "On Vietnam-ASEAN Relations", prepared for the Twentieth Diplomatic Conference (November 1995), p. 4.
76. Exchanges by the author with Pham Huu Chi, Deputy Director of MOFA ASEAN Department, 7 July 2003.
77. The Indonesian economist Hadi Soesastro at the Indonesian Center for Strategic and International Studies (CSIS) stressed this point in his exchanges with the author in Yangon, Myanmar (7 and 8 February 2003).

78. The Singaporean economist Chia Siow Yue at the Singapore Institute of International Affairs (SIIA) stressed this point in her exchanges with the author in Yangon, Myanmar, (7 and 8 February 2003).
79. Singapore Institute of Southeast Asian Studies (ISEAS), A Draft "Concept Paper on the ASEAN Economic Community", submitted for the ASEAN-ISIS review (February 2003), p. 9.
80. Interview by the author with Vu Duc Dam, 15 January 2003.
81. Foreign Minister Nguyen Manh Cam, "Two Years after Joining ASEAN", *Communist Review* (July 1997), p. 7. Foreign Minister Nguyen Dy Nien, "Five Years after Joining ASEAN", *Foreign Affairs Weekly*, Special Issues, p. 8. See also Carlyle Thayer, *Vietnam's Membership in ASEAN*, a report submitted to the Foreign Affairs and Trade Committee, Australian Parliament, 1996. ASEAN Department 1996 Report, "One Year after Joining ASEAN", p. 8.
82. MOFA ASEAN Department Report "On Vietnam-ASEAN Relations" (November 1999), p. 11.
83. The current account balance for the years of 1995, 1996, and 1997 were –7.3, –9.3, and –10.1 per cent, respectively. See Vo Hung Dzung, "Vietnam's Foreign Trades from 1991 to 2000: Achievements and Problems", in *Economic Studies*, no. 11 (294), November 2002, pp. 10 and 11.
84. Dao Huy Giam, "Swimming without Life Vest", *Foreign Affairs Weekly*, Special Issue, p. 28.
85. Vo Hung Dzung, "Vietnam's Foreign Trades from 1991 to 2000: Achievements and Problems", p. 10.
86. Dang Van Thang, MOT Multilateral Trade Policy Department Deputy Director, "A Report on Vietnam's Integration into ASEAN" (Báo cáo về hội nhập của Việt Nam vào ASEAN), July 2001, pp. 15–16.
87. Dang Van Thang, "A Report on Vietnam's Integration into ASEAN", July 2001, p. 16.
88. Ibid., p. 17.
89. MOFA, General Economic Department, *Globalization and Vietnam's Economic Integration*, p. 250.
90. Ibid.
91. Dang Van Thang, "A Report on Vietnam's Integration into ASEAN", July 2001, p. 16.
92. MOFA ASEAN Department Report, "On Vietnam-ASEAN Relations", November 1999, p. 11.
93. Ibid., p. 11.

94. Ibid., p. 12.
95. The Government Report, "On Our State's Foreign Affairs in 1997" (Về quan hệ đối ngoại của nhà nước ta năm 1977), submitted to the IXth National Assembly November 1997 Session, p. 16. The Government Report "On Our State's Foreign Affairs in 1998", submitted to the Fourth Session of the Xth National Assembly, October 1998 (p. 16) read: "The process of integrating Vietnam into the region and the rest of the world requires a full awareness of opportunities and challenges, strong efforts, and close coordination by all units of the system. The reality has, however, shown that our knowledge on integration is very limited, our cadres hardly grasp the nature of the matter, and the offices and departments, especially enterprises have not been active enough."

    The Government Report "On the World Situation and Our State's Foreign Affairs in 2002" (Về tình hình thế giới và quan hệ đối ngoại của nhà nước ta năm 2002), submitted to the Second Session of the XIth National Assembly, November 2002 (pp. 9–10) wrote: "The legal, personnel, and institutional preparation for our country's economic integration with the rest of the world has not kept pace with changes in the region and the world. Moreover, the institutional mechanisms and arrangements to coordinate the activities of ministries, sectors, and provinces are still incomplete and incompatible, thus limiting the effectiveness of our efforts as far as foreign affairs are concerned."
96. The CPV, *Major Documents of the IXth National Congress* (Hanoi: National Politics Publishing House, 2001), p. 14.
97. Interview by the author with Dang Dinh Quy, MOFA Foreign Policy Department Deputy Director, Hanoi, 19 January 2003.
98. MOFA ASEAN Department Report, "On Vietnam-ASEAN Relations", November 1999, p. 12

6

ASEAN MEMBERSHIP AND VIETNAM'S SHIFTING NATIONAL IDENTITY

In the absence of a detailed understanding of the ASEAN working procedures and principles as well as institutional arrangements to promote cooperation, the decision to join ASEAN was, according to many officials whom the author interviewed, "the political will" of Hanoi to further commit itself to the region.[1] What then was the nature of this political will? The decision to seek an early admission to the organization created additional pressures on the bureaucratic system, and brought about "new difficulties and challenges in the course of economic development".[2] Moreover, as discussed earlier, ASEAN membership did not ensure specific security benefits for Vietnam. What then were the real purposes of Vietnam's membership in ASEAN? This chapter will further trace the

---

* This chapter was adapted from the article entitled "Vietnam's Membership of ASEAN: A Constructivist Interpretation", *Contemporary Southeast Asia* 29, no. 3 (April 2007): 483–505. Reproduced with permission of the ISEAS – Yusof Ishak Institute.

official policy statements as well as the internal debates in Hanoi related to the question of ASEAN membership. Hopefully, tracing the internal debates among Hanoi's decision-makers on foreign policy in general and on the ASEAN membership in particular would shed light on the above-mentioned questions.

MORE ABOUT THE INTERNAL DEBATES

Only fourteen months elapsed between the February 1993 statement of "joining ASEAN at an appropriate time" and the April 1994 statement about "seeking an early membership". Then after another three months, that is in July 1994, Hanoi took the decision to join ASEAN. These developments showed that perceived differences between Vietnam and ASEAN did not prevent Hanoi from making the decision for an early ASEAN membership. And since the process of joining ASEAN was not so "long and complicated" as had been predicted,[3] we should look for more a plausible logic in the way Hanoi perceived the similarities between Vietnam and ASEAN as the underlying reasons for Vietnam to join the organization.

SIMILARITY IN POLITICAL STRUCTURES AND PRACTICES

National interests, according to the classical and structural realist as well as liberal institutionalist approaches, relate to the very survival of states existing in the anarchical environment of international politics that creates continuous wars and conflicts. Yet, the nature of international politics in the Third World has more to do with the survival of the ruling regimes that act in the name of their countries. The logics of international relations in Southeast Asia *à la* ASEAN should be seen in this perspective: the state of anarchy and interstate conflicts were gradually replaced by modes of regional cooperation aimed at enhancing the regime legitimacy and the resultant regime survival of the regional countries. To state in another way, a stable and cooperative environment in the region has been beneficial for regional countries to focus on stabilizing domestic politics and achieving socio-economic development so that the goal of keeping specific ruling regimes in power could be attained. This had become the nature of the regional order among ASEAN member countries since 1967, and furthermore, the approach that ASEAN countries wanted to apply to the ASEAN-Vietnamese relationship from the early 1970s. After 1986 and especially after 1990, detecting the genuine changes in the priorities in both domestic and international policies in Hanoi, ASEAN became more proactive in engaging Vietnam into the regional order and eager to admit Vietnam to ASEAN. For example, in 1991, Malaysian Prime Minister Mahathir stated that differences in socio-political systems between Vietnam and ASEAN would not prevent Vietnam from joining the association.[4]

The focus of inquiry, therefore, would be on the question of when leaders in Hanoi were able to grasp the nature of the ASEAN mode of regional politics. Great importance is attached to answering this question, for this would be definitive to the new perceptions of and subsequent policies by Hanoi towards ASEAN and the ASEAN membership.

It seems obvious that when faced with economic difficulties and resultant political challenges to regime legitimacy, Hanoi became more ready to learn ASEAN's economic and political lessons. In the late 1970s and early 1990s, when economic problems became increasingly salient, there were efforts at readjusting the developmental strategy to make it more compatible with non-socialist models. According to Gareth Porter, Foreign Minister Nguyen Co Thach was the first among Vietnamese leaders to begin studies on the merits of the market economy.[5] As Porter observed, based on the new knowledge Nguyen Co Thach initiated a debate in Hanoi on the need for coexistence between capitalist and socialist systems and participation in the international division of labour, which led to the adoption of the Resolution of the Sixth CPV CC Plenum in July 1984 in which Hanoi officially laid down the task of actively participating in the international division of labour influenced by the global capitalist system. The Resolution continued to serve as one of the most important documents guiding the economic reforms that officially began with the CPV Sixth National Congress in 1986.[6] Reflecting the Resolution, a MOFA Annual Report of 1986 also wrote,

> The production forces of mankind have achieved great leaps forward thanks to the progress of the new scientific and technological revolution, the high level of internationalization of economic activities, and the increased state of interdependence. The world economy, as a result,

has become a united whole of which our economy is an integral part. Regrettably, however, we have not linked our economic developments with these new trends, thus failing to combine our national strength with that of the era. For the last ten years, our five-year plans have been designed in isolation from the world economic environment that has undergone profound and rapid changes.[7]

In December 1996, at the Sixth National Congress, the CPV adopted a Political Report that read in part,

The scientific and technological revolution, the globalization of production forces, and the emergence of a single world market are the major characteristics of our era, forcing all the countries to readjust their economies in order to seek and protect their optimal niches in the international division of labour. And the internationalization of production forces has led to the inevitable need for economic cooperation and peaceful coexistence among countries with different political systems.[8]

These were indirect acknowledgements of the failures of the socialist mode of economic development and division of labour. What Hanoi wanted now was integration into the capitalist system and together with this, more cooperation with countries of different political systems and ideologies. This was a step forward in the thinking of Vietnamese leaders, less focused on the traditional worldview that divided the world into two mutually exclusive camps.[9] In that context, ASEAN's lessons became attractive to Hanoi.

The failed Soviet-style and the successful ASEAN developmental experiences in mid-1980s and thereafter altogether encouraged Hanoi to search for a new model of economic and political development that would help it to get out of its deep socio-economic crisis at home. The MOFA Annual Report of 1986 acknowledged,

Asia continues to be the most dynamic region of the world in economic terms. ASEAN countries are currently enjoying an economic growth that is many times higher than that of the Indochinese countries. Our country still remains in the group of about 100 backward countries. The economic gap between our country and other countries, especially our neighbouring countries has widened over the last ten years. And the gap will be wider.[10]

The Report then stressed, "Economic problems will become a threat, with political, security, and social dimensions that will affect domestic politics, Indochinese solidarity, our relations with other socialist countries, and the standing of our country. National defense, national security, and our political regime will only be strong if they are based on a strong economy."[11]

The new approach to security and threats also revealed that Hanoi's concern over regime stability and survival in the 1980s was even bigger than the concern of Vietnam in the past centuries with respect to foreign aggressions. The new focus on developmental needs, which became more clearly perceived in the post-Cold War context, marked by reduced global tensions and the collapse of socialist regimes, reflected the internal dimension of national security, namely, regime security. The Thirteenth Politburo Resolution of May 1988 held that economic backwardness and political isolation represented major threats to the security and independence of Vietnam, but did not name specifically the source of threat. Tran Quang Co, Deputy Foreign Minister, wrote in 1992, "At present, the enemies of Vietnam are poverty, famine, and backwardness; and the friends of Vietnam are all those who support us in the fight against these enemies."[12] In January 1994, when the CPV held a mid-term Congress, a list of Four Threats to national security was presented. These threats were identified as poverty and economic backwardness, corruption and inefficiency and bureaucratism, peaceful evolution, and the complex international situation. The list of threats also showed that by 1994, Vietnam was no longer isolated and the leadership felt that their regime was less vulnerable to outside dangers. The order of various items in the list and the relations among the threats also suggested that leaders in Hanoi were more concerned over regime legitimacy and believed that the threats of peaceful evolution and complex international situation would be less dangerous if the regime could improve the living conditions of the people and reduce corruption. Deputy Foreign Minister Vu Khoan argued that in the absence of an advanced economy, Vietnam could not have sufficient potential to defend the country and enhance its standing in the world.[13] He also stressed that without economic development the CPV's role would be seriously challenged. The lessons of the collapse of the socialist regimes in Eastern Europe and the Soviet Union were reflected in what he wrote:

> Reality in many countries has shown that the threats to security, sovereignty, and territorial integrity of a country lie within the national borders. Reality has also shown that in many cases, even without the element of foreign aggression, security and sovereignty were challenged and territories were divided because of mistakes in economic, cultural, ethnic, and religious policies. The developmental backwardness will reduce the people's belief, cause social problems, and inevitably, lead to threats to security, public order, and even regime survival.[14]

Poverty and economic backwardness, as well as corruption, inefficiency, and bureaucratism, not the threats from outside, directly challenged the legitimacy of the CPV leadership. Before the reforms started, the "grave socio-political crisis" in Vietnam had been recognized and openly mentioned in official documents.[15] The reforms that Hanoi started were, therefore, designed to ensure economic and social stability and also to protect the regime and the CPV ruling role from possible challenges from within.[16]

Such an approach to national security and threats clearly brought Hanoi's leaders closer to their ASEAN counterparts. This approach also indicated that the ASEAN models for domestic and foreign policies had now become more attractive to Vietnamese leaders. In a report in 1993, the then Deputy Prime Minister Phan Van Khai, wrote,

> In order to win the people's heart and their support, to strengthen and enhance the stability of the political structure, we must adopt the developmental strategy of the ASEAN countries. The key task is economic growth and social progress, and they become even more urgent as Vietnam is situated in a region marked by most dynamic economic activities in the world.[17]

Intellectual circles held similar views. Pham Nguyen Long, researcher at the Institute for Southeast Asian Studies, argued that the ASEAN developmental models were suitable for Vietnam and the study of these models was of great importance if Vietnam did not want to be left out of the mainstream of prosperity in Southeast Asia.[18] The more they learned about ASEAN, the more thinkers saw that the survival of ruling regimes was a major concern they shared with ASEAN governments.

Around the end of 1992, a group of IIR researchers were invited to take part in a comparative study of non-socialist political systems. The study, which was sponsored by the Ho Chi Minh National Political Academy—a major theoretical and training institution under the CPV—was designed to work out the theoretical ground for the continued maintenance of power by the CPV. The IIR researchers were asked to make a paper on the political systems and regimes in ASEAN countries. Their major findings were presented as follows,

- ASEAN governments are pro-West and anti-communist. Yet they are nationalist by nature, strive to defend their national independence and make their countries strong, especially in the economic field.
- They are determined to defend their ruling regimes, and refuse to share power with the people.
- Their nation-building formula is: export-oriented market economy, limited democracy, and even authoritarianism in some countries. This formula is different from the parliamentary democratic systems in the West, but is suitable in the Asian context. Thanks to this formula, most ASEAN countries have since the 1960s gained major economic achievements, stabilized their internal situation, and strengthened their ruling regimes.
- The nation-building formula of ASEAN is not totally different from ours, namely planned market economy under the leadership of the Communist Party, with some commonalities in political structures and practices. Therefore, our formula, if correctly applied, will bring about positive socio-economic and political results and would strengthen the position of the Party vis-à-vis the people.[19]

It was surprising that during the discussions the above findings did not elicit any objections from the other participants and a summary of the paper was sent to high-level decision-makers. IIR researchers even went to the length of suggesting to ASEAN diplomats in Hanoi to invite Vietnamese national leaders to visit ASEAN countries as a most effective way to improve Hanoi's awareness of the commonalities that existed between Vietnam and ASEAN countries in spite of their different political systems.[20]

In the meantime, ASEAN countries accelerated the process of reconciliation between Vietnam and ASEAN, thus making it easier for the learning process in Hanoi to gather strength. In mid-1989, Malaysian Prime Minister stated,

> We should be ready to launch the second phase of the regional reconciliation in order to achieve our ultimate objective, namely to build a system of Southeast Asian nations at peace with each other and closely linked to one another in a dynamic relationship of mutual respect and mutually beneficial cooperation.[21]

Leaders of Singapore and Malaysia held that differences between Vietnam and ASEAN countries in socio-political systems and levels of economic development were not obstacles to Vietnam's membership in ASEAN.[22]

From the late 1980s, many ASEAN officials began visiting Vietnam. According to the Southeast Asian Affairs Department annual report of 1989,

> all the ASEAN countries have sent delegations of officials, ranking from Deputy Foreign Minister to Deputy Prime Minister, to Hanoi. These visits have revived the political dialogues and exchanges, thus increasing the level of mutual understanding, narrowing down the knowledge gaps, building confidence, and laying the foundation for relations in the future.[23]

Hanoi even invited Singapore's former Prime Minister Lee Kuan Yew to become a special advisor on economic and political issues. In a MOFA report of a visit of Lee Kuan Yew to Hanoi on 23–27 April 1992, one could detect a sense of increasing friendship between Hanoi and ASEAN leaders. The report wrote:

> Mr Lee has closely studied the situation in Vietnam. Although the schedule was tight, he tried to have more exchanges of views with us in order to learn more about us. In his speeches, he was cautious and modest, but also candid, sincere, sharp, and informative. He was very pleased and moved by our leaders' sincerity, openness, and respect for him. In addition, all his entourage considered the visit "extremely good".[24]

The visits by Vietnamese leaders to ASEAN had even greater impacts. The CPV Seventh National Congress in 1991 stated in its Resolution, "We should establish relations with ruling parties in the region."[25] After the collapse of the Soviet Union, the CPV expanded its external relationships with United Malays National Organization (UMNO), People's Action Party (PAP) and Golongan Karya (Golkar) as the ruling parties in Malaysia, Singapore and

Indonesia, respectively. From 1993 to 1994, all the national leaders of Vietnam, including the CPV General Secretary, the President of the State, the Chairman of the National Assembly, and the Prime Minister, visited ASEAN countries. These high-level visits, as predicted, accelerated the learning process in Hanoi. A MOFA report on the 5–8 October 1993 visit by General Secretary Do Muoi to Singapore and Thailand stressed, "the visit is of great political significance. It shows that ideological differences are no longer obstacles to the development of Vietnam-ASEAN relations."[26] A report by the CERC on the same visit wrote, "This is the first visit by our General Secretary to a number of ASEAN countries. The General Secretary was received with the highest level of respect. The overall atmosphere was the one of openness, sincerity, and friendship. In one of the meetings, Mr Lee Kuan Yew said that Vietnam's policy of economic reforms and political stability was a correct one."[27] On 24–27 March 1994, General Secretary Do Muoi visited Malaysia. The CERC report on the visit stressed:

> The visit to Malaysia was successful. It contributed to enhance mutual understanding and confidence, thus further promoting the friendly and cooperative relations between the two countries in many fields. In the official and private talks, Prime Minister Mahathir and other national and provincial leaders were open, sincere, and showed respect to us. The two sides agreed to increase cooperation in all fields. We realize that Malaysia's developmental experience is more suitable to us as compared with other ASEAN countries.[28]

The May 1994 visit by President of State Le Duc Anh to Indonesia was seen in the same way. A MOFA report on the visit wrote, "more understanding about the political systems was acquired, and together with the Vietnam's withdrawal of troops from Cambodia and reforms at home, Vietnam-ASEAN relations are becoming better and better."[29]

When relations between leaders in ASEAN countries and Vietnam developed both in personal and institutional terms, it was no coincidence that Vietnam-ASEAN relations developed in qualitative terms. The MOFA SEA/SPA Department annual report of 1994 stressed, "1994 is the turning-point year, because Vietnam-ASEAN relations changed qualitatively. The relations of suspicion and hostility were transformed into all-sided cooperation, bilateral and multilateral." The report especially linked the improvement of relations with the visits to ASEAN countries by Vietnam's national leaders, "1994 is the year in which the highest leaders of Vietnam, including General Secretary Do Muoi and President Le Duc Anh, visited ASEAN countries and the CPV developed relations with the ruling parties in Southeast Asia."[30]

These visits had more profound effects than was immediately apparent. Speaking in private, a Cabinet Office official said that Hanoi leaders believed that their first-hand experience in dealing with ASEAN leaders and in visiting ASEAN countries helped to confirm what the reports had told them about ASEAN. They even confided that "the ASEAN countries are more similar to us than we have thought", and "ASEAN political documents and cooperative projects have proved that ASEAN is not an anti-communist military alliance and the ASEAN countries' objectives in terms of nation-building and external relations are 80 per cent similar to ours."[31] Note that in its first memo dated July 1992 arguing for Vietnam's joining ASEAN, MOFA said, "from a political grouping, ASEAN has been transformed into a regional politico-economic organization. In terms of military cooperation, ASEAN member countries promote bilateral military cooperation and have no ASEAN-wide cooperation in this field."[32] And in the above-mentioned series of MOFA memos, the following point was stressed, "ASEAN basic documents *do not have any point that is openly or tacitly suggestive of the anti-communist, anti-socialist, and anti-Vietnamese nature of the organization. ASEAN is not aimed at opposing any other country*," and its objectives "*are in principle in accordance with the principles in our Party's and State's foreign policy.*"[33] In short, only when Vietnamese national leaders visited ASEAN countries, held direct discussions with ASEAN leaders, and began to study the ASEAN developmental models, they became aware of the similarities and commonalities that existed between Vietnam and ASEAN countries and leaders. As a result, Vietnam-ASEAN relations developed rapidly and the last obstacles, namely the perceived differences in political and economic systems between Vietnam and ASEAN, were removed, thus making Vietnam's membership in ASEAN possible. According to a CERC official, "the development of Vietnam-ASEAN relations through the Party's channels has been instrumental in making a full political integration of Vietnam into the region possible."[34]

A key common point between Vietnam and ASEAN countries was the commitment to maintenance of the (de facto) one-party rule system.[35] By 1995, while Malaysia and Indonesia had several political parties, only one party (namely, UMNO and Golkar, respectively) dominated their internal politics. In Singapore, the PAP held an almost absolute majority in the Parliament. With the return to civilian rule, Thailand at the time was being described as soft authoritarianism. In order to enjoy legitimacy and to continue to stay in power, the ruling regimes in Southeast Asia found it imperative to achieve economic development through the market economy which first and foremost required stability in domestic settings (obtained largely by adopting authoritarian measures) and in regional settings (obtained largely by cultivating friendly and cooperative relations with other regional countries). Such policies have brought much success to the non-socialist countries of Southeast Asia, especially since the establishment of ASEAN in 1967 and furthermore gave rise to the plausibility of the non-democratic peace among ASEAN countries.

Since the mid-1980s, Hanoi started to see the merits of the ASEAN model and became more receptive to the ASEAN order of regional relations. Vietnamese top leaders' first-hand experiences with ASEAN countries and their leaders further consolidated the choice in Hanoi. Therefore, Hanoi's perception of differences in the nature of economic and political systems in Vietnam and ASEAN countries, which had been supposed to complicate the process of the country joining ASEAN, was diminished during 1994. Hanoi then was ready to join ASEAN, believing that ASEAN membership would help the regime to consolidate its legitimacy and power. The MOFA Review of the five-year period since Vietnam joined ASEAN wrote, "In essence, the ASEAN membership is designed to create a better environment for us to expand external relations in a proactive manner for the purpose of development and regime maintenance."[36] Kim Ninh also noted, "Socialism in Vietnam is increasingly similar to the one-party and authoritarian rule that is a common feature in Asia, namely liberal in economic development, but conservative in terms of social and political changes."[37]

In short, the argument that Vietnam should not seek an early membership in ASEAN due to differences in political systems was put forth at a time when Hanoi's top leaders had not visited ASEAN countries and had no direct contacts and discussions with their leaders. The high-level visits and discussions did serve to dispel the initial reluctance to join ASEAN. During the course of 1994, Hanoi's top leaders became aware of many similarities between Vietnam and ASEAN countries, and as a result, they became ready to join ASEAN. According to MOFA, the turning point was 1994.

COMMON FOREIGN POLICY OBJECTIVES

When leaders in Hanoi understood that regime survival was a common objective shared by Vietnam and ASEAN countries, they also became aware that regime survival mainly depended on economic growth, which in turn, was dependent on, among other things, the peaceful relationships among the regional states. Therefore, similar foreign policy objectives also served as an important factor for the promotion of Vietnam-ASEAN relations. To put it differently, when Hanoi understood that the foreign policy of ASEAN was similar to that of Vietnam, they became more ready to join ASEAN, thus downplaying the argument for a "long and complicated process of joining ASEAN" due to differences in levels of economic development between Vietnam and ASEAN. The differences in levels of economic developments were perceived and understood, but they did not prevent Vietnam from seeking an early ASEAN membership. In addition to this, as Funston pointed out, economic gaps, including levels of development and income per capita, had always existed among the original ASEAN members and could in no way be narrowed.[38] Besides, ASEAN cooperation did not require a high level of economic integration as compared with the EU experience, which meant that the economic entry barriers for prospective members were non-existent. Interestingly, the standard argument was turned around when Hanoi came to argue that ASEAN membership had contributed to narrowing down the developmental gaps between the original ASEAN states and the new members including Vietnam. A MOFA ASEAN document stated, "Vietnam now plays an active role in ASEAN in promoting the ASEAN cooperative projects designed to meet the new members' needs for narrowing down the developmental gaps among the members."[39]

While ASEAN was no longer concerned over Hanoi's alleged expansionist ambitions, Hanoi no longer had any serious reservations about ASEAN's foreign policy and the principles and objectives of the regional order the organization advocated. This was clearly seen in the way the Bali Treaty was viewed. In the 6 May 1992 memo sent to the State Council, Vo Van Kiet, on behalf of the Council of Ministers, proposed that the former ratify the treaty, which Foreign Minister Nguyen Manh Cam was going to sign in July. Vo Van Kiet stressed,

> On 25 February 1992, the Party Secretariat agreed with our accession to the Bali Treaty. After closely examining the Treaty, the Council of Ministers also realized that the contents of the Treaty, including its objectives and the principles for regional cooperation that ASEAN upholds, are compatible with the foreign policy of our Party and State. The accession to the Treaty will create conditions favorable for national construction and the promotion of cooperation among the parties to the Treaty.[40]

Since the end of 1991, ASEAN researchers in Hanoi had concluded that ASEAN countries' foreign policies, as reflected in the organization's policy, were designed to serve national interests. These were foreign policies of small- and medium-sized countries striving for peace, stability, and economic development.[41] Vu Khoan wrote in 1994:

> The ASEAN countries desire for peace, stability, and expanded cooperation is in keeping with our policy that tries to take advantage of the favourable international conditions and the emerging environment of peace and stability to construct and defend our country, thus realizing the objectives of building a strong country, a prosperous nation, and an advanced society. The ASEAN foreign policy, therefore, is compatible with the foreign policy of diversification and multilateralization of our external relations in which the primary focus is on cooperation with countries in Southeast Asia.[42]

In short, Hanoi believed that peace among Southeast Asian countries was possible thanks to the common need to ensure a peaceful regional environment conducive to economic growth, a derivative of the regime survival objective. As early as 1990, a MOFA policy analysis concluded, "Like us, ASEAN countries do not want to be caught up in the gears of Great Power confrontations and compromises as they want to keep their national independence and protect regional peace and stability. ASEAN countries also do not want Great Powers to impose arrangements in a way that violates ASEAN national interests."[43] From that perspective, Hanoi became more appreciative of the ASEAN leaders' efforts to preserve their national independence and stopped thinking that Vietnamese leaders had stronger nationalist credentials. For example, many began to appreciate Thailand's "bamboo diplomacy", which was in the past considered as opportunistic.[44] This shows that Hanoi had come to share ASEAN countries' foreign policy, both in terms of means and ends.

Further, Hanoi was also pleased with the organizational principles of ASEAN. Luu Doan Huynh, a former diplomat and researcher of the IIR, observed that Hanoi had experienced three types of alliances and the association with ASEAN seeming to be an optimal one. In the Soviet bloc, Hanoi was a junior partner, and its national interests were often infringed by the Soviet Union and particularly by China in their strategic calculations. The Indochinese alliance created and led by Hanoi did efficiently serve the cause of national liberation of all three countries but ended in bloodshed for both Vietnam and Cambodia, and in diplomatic isolation for Vietnam. These alliance patterns, according to Luu Doan Huynh, were short-lived for they produced hierarchies in interstate relations and the imposition of the will of the stronger parties and the manipulation by the weaker. But an equality-based association could promise sound and enduring cooperation. It is clear that ASEAN upholds, both in theory and practice, equality among its members, mutual respect for national independence, non-interference in domestic affairs, non-use of force in interstate relations, solution of disputes by peaceful means, and making decisions on the basis of consensus.[45] The 7 July 1995 MOFA Media Coverage Plan for the ceremony to celebrate Vietnam joining ASEAN instructed that the mass media should publicize that "equality is one of the most important principle in ASEAN cooperation. The ASEAN members cooperate with each other regardless of their geographical sizes and economic capabilities."[46] In his concluding remarks in one of the debates on the decision whether to join ASEAN, CERC Director Hong Ha said, "Regardless of what we have discussed, we can agree that national self-reliance and independence must be preserved when we join ASEAN."[47] Perhaps to clear any residual concerns over possible damage to the status of Vietnam following its entry into ASEAN, Vu Khoan stressed, "Vietnam's ASEAN membership will not create any obstacles, but provide an important impetus, to the implementation of the foreign policy of national independence, diversification, and multilateralization of relations of Vietnam."⁴⁸ The MOFA ASEAN Department Report covering the first half of 1996 stated that one year after joining ASEAN, it was clear that "the level of equality in relations between Vietnam and other member countries has improved."⁴⁹ Equality and respect for national independence were ideals dear to Vietnam, and satisfaction in regard to these matters was instrumental in making Hanoi more eager to strive for ASEAN membership. In making the final decision to join ASEAN, the Politburo stressed, "We join ASEAN in order to preserve our national self-reliance and independence."⁵⁰

Another common point was Hanoi's perception that ASEAN countries and Vietnam were all facing pressures from the West on the questions of democracy and human rights. An IIR paper on political structures in ASEAN countries concluded:

> It is noteworthy that Vietnam and ASEAN countries do not have conflicts on democracy and human rights issues. We can (1) learn from ASEAN on how to reject the demands by the US and other Western countries while maintaining good relations with them, (2) promote relations with ASEAN in order to have more supporters in facing pressures from the USA and other Western countries on such matters as democracy, political pluralism, and human rights.⁵¹

In fact, ASEAN countries proved that they could meet Hanoi's needs in this regard. In June 1993, Hanoi obtained substantial support from ASEAN countries in the UN-sponsored International Conference on Human Rights. According to the report submitted to the Politburo by Deputy Foreign Minister Le Mai, who led the Vietnamese delegation to the Conference, there was a de facto rally of forces between ASEAN countries and Vietnam against the pressures from the West. He wrote,

> Human rights are one of the main subjects in the ideological struggle of the post-Cold War era. This struggle is difficult (due to unfavourable international situations), intense (due to the direct linkage to national sovereignty), complicated (due to the overlapping zones between positive and negative elements as well as common and local interests), and protracted at both national and international levels. But at this Conference, the outcomes turned out to be better than we had expected, thanks to a large part to the rally of force among developing countries

against the pressures exerted by the West. The most active countries in this rally include Indonesia, Singapore, Malaysia, Vietnam, China, India, Yemen and Syria.[52]

One diplomat tried to examine the reasons why Vietnam and ASEAN countries could rely on one another in this field. He provided the following analysis, which was cabled to MOFA in May 1994:

> In the past, ASEAN countries were full of praise for the US and the West because they were economically weak and dependent on the latter for aid and perceived that the socialist countries were the main threat to them. At present, as they have achieved economic growth and political stability and the socialist bloc has collapsed, they think that the US and the West could use democracy and human rights as a pretext to interfere into and destabilize their domestic politics. This will create a favourable condition for us, because ASEAN and Vietnam have to face the same pressures on the same issues. After we normalize relations with the US, Washington will press us more on democracy and human rights issues. It may also demand us to hold free elections and invite foreign observers to the elections.[53]

In short, by 1994, Hanoi had a better understanding about ASEAN. Regime survival, a peaceful and cooperative environment for economic development, national independence, an equal status with other regional countries, and opposition to pressures by the West on human rights and democracy became the perceived commonalities between Vietnam and ASEAN countries. At first glance, it might have seemed that the decision to join ASEAN was made on the basis of purely traditional realist calculations about economic growth and political independence. But the facts show that it was precisely the socializing and learning process promoted by visits and exchanges of views between top leaders of Vietnam and ASEAN countries—which helped senior leaders in Hanoi become aware of the common points about regime survival and the maintenance of one-party rule, equality among ASEAN members and mutual respect for national independence, a regional environment of peace and stability—that was instrumental in making these leaders to decide to join ASEAN soon, somewhat forgetting the necessity to enquire more deeply into the intricacy of economic cooperation. To put in differently, Hanoi's new awareness of

ASEAN became a very important factor contributing to the decision to join ASEAN at an early date.

THE "ASSOCIATION MENTALITY" AND THE QUESTION OF STATE IDENTITY IN VIETNAMESE FOREIGN POLICY

As Cronin has observed, "a state that has no contact with other states cannot have an identity."[54] State identity formation, therefore, closely related to the external recognition by foreign countries, one country's position in the international society of states in the form of membership to specific international movements, forums, and organizations, etc. On 2 September 1945, the Democratic Republic of Vietnam (DRV) declared its independence, thus beginning the process of establishing its foreign relations and forming its identity. Since that time, Hanoi strived to design and conduct domestic and foreign policies in the capacity of an independent country and tried its best to obtain recognition by other countries of that independent status. Hanoi had made great efforts to secure external recognition but the choices open to it were very limited. In the period from 1945 to 1948, the focus of Vietnamese foreign policy was to win the sympathy of the Big Four, namely the US, Britain, China and the Soviet Union, to secure their recognition of the independence of Vietnam and frustrate French efforts to re-establish their colonial rule. Until 1950, Vietnam conducted its anti-French war of resistance largely alone. Its state identity, therefore, was mainly that of a country fighting for national independence as part of the anti-colonial movement. Gradually, however, in the context of an intensified Cold War, particularly following the outbreak of the Korean conflict, and partly due to the prevailing communist ideology of its leaders, the DRV found its state identity associated with the Soviet bloc. This crystallized when socialist countries extended diplomatic relations to Vietnam in January 1950. Ho Chi Minh wrote on this occasion,

> The Soviet Union and the People's Republic of China, the two biggest countries in the world, and other democratic countries have recognized the DRV as an equal member of the large democratic family of the world. That is to say, we have joined the democratic bloc and joined the 800-million-people bloc to oppose imperialism.[55]

Thereafter, Hanoi stuck to that communist identity, believing that the communist states built their relations on a novel ground, with great importance being attached to communist credentials and identity. According to Levine, the general principle that governed relations among them dictated, "Relations between socialist states are based on a common identity rather than transitory interests. Socialist international relations are relations of new type characterized by peace, long-term mutual interest, genuine cooperation, and fraternal solidarity."[56] The leaders in Hanoi, until the late 1970s remained convinced that their country stood in the vanguard of history and that it was charged with the responsibility of bringing the struggle of the proletariat against the forces of capitalism and imperialism to its epochal conclusion.[57] This kind of state identity suggested that Vietnam should adopt a policy of making a distinction between friends and foes, and that the struggle between 'the two roads,' namely socialism and capitalism would end with the victory of socialism.[58] Cultivating political relations with the Soviet Union and China, coupled with enjoying a great amount of assistance from them, all the more consolidated the notion of state identity within the Soviet bloc. A Vietnamese party leader thus said, "solidarity and all-round cooperation with the Soviet Union is the keystone of foreign policy, a matter of principle, strategy, and revolutionary sentiment of the state and the party."[59] As the previous chapters have shown, Hanoi's policies with regard to ASEAN from 1960s to sometime in the 1980s were based on this perception of state identity and the resultant foreign policy allowed very limited patterns of association with ASEAN.

Ironically, the issue of identity also suggested how relations between Vietnam and the PRC deteriorated in the 1970s. Hanoi believed in 1950 that in accordance with proletarian internationalism, there would be a new page in Sino-Vietnamese relations, free from the legacy of the tributary relationship of the past. Yet, with the 1954 Geneva Agreements and their disastrous consequences for Vietnam's national interest, Hanoi had to reassess its relations with two major socialist powers. Thereafter, it switched to a new policy of independence with respect to the growing Sino-Soviet rift, and with respect to the struggle for the liberation of South Vietnam. This new line, which effectively helped to secure victory for Vietnam in the second Vietnam War, constituted a change, through partial, of Vietnam's identity: still communist, but national communist.[60]

In short, state identity had always played an important role in Vietnam's foreign policy, as is the case with other countries in Southeast Asia. Seen in the historical context, if we trace the modern state identity of Vietnam since 1945, its role in the interstate relations in the region seemed to have been determined by the balance of forces and the definition of spheres of influence—the clearest application of the power game played by Big Powers since the end of World War Two. Yet, its state identity in the beginning was not the product of its leaders' consciousness of the power game but rather the desire for national independence and the belief that association with the Soviet bloc contributed to the realization of this desire. Such an association had always been identical with external recognition of the domestic regime, which in turn reflected the political nature of the leadership and the socio-economic patterns of development that leadership intended to follow. Moreover, the bipolarity of world politics during the Cold War also made the choices of political and economic paths a critical issue for countries like Vietnam, born, as it was, out of the struggle for national independence and wishing to chart a neutral course amid the superpowers' rivalries.

That Hanoi in the aftermath of the Cold War and especially in the early 1990s tried to approach Beijing about forming a new alliance based on communist ideology and then decided to join ASEAN in 1994 was strongly influenced by the need to seek state identity. This is known as "association mentality" in Vietnam: it has become an imperative for Hanoi to identify itself as a member of certain associations and organizations. According to a senior MOFA official, "As individuals need to be members of associations, countries cannot stay away from international organizations."[61] Therefore, the need to find a substitute membership became critical when the Soviet bloc, of which Hanoi had been a member for more than four decades, disintegrated. When the Soviet Union collapsed, many in Hanoi were concerned over how the world would be without the Soviets and other socialist friends and how Hanoi would face "political isolation". It should be noted again that the CPV Politburo Thirteenth Resolution considered political isolation and economic backwardness as major threats to Vietnam's security and independence. When asked what was actually meant by "political isolation", several policymakers and scholars in Hanoi said that the phrase implied a more limited range of external relations and the exclusion from an international grouping that had proved more effective in providing a viable political ideology and strong socio-economic credentials to serve as a firm ground for regime legitimacy and survival.[62] This had been the essence of the sense of belonging that foreign scholars observed when they analysed Vietnamese foreign policy, especially in the period Hanoi decided to join the Soviet bloc.[63] The collapse of the Soviet bloc and the refusal of Beijing to lead a new alliance of the remaining socialist countries was in fact the loss of the socialist/communist identity. Hanoi was then forced to find a new identity to replace the old one, that is to seek membership in another community of states. A senior MOFA official also told the author that in the early 1990s, Vietnamese diplomats found themselves isolated among the diplomatic corps in countries where they were posted. These personal experiences had greatly influenced their awareness of political isolation and subsequent recommendations for expanded foreign relations.[64] To join ASEAN, therefore, was to satisfy Hanoi's need for association. From this perspective, the decision to join ASEAN, which was made mainly because of Vietnamese leaders' awareness of commonalities between Vietnam and ASEAN countries concerning regime survival, foreign policy objectives, and particularly regional peace and stability, equality and mutual respect of national independence, although they had little detailed knowledge about the organization's working procedures and institutional arrangements, particularly on economic cooperation, was also clearly influenced by the association mentality and the need to find a new state identity. According to MOFA Foreign Policy Department Deputy Director Dang Dinh Quy, when the idea of joining ASEAN first emerged and when the decision was made, Hanoi knew little about ASEAN, its cooperative mechanisms, and the AFTA requirements and their possible impacts on the Vietnamese economy. The "association mentality" therefore was an important element behind the decision to join ASEAN.[65]

One, however, could argue that the association mentality was, in fact, based on calculations about possible and actual political and economic gains from the membership of international organizations. In this case, it would be natural for a country to seek memberships in new international organizations when the existing ones ceased to provide it with expected benefits. That would be a realist account of Vietnam's joining ASEAN.

When the Soviet Union stopped giving aid to Vietnam and bilateral trade in 1990 fell from 80 per cent to 14 per cent of Vietnam's total foreign trade,[66] Hanoi had to seek new recognition and establish new foreign relations so as to ensure the resources necessary for regime survival. View in this light, Vietnam's membership of the former Soviet bloc and its ASEAN membership, therefore, were not different in nature. That ASEAN countries joined the US-led system might also have been based on a similar logic. Seen in this way, there should be no contradiction between identity and interests: the adoption of a new identity was simply to replace the one that no longer produced benefits for any country. The author posed the following counterfactual question to decision-makers and scholars in Hanoi: what would have happened if Hanoi had not joined ASEAN but instead focused on improving bilateral relations with individual ASEAN member states? Vu Duc Dam answered that ASEAN countries had posed exactly the same question, fearing that Hanoi attached lesser importance to ASEAN as the regional organization. However, according to Dam, Hanoi thought that if it wanted to reap "full interests, then wearing the ASEAN hat was a must".[67] This suggested there was a close connection between identity and interest, and a perception that it would even be difficult to gain the latter without the former. The MOFA annual report of 1995 wrote,

> We join ASEAN to create more favourable conditions for national construction, to enlarge markets for our exports, to enhance Vietnam's attractiveness for businessmen from inside and outside the region, to have more economic partners, and to enhance our international status because ASEAN enjoys a high international posture and has a considerable political weight in international forums.[68]

In short, to some extent, for Hanoi, identity was a way to ensure interests as far as membership of ASEAN was concerned.

The point, however, is that even in the absence of ASEAN membership, improvements in Vietnam-ASEAN relations had brought about substantial political and economic benefits to Hanoi and had also generated additional pressures for further transformation of the Vietnamese economy. But most importantly, the focus on interests would run into trouble as one must answer the practical question about Hanoi's decision to join ASEAN at an early date based on the differentiation between state security and regime security. In other words, in case of Vietnam's membership of ASEAN, the logics of states seeking identity might not be influenced entirely by the logic of states seeking material interests, and the logic of states seeking interests might not entirely be identical with the logic of regimes protecting their legitimacy and survival. The 1994 decision to join ASEAN in 1995 was also due to the imperative necessity of presenting concrete foreign policy outcomes to the CPV National Congress to be held in 1996. Actually, foreign policy outcomes were considered one of the three majors achievements by the CPV between the Seventh and Eighth National Congresses (1991–96)—the other two being political stability and economic growth—thus justifying the effectiveness and correctness of the CPV leading role in Vietnam. The VIII National Congress Political Report said, "We have achieved socio-political stability, strengthened national security and defense, and widened our foreign relations, thus escaping from encirclement and isolation, expanding international cooperation and taking an active part in the international community."[69] Joining ASEAN, therefore, helped Hanoi to solve its identity crisis.

The ASEAN membership also shows the compatibility of Vietnam's state identity with the ASEAN identity. Note previously, Vietnam's ASEAN membership was materialized by the perception of leaders in Hanoi about the list of commonalities Vietnam had with the ASEAN countries and their perception about Vietnam's sharing the regional identity. In the early 1970s, when Hanoi thought that it was different from ASEAN countries, there had been an unwillingness to develop relations with ASEAN. But in the early 1990s, when it became clearer in the minds of Vietnamese leaders that ASEAN countries "were no different from us", membership of ASEAN became relatively easy to contemplate. On the one hand this showed the compatibility of identities between Vietnam and ASEAN countries, and on the other hand, the ease of international cooperation based on a collective and transnational identity. The leadership in Vietnam stressed the imperatives for the country's membership in ASEAN as follows:

> Our objectives in joining ASEAN should help consolidate our national independence, sovereignty, and territorial integrity. Our aims in joining ASEAN should include the improvement of friendly and cooperative

relations with the ASEAN countries on the basis of the principles of respect to national independence, sovereignty and territorial integrity, non-interference in each other's domestic affairs, peaceful resolution of disputes, non-use of force or threat of force, and mutually beneficial cooperation.[70]

These principles of interstate relations were quite common to the ASEAN's mode of regional cooperation in the region. Because of the commonalities in historical experiences, cultures, geography and interests, the stage had thus already been set for the identity-based process of Vietnam joining ASEAN. An observer therefore suggests that for the first time, an association of small- and medium-sized countries seemed to have overcome the syndrome of being tied to alliances with major powers to ensure national security and prosperity, and that

> The most noteworthy shift in Vietnam's conduct of external relations and its views of security in the past decade has been the reorientation from its intense preoccupation with great powers, particularly China, to a more balanced position in which regional cooperation with other Southeast Asian states plays a significant role.[71]

Yet this was not the first time identity played an important role in the Vietnamese foreign policy. As noted above, since the early 1950s, the communist/socialist identity had been the main basis for the country's foreign policy choices. The ASEAN membership, therefore, suggested that Hanoi's foreign policy had come to be influenced by a new state identity, which had the following characteristics:

(1) Timeliness: facing an identity crisis, Hanoi had found the ASEAN membership to replace the communist/socialist identity and to overcome the fear of being politically isolated. The search for the ASEAN identity was successful in 1994 when top leaders in Hanoi became aware of similarities and commonalities between Vietnam and ASEAN member states.
(2) Usefulness: Hanoi was able to find replacements for the Soviet sources of funds and markets. In addition, the membership helped to consolidate Vietnam's standing in the world community, especially to

place Vietnam on an equal footing with other countries in Southeast Asia. Moreover, the membership helped to consolidate the legitimacy of the CPV, thus enhancing the survival of the communist regime in Hanoi.

(3) Sustainability: due to the collective identity, common interests, and common sense of enjoying an equal international status, together with geographical proximity, Vietnam-ASEAN relations came to be based on a ground firmer than relations founded on ideology.

We could even say that ASEAN membership enabled Vietnam to realize its desired identity. The desire for national independence was always real and represents a consistent state preference. The country's contemporary history provided several examples. The decision to join the Soviet bloc was not an easy one even in the 1950s.[72] During the course of the Vietnam War, despite being heavily dependent on Soviet and Chinese economic and military aid, leaders in Hanoi had always tried to chart an independent course, endeavoring to limit efforts by Moscow and Beijing to influence Hanoi's strategy and conduct of the war.[73] Some in Hanoi had been cautious, even not entirely willing, about concluding the Treaty of Friendship and Cooperation with the Soviet Union in 1978. Pike observed, "In deeper analyses, the sentiment of independence was the thing that leadership in Hanoi would never trade. Vietnam can be a client state of the USSR but not a satellite," and the close Soviet-Vietnamese relationship, from that perspective, could be seen as "the marriage of convenience".[74] The decline of the Soviet Union in the late 1980s meant that the constraints on Hanoi's efforts to enjoy greater political independence were lessened. The process of changing the leadership's worldview thus started in earnest in the early 1980s and the drive for developing external relations with the non-communist states was in full swing in 1991 when the Soviet Union ceased to exist.[75]

As the emphasis on the identity of a small country wishing to enjoy independence from great powers' influence became stronger, Vietnam increasingly found that this type of state identity was identical to the way other Southeast Asian states behaved. In 1989, the leadership in Hanoi for the first time expressed its willingness to join ASEAN. ASEAN responded positively, starting the "process of reconciliation",[76] implying that social and political differences did not represent obstacles to Vietnam's membership in the organization. Joining ASEAN at first glance would be seen as the rational response to the changes in the post-Cold War world. Yet, deeper analyses would suggest that it was a result of a process of asserting a long-desired state identity that subsequently materialized in a policy shift in response to the incentives brought about by the end of the Cold War. ASEAN membership thus became optimal to overcome the "identity crisis" and to realize the desired state identity. From that perspective, the end of the Cold War was indeed a blessing in disguise, offering Hanoi the opportunity to view its own identity in a new light, to consolidate the process of identity shift and develop policies to take advantage of the relaxation of global tensions and the growing trend towards regional political and economic cooperation. Frost concluded that, "the end of the Cold War has involved severe costs and problems for Vietnam, but this development has simultaneously opened up greatly improved opportunities for wider and more beneficial foreign relationships."[77]

For some people, initially, joining ASEAN was only seen as the solution to a problem and the issue of state identity was not a strong focus. Yet, the benefits from the membership and the stability of the regional order that ASEAN had helped to build demonstrated that the ASEAN identity was the best choice for Hanoi. Moreover, since the ASEAN identity provided a guarantee for peace, security, development, and regime survival, Hanoi was willing to act in accordance with ASEAN norms and rules. To put it in a different way, identity in its turn was able to have its impact on Hanoi's international and regional behaviour.

In short, Hanoi joined ASEAN in order to overcome the identity crisis that followed its Cambodian trauma and the collapse of the Soviet bloc in the early 1990s. The decision to join a viable and successful organization such as ASEAN had been informed in part by calculation of benefits that membership of the organization would bring. Yet, to a greater extent, the decision was influenced by deepened understanding of leaders in Hanoi about commonalities between Vietnam and ASEAN member countries, centring on the imperatives of geographical proximity, historical and cultural experiences, as well as the common objectives of regime survival, economic development and political independence. The decision was also influenced by the need to overcome the collapse of the sense of belonging felt by leaders in Hanoi when the association with the Soviet bloc, which had conditioned the association mentality of Hanoi, came to an abrupt end. A senior diplomat and researcher thus observed that Vietnam's membership in ASEAN "would signify a return of Vietnam to its place of origin".[78]

Notes

1. Interviews by the author in Hanoi, August 2002–February 2003.
2. Document coded 3917/QHQT signed by Deputy Prime Minister Phan Van Khai on 17 July 1995.
3. With the unconditional withdrawal of Vietnamese troops and the conclusion of the Paris Agreement on Cambodia, conditions were fulfilled for the normalization of relations between ASEAN and Vietnam. In this situation, ASEAN countries, or most of them, thought that it was necessary to bring Vietnam into ASEAN in due course, for the following reasons: (1) with the collapse of the socialist regimes in the former Soviet Union and Eastern Europe, Vietnam was then without friends. It was thus appropriate for ASEAN countries to show Vietnam that they were the true friends of Vietnam provided Hanoi behaved, and it was hoped that Hanoi would understand that a friend in need is a friend indeed. (2) In the case of Indonesia, ASEAN membership had been a long-term measure designed to contain Indonesia's expansion. In the case of Vietnam, ASEAN membership would also serve the purpose of containing Hanoi's possible future expansionist ambitions, and preventing it from sliding back into the sphere of Chinese influence, a development that would be most harmful to Southeast Asia security. (3) In the long run, ASEAN should cover the whole of Southeast Asia, and Vietnam should be a good start for the subsequent entry of Laos, Myanmar, and Cambodia.

   The MOFA Report "On the Outcomes of the Visit to Vietnam by Lee Kuan Yew, 23–27 April 1992" (Về kết quả chuyến thăm Việt Nam của Lý Quang Diệu), quoted Lee's comment that it would take between fifteen and twenty years for Vietnam to join ASEAN, because the differences between Vietnam and ASEAN were still many and vast. Analysts in Hanoi, however, held that such a statement only reflected the fact that ASEAN countries had not been able to reach a consensus among themselves on the issue. According to the SEA/SPA Department report covering August 1994, the Singaporean Ambassador in Bangkok was instructed to meet his Vietnamese counterpart to "confirm that Singapore was very eager to support an early membership for Vietnam".

4. Texts of Foreign Minister Nguyen Manh Cam's Speech at the Fourth Vietnam Fatherland Organization National Congress, October 1995, p. 7.
5. Gareth Porter, "The Transformation of Vietnam's Worldview: From Two Camps to Interdependence", *Contemporary Southeast Asia* 12, no. 1 (June 1990), p. 1.
6. Ibid., p. 5.
7. MOFA Annual Report of 1986, "On the World Situation and Our People's Struggle on the Foreign Relations Front," (Về tình hình thế giới và cuộc đấu tranh của nhân dân ta trên mặt trận đối ngoại), p. 36.
8. Porter, "The Transformation of Vietnam's Worldview: From Two Camps to Interdependence", p. 6.
9. Eero Palmujoki, *Vietnam and the World: Marxist-Leninist Doctrine and the Changes in International Relations, 1975–1993* (London: Macmillan Press, 1997), p. 30.
10. MOFA Annual Report of 1986, "On the World Situation and Our People's Struggle on the Foreign Relations Front", pp. 39–40.
11. Ibid.
12. Tran Quang Co, "The post-Cold War World and Asia-Pacific", *IIR International Studies Review*, December 1992, p. 7.
13. Vu Khoan, "Security, Development, and Influence in Foreign Relations", in MOFA, *Integrating into the World and Preserving Our Characteristics* (Hanoi: National Politics Publishing House, 1995), p. 210.
14. Ibid., pp. 209–10.
15. Luu Van Loi, *50 Years of Vietnamese Diplomacy, Vol. 2, 1975–1995* (Hanoi: Public Order Publishing House, 1998), p. 223.
16. Nguyen Vu Tung, "Vietnam's New Concept of Security", in *Comprehensive Security in Asia: Views from Asia and the West on a Changing Security Environment*, edited by Kurt Radtke and Raymond Feddema (Boston: Brill, 2000), pp. 415–20.
17. Deputy Prime Minister Phan Van Khai, 20 August 1993 Report, "On the Prospects of Vietnam's Economy for the Coming Years" (Về triển vọng kinh tế Việt Nam trong các năm tới), p. 6.
18. Pham Nguyen Long, (The Institute for Southeast Asian Studies) Proposal for a ministerial-level study on "Regional Integration in Southeast Asia", 1993, p. 9.
19. The IIR Group Study Report on "ASEAN Political Structures and Systems", in the Nguyen Ai Quoc National Academy of Politics Study Program coded KX 05.02, December 1992.
20. For example, Luu Doan Huynh, a researcher at the IIR, suggested to the

Malaysian Ambassador in Hanoi to organize high-level visits between the two countries including CPV and UMNO leaders.
21. Mahathir was quoted by Malaysian Foreign Minister Hassan Omar in his keynote address for the opening of the Conference on "A New Southeast Asia". Proceedings of the Conference, Kuala Lumpur, 6–9 January 1991.
22. Texts of Foreign Minister Nguyen Manh Cam's Speech at the Fourth Vietnam Fatherland Organization National Congress, October 1995, p. 7. Ramses Amer recently stressed that ASEAN did not consider the change of the Vietnamese political system a prerequisite for the ASEAN member nor did it wish to impose a particular political system on Vietnam. Thus, Vietnam joined ASEAN although it was and still is governed by the Communist party of Vietnam. Ramses Amer, "Regional Integration and Conflict Management: The Case of Vietnam", in the Third Asia-Europe Roundtable, *Peace and Reconciliation: Success Stories and Lessons in Asia and Europe* (Hanoi, 20–21 October 2003). I am thankful for Luu Doan Huynh who alerted me of this conference and offered the notes of his exchanges with Ramses Amer in the conference. Huynh said: "He [Ramses] explained to me that the EU always required new member countries to do away with socialist systems and communist party rules as a prerequisite for admission. But ASEAN was more flexible. The passage should be seen as praise for ASEAN and indirect criticism of the other."
23. SEA/SPA Department Annual Report of 1989 (Vụ Đông nam Á và Nam Thái bình dương, Báo cáo tổng kết năm 1989), p. 5.
24. MOFA Report on Lee Kuan Yew's visit to Vietnam, 23–27 April 1992, p. 3.
25. The CPV, *Documents of the VII National Congress* (Hanoi: Truth Publishing House, 1991), p. 88. See also The CPV, *Documents of the VIII National Congress* (Hanoi: National Politics Publishing House, 1996), p. 62.
26. A Report dated 10 December 1993 by the Vietnam-ASEAN Liaison Office attached to the Vietnamese Embassy in Jakarta, p. 5. Foreign Minister Nguyen Manh Cam stressed in his speech at the Fourth Fatherland Organization National Congress held in Hanoi in October 1995, "when leaders of some ASEAN countries stated that ASEAN wanted to admit Vietnam soon, other ASEAN leaders were still hesitant on the ground that there were differences in political systems and levels of economic development between Vietnam and ASEAN countries. Yet, ASEAN could solve this issue among them. Malaysian and Singaporean Prime Ministers stressed that these differences were not creating obstacles for Vietnam's membership in ASEAN."
27. The CERC Report dated 10 October 1993, pp. 1 and 3.
28. The CERC Report dated 28 March 1994, pp. 3–7.

29. MOFA 5 May 1994 Report, "On the Outcomes of the Visit by President Le Duc Anh to Indonesia" (Về kết quả chuyến thăm của của tịch Lê Đức Anh tai Indonesia), p. 6.
30. SEA/SPA Annual Report for 1994, p. 6.
31. Interview by the author with Vu Duc Dam, Hanoi, 15 January 2002.
32. The MOFA, 8 July 1992 submitted to the CPV Politburo on Vietnam membership in ASEAN, pp. 1 and 3–4.
33. The MOFA Additional Memo dated 16 January 1993 "On Vietnam-ASEAN Relations", p. 2. Emphasis as in original. In November 1994, Vu Khoan stressed in the *Communist Review* article, "I would like to reiterate that so far, military cooperation in ASEAN is of bilateral nature". See Vu Khoan, "Vietnam and ASEAN", p. 30.
34. Interviews by the author with the CERC officials, January–February 1999. In the period between 1991 and 1994, relations with the CPV and ruling parties in ASEAN countries developed strongly. The CPV established official relations with the PAP in Singapore, and UMNO in Malaysia. After Vietnam joined ASEAN, CPV-Golkar relations also improved. In October 1996, the CERC Director was sent to observe the Thirty-Second Anniversary of Golkar's establishment. This was the first time Golkar had invited foreign delegations to the anniversary. The CPV, PAP, UMNO, the National Party of the Philippines and the Democratic Party of Thailand were the only other parties invited by Golkar. According to CERC officials, after 1996, Hanoi sought to establish relations with ruling parties in Thailand and the Philippines.
35. The National Security Act was used in ASEAN countries to oppress dissidents. Similarly, internal aspects have been stressed in the "national security" concept in Vietnam. For example, the crimes in violation of national security include those directly threatening the survival and the consolidation of the people's government. See *New Hanoi*'s Law Study Section, 26 October 2002, p. 2.
36. MOFA ASEAN Department Report, "On Vietnam-ASEAN Relations", prepared for the Twenty-Second Diplomatic Conference, November 1999, pp. 10–11.
37. Kim Ninh, "Vietnam: Struggle and Cooperation", in *Asian Security Practice: Material and Ideational Influence*, edited by Muthiah Alagappa (Stanford, CA: Stanford University Press, 1998), p. 476.
38. John Funston, "Challenges Facing ASEAN in a More Complex Age", *Contemporary Southeast Asia* 21, no. 2 (August 1999), p. 220. Similar arguments can be seen in Marty Natalegawa, *Does ASEAN Matter? A View from Within* (Singapore: ISEAS – Yusof Ishak Institute); Mari Elka Pangestu

and Rastam Mohd Isa, eds., *ASEAN Future Forward: Anticipating the Next 50 Years* (Kuala Lumpur: ISIS Malaysia, 2017).
39. MOFA ASEAN Department Report, "On Vietnam-ASEAN Relations", July 2003, prepared for the Twenty-Fourth Diplomatic Conference (Hanoi, August 2003).
40. The Council of Ministers Document coded 1821-KT§N, p. 2. The 1821-KT§N Document was the reply to the MOFA 25 March 1992 document coded 624/NG-LPQT that suggested, "because all the ASEAN members have officially supported Vietnam's accession to the Bali Treaty, it is likely that we can sign the Treaty in June 1992 when the AMM meets in Manila. Earlier, the CPV Secretariat, in the 25 February 1992 document coded 153-CV/VPTW, agreed that we would be a party to the Bali Treaty. As a matter of procedure, however, we have to submit the accession proposal to the Council of State. Therefore, MOFA would like to ask the Chairman of the Council of Ministers to seek the approval by the Council of State before we could sign the Treaty."
41. Nguyen Vu Tung, "ASEAN: New Adjustments in Foreign Policy", *The IIR Bulletin of International Relations*, Vol. 2, December 1991, p. 22.
42. Vu Khoan, "Vietnam and ASEAN", *Communist Review*, p. 31.
43. MOFA 21 December 1990 Report, "On Some Strategic and Tactical Issues in Our Struggle for a Solution to the Cambodia Problem and Improvement of International Relations", p. 21.
44. MOFA Group for Vietnam's Diplomatic History, *Characteristics of Major Diplomatic Schools of the World*, Hanoi, December 2000, pp. 35–45.
45. Exchanges with Luu Doan Huynh by the author, Hanoi, January 2003. On another occasion, Huynh said, "ASEAN countries were motivated by a strong will for independence, which is no less than that of Vietnam." The Third Asia-Europe Roundtable, *Peace and Reconciliation: Success Stories and Lessons in Asia and Europe*. (Hanoi, 20–21 October 2003).
46. The 7 July 1995 MOFA Suggested Media Plan for the Vietnam joining ASEAN celebrations, p. 3. Equality, however, also required that Hanoi had to share equal responsibilities, especially financial ones. The same plan (p. 3) said, "ASEAN cooperation does not involve grants and aid. We therefore have to equip ourselves with a high sense of self-reliance and be more proactive in initiating the projects that could ensure mutual interests."
47. Transcripts of the CERC Discussions in March 1994.
48. Vu Khoan, "Vietnam and ASEAN", p. 31.
49. SEA/SPA Department Report covering first half of 1996, p. 5.
50. Transcripts of the Politburo Meeting on the question of Vietnam's membership of ASEAN (8:00–10:30 a.m., 22 July 1994) coded 229/BBK/BCT.

51. The IIR Group Study Report on "ASEAN Political Structures and Systems", in the Nguyen Ai Quoc National Academy of Politics Study Program coded KX 05.02, December 1992.
52. The June 1993 Report by Deputy Foreign Minister Le Mai on the outcomes of the UN-sponsored International Conference on Human Rights, p. 3.
53. 31 May 1994 Cable by Chargé d'Affaires Phan Doan Nam from Mexico to Deputy Foreign Minister Tran Quang Co in reply to the latter's question about ASEAN-US relations, p. 2.
54. Bruce Cronin, *Community under Anarchy: Transnational Identity and the Evolution of Cooperation* (New York: Columbia University Press, 1999), p. 26.
55. Ho Chi Minh, *Selected Writing*, Vol. 5 (Hanoi: Truth Publishing House, 1985), p. 411.
56. Steven Levine, "Perception and Ideology in Chinese Foreign Policy", in *Chinese Foreign Policy: Theory and Practice*, edited by Thomas Robinson and David Shambaugh (Oxford: Clarendon Press, 1994), pp. 37–38.
57. James A. Gregor, *In the Shadow of Giants: The Major Powers and the Security of Southeast Asia* (California: The Hoover Institution Press, Stanford University Press, 1989), pp. 55–56.
58. See Eero Palmujoki, *Vietnam and the World*, p. 30.
59. See Douglass Pike, *Vietnam and the Soviet Union: Anatomy of an Alliance* (Boulder, CO: Westview Press, 1978), p. 182.
60. See Chen Jian, "China's Involvement in the Vietnam War, 1964–1969", *China Quarterly* 142 (June 1995): 356–87. See also Odd Westad et al., "77 Conversations between Chinese and Foreign Leaders on the Wars in Indochina, 1964–1977", *Working Paper No. 22*, Cold War International History Project (Woodrow Wilson Center for Scholars, Washington, DC, 1998). Alagappa has notices the question of "identity dilemma" that stems from historical contexts and still underlines the deep distrust and suspicion in some bilateral relations, such as those between Vietnam and Cambodia, and Vietnam and China.
61. Interviews by the author with senior MOFA officials, Hanoi, 1999 and 2003.
62. Ibid.
63. Eero Palmujoki, *Vietnam and the World*, pp. 30–40.
64. Interviews by the author with senior MOFA officials, Hanoi, 1999 and 2003.
65. Interview by the author with Deputy Director of MOFA Foreign Policy Department Dang Dinh Quy, 20 January 2003.
66. Richard Betts et al., *Time for a Critical Decision on Vietnam: It Is Time for the US to End Its Economic Embargo on Vietnam and Establish Diplomatic*

Relations (New York: Columbia University, East Asian Institute, 1992), pp. 6–7.

67. Interview by the author with Vu Duc Dam, 15 January 2003. Texts of Foreign Minister Nguyen Manh Cam's Speech at the Fourth Vietnam Fatherland Organization National Congress, October 1995 (p. 7): "After considering all aspects, we hold that once we become an ASEAN observer, it is natural and logical that we will become an official ASEAN member."
68. The Government Report "On Our State's Foreign Relations and Directions for the Coming Period" (Về quan hệ đối ngoại của nhà nước ta và định hướng giai đoạn tới), submitted to the IX National Assembly Eighth Session, 20 October 1995, p. 21.
69. The CPV, *Documents of the VIIIth National Congress*, p. 11.
70. Transcripts of the Politburo Meeting on the question of Vietnam's membership in ASEAN (8:00–10:30 a.m., 22 July 1994) coded 229/BBK/BCT.
71. Kim Ninh, "Vietnam: Struggle and Cooperation", p. 454.
72. See, Andrew Rotter, *The Path to Vietnam: Origins of the American Commitment to Southeast Asia* (Ithaca: Cornell University Press, 1987); Anthony Short, *The Origins of the Vietnam War* (London: Longman, 1989).
73. Donald Zagoria, *Vietnam Triangle: Moscow, Peking, Hanoi* (New York: Pegasus, 1967); Ilya Gaiduk, *The Soviet Union and the Vietnam War* (Chicago: Ivan R. Dee, 1996), and Westad, "77 Conversations between Chinese and Foreign Leaders on the Wars in Indochina, 1964–1977".
74. Pike, *Vietnam and the Soviet Union: Anatomy of an Alliance*, p. 245.
75. Porter, "The Transformation of Vietnam's Worldview: From Two Camps to Interdependence", p. 1. Discussions of the identity-finding process will be presented later.
76. Mahathir was quoted in Nguyen Vu Tung, "Vietnam-ASEAN Cooperation in Southeast Asia", *Security Dialogue* 4, no. 1 (March 1993), p. 92.
77. Frank Frost, *Vietnam's Foreign Relations: Dynamic of Change* (Singapore: Institute of Southeast Asian Studies, 1993), p. 78.
78. Luu Doan Huynh at the Third Asia-Europe Roundtable, *Peace and Reconciliation: Success Stories and Lessons in Asia and Europe* (Hanoi, 20–21 October 2003).

7

CONCLUSION

From the time of the 1986 Thirteenth Politburo Resolution that stated, "We will support peaceful coexistence between the Indochinese and ASEAN countries and will not see relations between Vietnam, Laos, and Kampuchea and ASEAN countries as socialism versus capitalism" to Hanoi's enhanced interaction and socialization with ASEAN countries between 1990 and 1994, the following factors seemed to have influenced the Vietnam-ASEAN relations in a decisive way.

(1) The disintegration of the Soviet bloc and the collapse of the Soviet Union, which made Vietnam's search for a new identity to protect its survival of the communist regime in Vietnam an urgent task.
(2) Beijing's rejection of Hanoi's proposal to establish a new mode of Sino-Vietnamese relations based on communist identity, which made the search for a new and non-communist identity imperative.
(3) New understanding and awareness of ASEAN's importance to the overall developmental and foreign policy of Vietnam as well as the enhancement of the new posture of Vietnam in its regional and international relations.
(4) New awareness of commonalities between Vietnam and ASEAN countries in terms of history and culture as well as developmental goals

and regime survival, gained through a process of intense interactions and socialization between Vietnam and ASEAN member states.

These are the four main factors, which formed a "matrix of dynamics" that involved new ideas, choices, and processes and in fact informed the decision by Hanoi first to improve relations with ASEAN countries and then to join ASEAN.

At first glance, it might seem that Hanoi's policymakers based their decision to join ASEAN on the considerations that attached great importance to nationalism, and national and regime interests. Yet a closer look suggests a more complicated picture. As previous chapters have shown, Hanoi did not hope, and could not hope, to turn ASEAN into a military alliance and help to improve its position vis-à-vis Beijing. Moreover, there was no substantial surge in economic and political gains in the period between the improvement of Vietnam-ASEAN relations and Vietnam's membership in ASEAN. Further, additional economic pressures and challenges were exerted on Vietnam due to its ASEAN membership. More than anything else, the ASEAN membership helped to provide Hanoi with a better chance for regime legitimacy and survival. In addition to this, the decision to join ASEAN was in part due to the loose and socialization-based nature of ASEAN institutional arrangements. This then suggested that the decision to join ASEAN reflected major changes in Hanoi's view about itself and ASEAN countries, the improved awareness of commonalities between Vietnam and ASEAN countries forged by cooperation in many fields and by Vietnam-ASEAN friendly interactions and socialization (especially those between top leaders), the break away from the old identity and commitments attached to this identity, the formation of a new state identity climaxed by the ASEAN membership, and continued cooperation within ASEAN. Indeed, the collapse of the Soviet Union and Beijing's refusal to return to the 1960s pattern of Sino-Vietnamese relations may put the regime in Hanoi at risk. Yet, they also resulted in the disappearance of pre-existing constraints over the process of Hanoi's search for new means to protect the regime and to attain its desired identity. And when these constraints were removed, there was also a break away from the commitments attached to the old identity. Therefore, the author claims that the changes in the thinking of Vietnamese leaders about ASEAN were more important in explaining the Hanoi's choice to associate itself with ASEAN and the parallel emergence of a new state identity.

Therefore, while the decision to join ASEAN was influenced by the actual and projected interests associated with the membership, to a greater extent however, it was also influenced by the enhanced awareness of leaders in Hanoi about commonalities between Vietnam and ASEAN. When the MOFA Annual Report of 1992 stated that "we do not have sufficient understanding about the nature of ASEAN and ideology is still influencing our efforts to understand ASEAN", this was a considerable advance as compared with the perceived "difference in nature between Vietnam and ASEAN" that leaders in Hanoi held from the early 1970s to the mid-1980s. And when the MOFA Annual Report of 1994 stated, "we have had a conceptual change about ASEAN," it was believed that Vietnam-ASEAN relations would change, too. This statement, therefore, serves to justify another statement in the 1994 Report, which said, "1994 is the turning-point in Vietnam-ASEAN relations." In short, the decision to join ASEAN was in the first place based on the perception that "the ASEAN members were like us."[1]

There are two points that need to be stressed here. Firstly, the construction of a state identity is a matter of choice. Based on the perception of common objectives and priorities in domestic and foreign policies, on the acknowledgement of commonalities in political structures and practices, as well as on the need to secure regime legitimacy and survival that also required reduction of military spending and a peaceful and stable regional environment for economic development, Hanoi accepted the ASEAN regional order by acceding to the Bali Treaty in 1992 and joining ASEAN in 1995. The collapse of the Soviet bloc, the Chinese refusal to return to the Sino-Vietnamese communist alliance of the 1950s and 1960s, and interests associated with the improvements of Vietnam-ASEAN relations did help to make it easier for Hanoi to make the choice of ASEAN identity.

Secondly, interactions and socialization contributed to a great extent to the changes in perception and changes in identity. In a very real sense, increased interactions, especially those at the highest level, helped Hanoi to come to a better understanding of ASEAN, then to a realization of commonalities between Vietnam and ASEAN countries, and to the adoption of the ASEAN's identity. Socialization in the form of exchanges and meetings between Vietnamese and ASEAN leaders clearly influenced the formation of the new perception on ASEAN in Hanoi. The period from 1993 to 1994 was marked by visits to ASEAN countries by highest Vietnamese leaders. The pattern of development and improvement of Vietnam-ASEAN relations then suggested that increased interactions served to consolidate the positive perception about each other and better relations that followed. Thu My observed,

> regular meetings and innumerable exchanges, talks, and conferences at all levels help ASEAN countries have sufficient and correct information about each other. They contribute to the removal of suspicions and doubts and help build confidence, which serve as the basis for good relations among ASEAN members for the last several decades.[2]

In short, the changed perceptions about each other suggested new opportunities for developing cooperative relations based on the realization of commonalities among states. These commonalities may include common national and regime interests. They may also include the common sense of historical experiences, geographical proximity and cultural values. Therefore, Vietnam's relations with other states in Southeast Asia in general and its membership of ASEAN were involving in a broader socio-historical context.

As the definition of identity—namely a set of behavioural or personal characteristics by which an individual is recognizable as a member of a group[3]—suggests, the following points now help define the new identity of Vietnam in the aftermath of the Cold War. As a matter of fact, these are also the points the leadership and the elites in Hanoi stress when explaining how they have come to understand the ASEAN countries and why they want Vietnam to be seen as one of them.

Firstly, there has been a greater emphasis on archaeological, cultural, religious, anthropological and ethnic similarities between Vietnam and other Southeast Asian states.[4] The consensus among elite circles in Vietnam about these similarities has served to improve the country's positive images about ASEAN states. It has also helped realize the possibility that Vietnam could forge closer relations with countries of different political regimes in Southeast Asia.

Secondly, the stress on geographical proximity and a common history with other Southeast Asian countries refers to their similarities in sizes and historical experiences of seeking national independence and building nation-states in the era of decolonialization. The notion of ASEAN states as countries with similar sizes and concerns has made Hanoi more comfortable in dealing with the ASEAN states, a mentality totally different from the past experiences of association with the great and powerful allies. Moreover, Hanoi came to appreciate the way of working of ASEAN which involves rotations in hosting regular meetings of foreign ministers and heads of states, equal contributions, real consultations, and consensus seeking, among other things, because these practices put all the members on an equal footing. This differed from the past experiences of Vietnam when it was a "little brother" of both the Soviet Union and China with their sense of superiority.

In addition to this, Vietnam also started to recognize the merits of the developmental experiences of the ASEAN states, in the economic and political field and in foreign policy. The role of an embedded state played in economic development as well as the emphasis on social and political stability at the national and regional levels as a necessary condition for it—as the case of ASEAN shows—suggested to the leadership in Hanoi the applicability of the model that had been successful in these neighbouring countries. In other words, Hanoi came to believe in the ASEAN model of newly independent states charting an effective way to modernization but not at the expense of national independence and leadership legitimacy.

Finally, the emphasis on geography also reinforced the sense of belonging to Southeast Asia. Other Southeast Asian countries then became "long-lost friends" who had been separated by the conditions of the Cold War. Hanoi then came to accept ASEAN as the best substitute for the loss of membership in the Soviet bloc. It therefore seems that by emphasizing geographical proximity, cultural and social affinity, Hanoi had been going through a process of self-reflection to redefine its role in the regional social and cultural contexts in which it relates with other states. Therefore, in the association and socialization with other Southeast Asian states, Vietnam no longer faced a crisis of identity. Pragmatic regionalism now seemed to replace socialist internationalism. Moreover, the country's economic prosperity, domestic stability, and national security also came to be closely linked with its ASEAN membership. To put it differently, when Hanoi found that its state identity could be found in association with other Southeast Asian states, it felt more secure within its immediate geographic space and more confident to act as a member of the regional community. This sense of belonging, this newly found state identity, which led to a sense of enhanced state security, achievable equality, and economic prosperity, gradually began to serve as a long-lasting link in the new type of association Vietnam sought to forge with other ASEAN states.[5] In the final analysis, alliance with other Southeast Asian states also meant that Vietnam's foreign policies in the aftermath of the Cold War would be similar to those of the other ASEAN members especially with regard to the pursuit economic integration and growth, non-interference in domestic affairs, and maintenance of friendly relations with all countries.

This also means that in its turn, state identity would be informative to future state behaviours. Some scholars have argued that ASEAN countries needed to offer Vietnam the ASEAN membership in order to utilize the ASEAN norms and principles of interstate relations to contain Hanoi's perceived regional ambitions, in the analogy of using the iron cage to tame a tiger.[6] The same logic might be detected in the arguments for the necessity to invite Indonesia to join ASEAN in 1967. But empirically, Hanoi's wish to enter ASEAN was influenced by the need to have an ASEAN identity, and the ASEAN rules and norms were indicative of desired behaviours of states sharing a collective identity. In other words, records have shown that the willingness to accept a new role and to abide by the ASEAN Way had emerged *prior* to joining ASEAN. Besides, the decision to join ASEAN was partly influenced by the understanding that ASEAN institutional frameworks were weak and ASEAN was far from being institutionalized by Western standards.

The idea of Vietnam and ASEAN sharing a collective identity, however, has not been an issue broadly publicized and discussed in Hanoi, for several reasons. In the first place, the reorientation of priorities that separated ideology from the actual design and implementation of foreign policy seems to run counter to the Marxist and Leninist doctrines still held in high regard by the CPV. Anyway, the ASEAN membership indicated that the socialist/communist vision and concept of regional had failed, while the capitalist one had prevailed, something which orthodox ideologues in the CPV still found hard to accept. In addition to this, as the residual impact of the decades-long negative propaganda about ASEAN still lingered, the stress on the similarity and sharing a collective identity with ASEAN countries might have faced negative reactions from officials and some sectors of the population still sentimentally attached to socialism. Some in Hanoi still believed that the differences between Vietnam and ASEAN countries were matters of substance, not only form, according to Vu Duc Dam.[7] Finally, the notion of sharing a collective identity with ASEAN could not be stressed in the absence of guarantees that ASEAN membership would entail only benefits. Hanoi, as noted earlier, was quite uncertain about the specific benefits related to the ASEAN membership and it was already aware that the membership would involve major challenges, especially in economic terms, although the magnitude of these challenges had still not been adequately assessed. The hesitation to publicize the new Vietnam-ASEAN relationship based on the concept of collective identity, therefore, was reflected in several major documents issued around the time the ASEAN membership decision was made. In July 1994, the Politburo instructed,

- We have to do much work in explaining the decision to the Party members, cadres, as well as the people at large so as to clear their doubts and build a broad consensus on the decision to join ASEAN. We are going to join ASEAN but we are firmly defending national independence, sovereignty, territorial integrity and socialist orientations. The objectives of joining ASEAN are to increase friendly and cooperative relations with ASEAN countries, mainly in the economic, trade, and scientific-technological fields.
- Mass media of Vietnam should report the decision and the admission ceremony in an appropriate way.[8]

In other words, Hanoi did not want to publicize widely the many commonalities that were behind the decision to join ASEAN, a factor that made it a political decision, mainly serving political objectives. To reflect the Politburo instructions, the MOFA Suggested Media Plan for the Admission Ceremony wrote,

> Vietnam's joining ASEAN is a topic that draws great interest at home and abroad. While covering the event, we should help the public opinion understand better the significance of the event, our policy towards the region in the context of the overall policy of diversification and multilateralization. In general, we should cover it in an appropriate way, not giving it excessive publicity, mentioning both advantages and disadvantages of the membership. At the same time, we should not create the impression in the international community that internally we still have disagreements and hesitations about joining ASEAN.[9]

Commenting on the above Plan, the Cabinet Office said,

> We agree with the MOFA Suggested Media Plan. The following points should be stressed in the coverage of the event:
>
> - The significance of the event to our foreign policy, including the policy toward ASEAN and its member countries
> - The advantages and opportunities, as well as new difficulties and challenges in the course of economic development after we will have joined ASEAN
> - The necessity to provide more information about ASEAN cooperative fields and mechanisms, especially regarding economic cooperation in order to help our enterprises compete on equal footings at home and in the region.[10]

Obviously, there were efforts to play down in internal public relations the nature and the significance of the Vietnam's ASEAN membership.

Deeds, however, are more important than words. ASEAN membership helped Hanoi to overcome the residual mentality of stressing the differences with other ASEAN members and look forward to the construction of a new Vietnam-ASEAN relationship based on commonalities. Increased interactions and cooperation after joining the organization helped to further reduce the remaining concerns and to enhance the understanding of ASEAN by Hanoi. As a result, there had been changes in the way ASEAN was addressed and covered. The notions of "the ASEAN family", or "the ASEAN community" increasingly came to be accepted. For example, in welcoming the Thai Prime Minister, his Vietnamese counterpart Phan Van Khai said, "We are bathed in the affectionate atmosphere of family members."[11] Such words closely reflect the actual thinking of Hanoi about

ASEAN countries. The word "friend" (*bạn*) was used to refer to ASEAN countries in public and in internal documents. The same word was rarely used to refer to other countries.[12] For example, the MOFA report on the visit to Vietnam by Indonesian president Soeharto said, "our Indonesian friends welcome us to join regional cooperation and suggest that we accede to the Bali Treaty."[13] The speech by Foreign Minister Nguyen Manh Cam at the opening session of the Twenty-Seventh AMM on 22 July 1994 wrote, "In the cause for peace and prosperity, the ASEAN friends can find in Vietnam a good friend."[14] By the end of 1999, an ASEAN MOFA report wrote, "The ASEAN membership increasingly provides us with the feeling of being on the same boat (*cùng hội cùng thuyền*) with other ASEAN countries, which promotes better mutual understanding and sympathy."[15] Such words reflected a positive attitude towards Vietnam's ASEAN identity.

In the final analysis, Vietnam's increased cooperation with and membership in ASEAN was based on calculations about the benefits and advantages of improved relations. It might seem, therefore, that Vietnam-ASEAN relations since 1986 could to be more plausibly understood within the traditional realist framework. Yet, the very perception about common interests and similarities in political nature and practice, as well as foreign policy objectives, between Vietnam and ASEAN countries, which was further supported by the perceived geographical proximity, cultural affinity and shared historical experiences, had created a social context out of which a common identity among regional countries and the resultant regional cooperation were built and developed. The decision to join ASEAN was, as the author has tried to show, made when leaders in Hanoi obtained a better understanding of the commonalities in political nature and practices, regime survival, developmental and foreign policy experiences and goals between Vietnam and ASEAN countries. Of course, Hanoi's altered perception was facilitated by the relaxation of global tensions and superpower constraints on small countries' behaviour following the end of the Cold War, political and economic reforms by Hanoi, and efforts at regional reconciliation on the part of the ASEAN countries themselves. However, the simple fact is that the decision to join ASEAN was made when Hanoi came to understand that there was great similarity and close affinity between Vietnam and ASEAN countries and that ASEAN was an equality-based regional organization. As a result, the ASEAN membership did not bring about major changes in the overall foreign policy of Vietnam while Vietnam-ASEAN cooperative relations were able to flourish even with remaining differences in political structures/regimes and levels of socio-economic developments between Vietnam and other ASEAN countries.

Because of this common identity, Vietnam-ASEAN relations, formed in this way after the Cold War, continue to strongly evolve in a mutually beneficial and harmonious fashion while ASEAN continues to play a more important role in the overall foreign policy of Vietnam.

Notes

1. Interview by the author with Vu Duc Dam on 15 January 2003.
2. Thu My, "ASEAN and the Regional Security", *Southeast Asia Today*, September 1995, p. 10.
3. Bruce Cronin, *Community under Anarchy: Transnational Identity and the Evolution of Cooperation* (New York: Columbia University Press, 1999), p. 5.
4. Ibid., p. 455. Kim Ninh also observed that since early 1990s, the Institute for Southeast Asian Studies had been conducting research projects and producing publications on these themes. Kim Ninh, "Vietnam: Struggle and Cooperation", in *Asian Security Practice: Material and Ideational Influence*, edited by Muthiah Alagappa (Stanford, CA: Stanford University Press, 1998), p. 734, fn 9.
5. Vietnam Foreign Minister Nguyen Dy Nien's Interview on the Fifth Anniversary of Vietnam's Membership in ASEAN, at http://www.mofa.gov.vn:8080/tbqt/2000
6. Hoang Anh Tuan, "ASEAN Dispute Management: Implications for Vietnam and an Expanded ASEAN", *Contemporary Southeast Asia* 18, no. 1 (June 1996), pp. 74–76.
7. Interview with Vu Duc Dam by the author, 15 January 2003.
8. Transcripts of the Politburo Meeting on the question of Vietnam's membership in ASEAN (8:00–10:30 a.m., 22 July 1994) coded 229/BBK/BCT.
9. MOFA, Suggested Media Plan, (Đề án tuyên truyền) dated 7 July 1995, pp. 2–3. Similar contents were found in the cable by Deputy Foreign Minister Vu Khoan dated 1 August 1994 to Vietnamese Ambassadors and Director of the Department of External Relations in Ho Chi Minh City in which Vu

Khoan instructed the latter on how to conduct exchanges and explain the decision by the Twenty-Seventh AMM Meeting to admit Vietnam to ASEAN in 1995.
10. Document coded 3917/QHQT signed by Deputy Prime Minister Phan Van Khai on 17 July 1995.
11. Phan Van Khai's Welcome Speech at the State Banquet in honour of the Thai Prime Minister during his Vietnam visit in November 2000.
12. For other countries, the specific words including "the other side" or "they" (*họ*) were used. For example, the MOFA report dated 1 September 1994 on the outcomes of the Vietnam visit by the Japanese Prime Minister Tomiichi Murayama on 25 and 26 August 1994 wrote, "The Japanese side (*phía Nhật*) is supportive of economic reforms in Vietnam; they have promised to support reforms in Vietnam.
13. MOFA Report dated 25 November 1990 submitted to the CPV Politburo on the outcomes of the Vietnam visit by the Indonesian President Suharto on 19 and 21 November 1990. MOFA reports dated 25 January 1992 and 3 March 1992 on visits by Prime Minister Vo Van Kiet to Malaysia on 20–23 January 1992 and the Philippines on 26 February and 1 March 1992 also used the word of "friend" to refer to the Malaysian and Philippine officials. In 1994, some internal documents in Hanoi started to include Thailand and Singapore in the category of "friends".
14. Nguyen Manh Cam's Speech at the Opening Session of the Twenty-Seventh AMM, p. 2.
15. MOFA ASEAN Report, "On Vietnam-ASEAN Relations", November 1999, p. 11.

REFERENCES

Abuza, Zachary. 1996. "International Relations Theory and Vietnam". *Contemporary Southeast Asia* 17, no. 4 (March): 410–15.
———. 1997. "Institutions and Actions in Vietnamese Foreign-Policy Making: A Research Note". *Contemporary Southeast Asia* 19, no. 3 (December): 309–33.
Acharya, Amitav. 1998. "Collective Identity and Conflict Management in Southeast Asia". In *Security Communities*, edited by Emmanuel Adler and Michael Barnett. Cambridge, MA: Cambridge University Press.
———. 2000. *The Quest for Identity: International Relations of Southeast Asia*. Singapore: Oxford University Press.
———. 2001. *Constructing a Security Community in Southeast Asia: ASEAN and the Problem of Regional Order*. New York: Routledge.
Ahmad, Zakaria Haji. 1993. "Question for Greater Communality in Southeast Asia: A Political and Security Perspective". Paper presented at the Third International Symposium on Interaction for Progress: ASEAN-Vietnam All-Round Cooperation, Manila, 4–9 December 1993.
Alagappa, Muthiah, ed. 1998. *Asian Security Practice: Material and Ideational Influence*. Stanford, CA: Stanford University Press.
Amer, Ramses. 1991. *The Ethnic Chinese in Vietnam and Sino-Vietnamese Relations*. Kuala Lumpur: Forum.
———. 1999. "Sino-Vietnamese Relations: Past, Present, and Future". In *Vietnamese Foreign Policy in Transition*, edited by Carlyle Thayer and Ramses Amer. Singapore: Institute of Southeast Asian Studies.
Anderson, Benedict. 1991. *Imagined Community: Reflections on the Origin and Spread of Nationalism*. London: Vecto.
Anderson, Desaix. 2002. *An American in Hanoi: American's Reconciliation with Vietnam*. New York: EastBridge.

Ang, Cheng Guan. 1998. "Vietnam-China Relations Since the End of the Cold War". *Asian Survey* XXXVII, no. 12 (December): 1122–41.

———. 2013. *Singapore, ASEAN and the Cambodia Conflict, 1978–1991*. Singapore: National University of Singapore Press.

Antolik, Michael. 1990. *ASEAN and the Diplomacy of Accommodation*. New York: M.E. Sharpe.

Ball, Desmond, ed. 1987. *Transformation of Security in the Asia/Pacific Region*. Portland: Washington University.

Betts, Richard, et al. 1992. *Time for a Critical Decision on Vietnam: It Is Time for the US to End Its Economic Embargo on Vietnam and Establish Diplomatic Relations*. Columbia University: East Asian Institute.

———. 1995. "Vietnam's Strategic Predicament". *Survival* 37, no. 3 (Autumn).

———. 1995. "Wealth, Power, and Conflict: East Asia after the Cold War". *International Security* 18, no. 3: 3–47.

———, and Thomas Christensen. 2000/2001. "China: Getting the Question Right". *National Interests*, no. 62 (Winter): 17–29.

Brown, Frederick. 1997. "U.S.-Vietnam Normalization: Past, Present, Future". In *Vietnam Joins the World*, edited by James Morley and Masashi Nishihara. New York: M.E. Sharpe.

Bui Thanh Son, 2000. "50 Years of Sino-Vietnamese Relations". *The IIR Proceedings of the Seminar on 50 Years of Sino-Vietnamese Relations* (January), Hanoi.

Bull, Hedley, ed. 1975. *Asia and the Western Pacific: Toward a New International Order*. Canberra: Thomas Nelson Publisher.

Busse, Nicholas. 1999. "Constructivism and Southeast Asia Security". *Pacific Review* 12, no. 3.

Buszynski, Leszek, 1983. *SEATO: The Failure of an Alliance Strategy*. Singapore: Singapore University Press.

Buzan, Barry, and Gerald Segal. 1994, "Rethinking East Asian Security". *Survival* 36, no. 2: 3–21.

Cao Xuan Pho. 1990. *Cultural Similarity: Vietnam and Other Countries in South East Asia*. Hanoi: National Politics Publishing House.

Chalmer, Malcom. 1996. "Openness and Security Policy in Southeast Asia". *Survival* 38, no. 3 (Autumn): 82–98.

Chanda, Nayan. 1986. *Brother Enemy: The War after the War*. New York: Collier Book.

Chapman, Nicholas. 2017. "Mechanisms of Vietnam's Multidirectional Foreign Policy". *Journal of Current Southeast Asian Affairs* 36, no. 2: 31–69.

Chen Jian. 1995. "China's Involvement in the Vietnam War, 1964–1969". *China Quarterly* 142.

Christensen, Thomas. 2001. "Posing Problems Without Catching Up: China's Rise and Challenges for US Security Policy". *International Security* 25, no. 4 (Spring): 5–40.

Collins, Alan. 2000. *The Security Dilemma of Southeast Asia*. New York: St. Martin's Press.

Constantine, Gus. 1995. "Vietnam Sees Boon in ASEAN". *Washington Times*, 3 August 1995, p. A17.

CPV. 1991. *Documents of the VII National Congress*. Hanoi: Truth Publishing House.

———. 1996. *Documents of the VIII National Congress*. Hanoi: National Politics Publishing House.

———. 2001. *Major Documents of the IXth National Congress*. Hanoi: National Politics Publishing House.

———. 2006. *Major Documents of the Xth National Congress*. Hanoi: National Politics Publishing House.

———. 2011. *Major Documents of the XIth National Congress*. Hanoi: National Politics Publishing House.

Cronin, Bruce. 1999. *Community under Anarchy: Transnational Identity and the Evolution of Cooperation*. New York: Columbia University Press.

Da Cunha, Derek Martin. 1988. "Aspects of Soviet-Vietnamese Economic Relations, 1979–1984". *Contemporary Southeast Asia* 12, no. 3 (December): 306–19.

Dang Cam Tu. 2011. "Vietnam in ASEAN Community Building". Thesis submitted to the University of New South Wales in Fulfillment of the Requirements of the Degree of Doctor of Philosophy.

———. 2020. "Vietnam in ASEAN: The Past 25 Years and the Way Forward" (Việt Nam trong ASEAN: 25 năm qua và chặng đường phía trước). *The Communist Review* 7, no. 321 (July): 8–17.

Dao Huy Giam. 2000. "Swim without Life Vest". *Foreign Affairs Weekly*. Special Issues Marking the Fifth Anniversary of Vietnam's Joining ASEAN (July).

Dao Huy Ngoc, and Matsunaga Nobuo, eds. 1994. *Asia-Pacific and Vietnam-Japan Relations*. Hanoi: Institute of International Relations.

Dibb, Paul. 1995. "Toward a New Balance of Power in Asia". *Adelphi Paper*, no. 295. London: International Institute for Strategic Study.

Dosch, Jorn, and Ta Minh Tuan. 2004. "Recent Changes in Vietnam's Foreign Policy: Implications for Vietnam-ASEAN Relations". In *Rethinking Vietnam*, edited by Duncan McCargo. London: Routledge Curzon.

Duiker, William. 1986. *China and Vietnam: Roots of Conflict*. Berkeley: Institute of East Asian Studies, University of California.

———. 1987. "Vietnam Moves toward Pragmatism". *Current History* 86, no. 519 (April): 148–51.
East Asian Institute, Columbia University. 1991. *A Critical Year for Indochina: First-Hand Observations of American and Japanese Analysts*. Report no. 2, March.
———. 1993. *Vietnamese Reforms and Cambodia Peace: Concerns and Observations of American And Japanese Analysts*. Report no. 4, March.
Elliot, David W. 2012. *Changing Worlds: Vietnam's Transition from Cold War to Globalization*. New York: Oxford University Press.
Emmerson, Donald K. 1984. "'Southeast Asia': What's in a Name?". *Journal of Southeast Asian Studies* XV, no. 1 (March).
Fifield, Russell H. 1973. *Americans in Southeast Asia: The Roots of Commitment*. New York: Thomas Crowell Company.
Fisher, Charles A. 1964. *Southeast Asia: A Social, Economic and Political Geography*. London: Methuen & Co. Ltd.
Friedberg, Aaron. 1995. "Ripe for Rivalry: Prospects for Peace in a Multipolar Asia". *International Security* 18, no. 3.
Frost, Frank. 1993. *Vietnam's Foreign Relations: Dynamic of Change*. Singapore: Institute of Southeast Asian Studies.
Funston, John. 1999. "Challenges Facing ASEAN in a More Complex Age". *Contemporary Southeast Asia* 21, no. 2 (August): 217–18.
———, ed. 2001. *Government and Politics in Southeast Asia*. Singapore: Institute of Southeast Asian Studies.
Gaiduk, Ilya. 1996. *The Soviet Union and the Vietnam War*. Chicago: Ivan R. Dee.
Goodman, Alan. 1995. "Vietnam in 1994: With Peace at Hand". *Asian Survey* XXXV, no. 1 (January): 92–111.
———. 1996. "Vietnam in 1995: It Was a Very Good Year". *Washington Quarterly* 19, no. 2 (Spring): 137–50.
Gregor, James. 1989. *In the Shadow of Giants: The Major Power and the Security of Southeast Asia*. California: The Hoover Institution Press, Stanford University Press.
Ha Van Tan. 1992. *Ethnological Roots of the Ancient Viet Race*. Hanoi: Truth Publishing House.
Hall, D.G.E. 1981. *History of South East Asia*. 4th ed. New York: Red Globe Press.
Hanh Phuong. 2003. "The AFTA Roadmap: Challenges to the Vietnamese Economy". *Lao Dong*, 4 January 2003.
Heng, Russell. 1993. "Leadership in Vietnam: Pressure for Reform and Their Limits". *Contemporary Southeast Asia* 15, no. 1 (June).

Ho Chi Minh. 1985. *Selected Writing*, vol. 5. Hanoi: Truth Publishing House.

Hoang Anh Tuan. 1994. "Vietnam's Membership in ASEAN: Economic, Political, and Security Implications". *Contemporary Southeast Asia* 16, no. 3 (December).

———. 1996. "ASEAN Dispute Management: Implications for Vietnam and an Expanded ASEAN". *Contemporary Southeast Asia* 18, no. 1 (June): 61–79.

Holsti, K.J. 1991. *Change in the International System: Essays on the Theory and Practice of International Relations*. Brookfield, VT: Edward Elgar.

Horn, Robert. 1987. *Alliance Politics between Comrades: The Dynamics of Soviet-Vietnamese Relations*. RAND/University of California: Center for the Study of Soviet International Behavior.

Huxley, Tim. 1983. *Indochina and Insurgency in the ASEAN States, 1975–1981*. Working Paper no. 67. Canberra: The Research School of Pacific Studies, Australian National University.

———. 1985. *ASEAN and Indochina: A Study of Political Responses, 1955–1981*. Canberra: Department of International Relations, Australian National University.

———. 1996. "Southeast Asia in the Study on International Relations". *Pacific Review* 9, no. 2: 199–228.

Jeshurun, Chandran, A. Terry Rambo, and Tunku Shamsul Bahrin, eds. 1981. *A Colloquium on Southeast Asian Studies*. Singapore: Institute of Southeast Asian Studies.

Johnston, Alastair Iain. 1999. "The Myth of the ASEAN Way? Explaining the Evolution of the ASEAN Regional Forum". In *Imperfect Unions: Security Institutions over Time and Space*, edited by Helga Haftendorn, Robert Keohane, and Celeste Wallader. London: Oxford University Press.

Jones, Martin, and Michael Smith. 2001. "Is There a Sovietology of Southeast Asian Studies?". *International Affairs* 77, no. 4.

Kang, David. 2003. "Getting Asia Wrong: The Need for New Analytical Frameworks". *International Security* 27, no. 4 (Spring): 57–85.

Katzenstein, Peter. 1996. "Regionalism in Comparative Perspective". *Cooperation and Conflict* 31, no. 2.

Kim Ninh. 1998. "Vietnam: Struggle and Cooperation". In *Asian Security Practice: Material and Ideational Influence*, edited by Muthiah Alagappa. Stanford, CA: Stanford University Press.

Kim, Shee Poon. 1980. *The ASEAN States' Relations with the Socialist Republic of Vietnam*. Singapore: Chopmen Publisher.

Kuah Guan Oo, ed. 1997. *ASEAN: One Region One Vision*. Kuala Lumpur: Bernama.

Le Hong Hiep, and Anton Tsvetov, eds. 2018. *Vietnam's Foreign Policy under Doi Moi*. Singapore: ISEAS – Yusof Ishak Institute.

Le Van Lan, and Pham Van Kinh. 1986. *Cultural Exchanges with Southeast Asia: Vietnam and the Region*. Hanoi: National Politics Publishing House.

Le Viet Duyen. 2017. *The Development of the Foreign Policy of Viet Nam with the Association of Southeast Asian Nations (ASEAN) in the Doi Moi Period (from 1986 to the present)*, Dissertation submitted for the degree of Doctor of Philosophy at the Diplomatic Academy of Vietnam.

Leifer, Michael. 1974. *The Foreign Relations of the New States*. London: Longman.

———. 1989. *ASEAN and the Security of Southeast Asia*. London: Routledge.

———. 1996. *The ASEAN Regional Forum*, Adelphi Paper 302. Oxford: Oxford University Press.

Lowe, Pete, ed. 1998. *The Vietnam War*. London: Longman.

Luu Van Loi. 1998. *50 Years of Vietnamese Diplomacy, 1945–1995*. Hanoi: National Politics Publishing House.

Lyon, Peter. 1969. *War and Peace in Southeast Asia*. London: Oxford University Press.

Mahbubani, Kishore, and Jeffrey Sng. 2017. *The ASEAN Miracle: A Catalyst for Peace*. Singapore: Ridge Books.

McCargo, Duncan, ed. 2004. *Rethinking Vietnam*. London: Routledge Curzon.

McCloud, Donald G. 1986. *System and Process in Southeast Asia: The Evolution of a Region*. Boulder, CO: Westview Press.

Menetrey-Monchau, Cecil. 2003. "The Changing US Strategy in Indochina". Paper presented at the London School of Economics and Political Science Cold War Study Program Conference entitled "Tripartite Diplomacy and the Third Indochina War", Cumberland Lodge, London, 14–16 May 2003.

———. 2006. *American-Vietnamese Relations in the Wake of War: Diplomacy after the Capture of Saigon, 1975–1979*. Jefferson, NC: McFarland & Co.

MOFA. 1980. *The White Book on the 30 Years of Vietnam-China Relations*. Hanoi: Truth Publishing House.

———. 1981. *Conferences of Foreign Ministers of Vietnam, Laos, and Kampuchea: 1980–1981*. Hanoi: MOFA Information and Press Department.

———. 1994. *President Ho Chi Minh and Foreign Relations*. Hanoi: National Politics Publishing House.

———. 1995. *Integrating into the World and Preserving Our Characteristics*. Hanoi: National Politics Publishing House.

———. 2002. *The Vietnamese Diplomacy, 1945–2000*. Hanoi: National Politics Publishing House.

———. ASEAN Department's Reports.
———. Asia 2 Department's Reports.
———. Southeast Asia and South Pacific Affairs Department's Reports.
———. Policy Planning Department's Reports.
———. Americas Affairs Department's Reports.
MOFA Economic Affairs Department. 1999. *Globalization and Vietnam's Economic Integration*. Hanoi: National Politics Publishing House.
Morley, James, and Bernstein Thomas. 1993. *Driven by Growth: Political Change in the Asia-Pacific Region*. Armonk, NY: M.E. Sharpe.
Morley, James, and Masashi Nishihara, eds. 1997. *Vietnam Joins the World*. New York: M.E. Sharpe.
Morris, Stephen. 1999. *Why Vietnam Invaded Cambodia: Political Culture and the Cause of War*. California: Stanford University Press.
Morrison, Charles, ed. 2001. *East Asia and the International System: Report of a Special Study Group*. New York: The Trilateral Commission.
———, and Astri Suhrke. 1979. *Strategy of Survival: The Foreign Policy Dilemmas of Small Asian States*. New York: St. Martin's Press.
Murphy, Ann Marie. 2002. *From Conflict to Cooperation in Southeast Asia, 1961–1967: The Disputes Arising Out of the Creation of Malaysia and the Establishment of the Association of Southeast Asia (ASEAN)*. Unpublished PhD dissertation submitted to the Political Science Department, Columbia University.
Natalegawa, Marty. 2018. *Does ASEAN Matter? A View from Within*. Singapore: ISEAS – Yusof Ishak Institute.
Nguyen Duy Trinh. 1978. *Taking Advantages of Favorable International Conditions and Contributing to the Construction of Socialism and Fulfillment of International Obligations*. Hanoi: Truth Publishing House.
Nguyen Dy Nien. 2000. "Five Years after Joining ASEAN". *Foreign Affairs Weekly*. Special Issues Marking the Fifth Anniversary of Vietnam's Joining ASEAN (July).
Nguyen Hung Son. 2010. "Việt Nam sau 15 năm là thành viên ASEAN: Hướng tới một Việt Nam chủ động, tích cực, và có trách nhiệm trong ASEAN". (Vietnam after 15 Years in ASEAN: Toward a Proactive and Responsible Member). In *Vietnam's Foreign Policy Orientations toward 2030*, edited by Pham Binh Minh, pp. 223–36. Hà nội: Nhà xuất bản Chính trị Quốc gia, National Political Publishing House.
Nguyen Huy Quyet. 2013. "Vietnam's ASEAN Strategic Objectives since the 1986 Doi Moi Reform". Dissertation submitted for the degree of Doctor of Philosophy in the National Graduate Institute for Policy Studies.

Nguyen Manh Cam. 1992. "On the Implementation of the New Foreign Policy". *Communist Review* (August).

———. 1994. Interview given to *Nhan Dan*, 29 July 1994.

———. 1997. "Two Years after Joining ASEAN". *Communist Review* (July).

———. 2010. "Vietnam's Membership in ASEAN: A Right Decision of History-Making Significance" (Việt Nam tham gia ASEAN – một quyết sách đúng đắn có ý nghĩa lịch sử quan trọng). *Vietnam and the World* (*Báo Thế giới và Việt Nam*) (July).

Nguyen Nam Duong. 2010. "Vietnam Foreign Policy since Doi Moi: The Dialectic of Power and Identity". Dissertation submitted for the degree of Doctor of Philosophy in the School of Humanities and Social Sciences, UNSW@ADFA.

Nguyen Ngoc Son. 2000. "Those Unforgettable Days". *Foreign Affairs Weekly*, Special Issues for the Fifth Anniversary of Vietnam's Joining ASEAN (July).

Nguyen Phuc Luan, et al. 2001. *Contemporary Vietnamese Diplomacy for Independence and Freedom*. Hanoi: National Politics Publishing House.

Nguyen Thi Que, and Nguyễn Hoàng Giáp. 2012. *Việt Nam gia nhập ASEAN từ 1995 đến nay: Thành tựu, Vấn đề và Triển vọng* (*Vietnam's ASEAN Membership from 1995 to the Present: Achievement, Issues, and Prospects*). Hanoi: Nhà xuất bản Chính trị Quốc gia, National Political Publishing House.

Nguyen Vu Tung. 1991. "ASEAN: New Adjustments in Foreign Policy". *IIR Bulletin of International Relations* 2 (December).

———. 1993. "Vietnam-ASEAN Cooperation in Southeast Asia". *Security Dialogue* 4, no. 1 (March).

———. 1994. "On the ASEAN Activities since the Establishment". *IIR International Studies*, no. 3 (July).

———. 1997. "Vietnam's Perspective on Security". *CSCAP Working Paper Series on Comprehensive Security*. Institute of Security and International Studies, Kuala Lumpur.

———. 1998. "Coping with the United States: Hanoi's Search for an Effective Strategy". In *The Vietnam War*, edited by Peter Lowe, pp. 30–61. London: Longman.

———. 1998. "Interpreting Beijing and Hanoi: A View of Sino-Vietnamese Relations, 1965–1970". In *77 Conversations between Chinese and Foreign Leaders on the Wars in Indochina, 1964–1977*, edited by Odd Arne Westad et al., Cold War International History Project (Woodrow Wilson International Center for Scholars, Washington D.C., May).

———. 2000. "Vietnam's New Concept of Security". In *Comprehensive Security* in *Asia: Views from Asia and the West on a Changing Security Environment*, edited by Kurt Radtke and Raymond Feddema. Boston: Brill.

———. 2002. "Vietnam: ASEAN Cooperation after the Cold War and the Continued Search for a Theoretical Framework". *Contemporary Southeast Asia* 24, no. 1 (April).

———. 2004. "The Paris Agreement and Vietnam-ASEAN Relations in the Early 1970s". In *The Third Indochina War: Domestic, Regional, and International Aspects*, edited by Odd Arne Westad. London: Longman.

———. 2007. "Testing the Institutionalist Approach: Cooperation between Vietnam and ASEAN". In *Vietnam's New Order: International Perspectives on the State and Reform in Vietnam*, edited by Stephanie Balme and Mark Sidel, pp. 51–70. New York: Palgrave Macmillan.

———, ed. 2007. *Chính sách đối ngoại Việt Nam (Vietnam's Foreign Policy)*, vol. 2. Hanoi: Nhà xuất bản Thế giới, World Publishing House.

———. 2007. "Vietnam's Membership of ASEAN: A Constructivist Interpretation". *Contemporary Southeast Asia* 29, no. 3 (December): 483–505.

———. 2010. "Vietnam-Thailand Relations after the Cold War". In *International Relations in Southeast Asia: Between Bilateralism and Multilateralism*, edited by Ganesan and Ramses Amer, pp. 67–91. Singapore: Institute of Southeast Asian Studies.

———. 2017. "Vietnam-Cambodia Relations: An Analysis from a Vietnamese perspective". In *Cambodia's Foreign Relations in Regional and Global Context*, edited by Deth Sok Udom, Sun Suon, and Serkan Bulut, pp. 85–99. Phnom Penh: Konrad Adenauer Stiftung.

———, and Dang Cam Tu. 2018."Vietnam's Decision to Join ASEAN: The South China Sea Disputes Connection". In *Vietnam's Foreign Policy under Doi Moi*, edited by Le Hong Hiep and Anton Tsvetov. Singapore: ISEAS – Yusof Ishak Institute.

Nischalke, Tobias. 2002. "Does ASEAN Measure Up? Post-Cold War Diplomacy and the Idea of Regional Community". *Pacific Review* 15, no. 1: 89–117.

Odgaard, Liselotte. 2002. *Maritime Security between China and Southeast Asia: Conflict and Cooperation in the Making of Regional Order*. Burlington, VT: Ashgate Publishing Company.

Osborne, Milton. 1985. *Southeast Asia: An Illustrated Introductory History*. Boston: Allen & Unwin.

Palmer, Ronald, and Thomas Reckford. 1987. *Building ASEAN: 20 Years of Southeast Asian Cooperation*. New York: Praeger.

Palmuljoki, Eero. 1999. "Ideology and Foreign Policy: Vietnam's Marxist-Leninist Doctrine and Global Change, 1986–1996". In *Vietnamese Foreign Policy in*

Transition, edited by Carlyle Thayer and Ramses Amer, pp. 38–39. Singapore: Institute of Southeast Asian Studies.

———. 1997. *Vietnam and the World: Marxist-Leninist Doctrine and the Changes in International Relations, 1977–1993*. New York: St. Martin Press.

Pangestu, Mari Elka, and Rastam Mohd Isa, eds. 2017. *ASEAN Future Forward: Anticipating the Next 50 Years*. Kuala Lumpur: ISIS Malaysia.

Peffer, Nathaniel. 1954. "Regional Security in Southeast Asia". *International Organization*, vol. 8.

Peou, Sorpong. 2002. "Realism and Constructivism in Southeast Asian Security Studies Today: A Review Essay". *Pacific Review* 15, no. 1: 119–38.

Pfennig, Werner, and Mark M. B. Suh, eds. 1984. *Aspects of ASEAN*. Munchen: Weltforum Verlag.

Phạm Bình Minh, ed. 2010. *Định hướng chiến lược đối ngoại Việt Nam đến 2020* (*Vietnam's Foreign Policy Orientations toward 2030*). Hà nội: Nhà xuất bản Chính trị Quốc gia, National Political Publishing House.

———. 2015. "Việt Nam tham gia ASEAN: 20 năm qua và con đường đi tới" (Vietnam's Participation in ASEAN: The Past 20 Years and Beyond). In *Ngoại giao Việt Nam: Quá trình triển khai đường lối đối ngoại đại hội toàn quốc lần thứ XII của Đảng (Vietnamese Diplomacy: On the Process of Implementation of Foreign Policy adopted by the Party's XIIth Congresss)*, by Phạm Bình Minh, pp. 149–58. Hanoi: Nhà xuất bản Chính trị Quốc gia, National Political Publishing House.

Phạm Đức Thành, and Trần Khánh, eds. 2006. *Việt Nam trong ASEAN: Nhìn lại và hướng tới* (*Vietnam in ASEAN: Looking Back and Forward*). Hà nội: Nhà xuất bản Khoa học Xã hội (Social Science Publishing House).

Phạm Gia Khiêm, 2008. "ASEAN in a New Phase of Development and the Participation of Vietnam". *International Studies* 78 (August): 7–10.

———. 2011. "Vietnam's ASEAN Chairmanship in 2010: ASEAN's Success and Vietnam's Imprints" (Vai trò chủ tịch ASEAN của Việt Nam năm 2010: Những thành tựu của ASEAN và dấu ấn của Việt Nam). *Communist Review* 1, no. 217 (January): 15–18.

Pike, Douglas. 1987. *Vietnam and The Soviet Union: Anatomy of an Alliance*. Boulder: Westview Press.

Porter, Gareth. 1990. "The Transformation of Vietnam's Worldview: From Two Camps to Interdependence". *Contemporary Southeast Asia* 12, no. 1 (June).

———. 1993. *Vietnam: The Politics of Bureaucratic Socialism*. Ithaca, NY: Cornell University Press.

Radtke, Kurt, and Raymond Feddema, eds. 2000. *Comprehensive Security in East*

Asia: Views from Asia and the West on a Changing Security Environment. The Netherlands: Brill Publishers.

Robinson, Thomas, and David Shambaugh, eds. 1994. *Chinese Foreign Policy: Theory and Practice*. Oxford: Clarendon Press.

Ross, Robert, ed. 1995. *East Asia in Transition: Toward a New Regional Order*. New York: M.E. Sharpe.

Rotter, Andrew, 1987. *The Path to Vietnam: Origins of the American Commitment to Southeast Asia*. Ithaca: Cornell University Press.

Roy, Denny. 1994. "Hegemon on the Horizon? China's Threat to East Asian Security". *International Security* 19, no. 1 (Summer): 149–68.

Segal, Gerald. 1996. "East Asia and the 'Constraintment' of China". *International Security* 20, no. 4 (Spring): 107–35.

Short, Anthony. 1989. *The Origins of the Vietnam War*. London: Longman.

Sidel, Mark, and Stephanie Balme, eds. 2007. *Vietnam's New Order: International Perspectives on the State and Reform in Vietnam*. New York: Palgrave Macmillan.

Simon, Sheldon. 1979. "China, Vietnam, and ASEAN: The Politics of Polarization". *Asian Survey* XIX, no. 12.

———. 1995. "Realism and Neoliberalism: International Relations Theory and Southeast Asian Security". *Pacific Review* 8, no. 1: 5–24.

Singh, Bilveer. 1989. *Soviet Relations with ASEAN: 1968–88*. Singapore: National Singapore University Press.

———. 1992. *Moscow and Southeast Asia since 1985: From the USSR to the CIS*. Singapore: Institute of International Affairs.

Steinberg, David, ed. 1971. *In Search of Southeast Asia: A Modern History*. London: Oxford University Press.

Tan See Seng, and Ralph Cossa. 2001. "Rescuing Realism from the Realists: A Theoretical Note on East Asian Security". In *The Many Faces of Asian Security*, edited by Sheldon Simon. New York: National Bureau of Asian Research.

Tanham, George K., and Alvil Bernstein, eds. 1989. *Military Basing and the US/Soviet Military Balance in Southeast Asia*. New York: Crane Russak.

Thai Quang Trung. 1989. "The Ties that Bind". In *Military Basing and the US-Soviet Military Balance in Southeast Asia*, edited by George K. Tanham and Alvil Bernstein. New York: Crane Russak.

Thayer, Carlyle. 1985. "United States Policy towards Revolutionary Regimes: Vietnam (1975–1983)". In *U.S. Foreign Policy: Adjusting to Change in the Third World*, edited by Dick Clark. No. 85-W441, pp. 121–28. Wye Plantation, Queenstown, MD: Aspen Institute for Humanistic Studies.

———. 1987. "Vietnam's Sixth Party Congress: An Overview". *Contemporary Southeast Asia* 9, no. 1 (June): 12–22.

———. 1992. "Comrade Plus Brother: The New Sino-Vietnamese Relations". *Pacific Review* 5, no. 4 (September): 402–6.

———. 1994. *The Vietnam People's Army under Doi Moi*. Singapore: Institute of Southeast Asian Studies.

———. 1997. "Force Modernization: The Case of the Vietnam People's Army". *Contemporary Southeast Asia* 19, no. 1 (June): 1–18.

———. 1998. "ASEAN and Indochina: The Trends toward Dialogue". A monograph dated 13 May 1998.

———. 2007. "Vietnam's Regional Integration: Domestic and External Challenges to State Sovereignty". In *Vietnam' New Order: International Perspectives on the State and Reform in Vietnam*, edited by Stephanie Balme and Mark Sidel, pp. 31–50. New York: Palgrave Macmillan.

———. 2015. "Vietnamese Diplomacy, 1975–2015: From Member of the Socialist Camp to Proactive International Integration". Paper presented at International Conference on Vietnam: 40 Years of Reunification, Development and Integration (1975–2015), Thu Dau Mot University, Binh Duong province, Vietnam, 25 April 2015.

———. 2017. "Vietnam's Foreign Policy in an Era of Rising Sino-US Competition and Increasing Domestic Political Influence". *Asian Security* 13, no. 3 (July): 1–17.

———, and Ramses Amer. 1999. *Vietnamese Foreign Policy in Transition*. New York: St. Martin's Press.

———, and Ramesh Thakur. 1992. *Soviet Relations with India and Vietnam*. London: Macmillan Press; New York: St. Martin's Press.

Thu My. 1995. "ASEAN and the Regional Security". *Southeast Asia Today*, September.

Tinker, Hugh, 1980. "The Search for the History of Southeast Asia". *Journal of Southeast Asian Studies* XI, no. 2 (September): 369–82.

Ton That Thien. 1989. *The Foreign Politics of the Communist Party of Vietnam: A Study of Communist Tactics*. New York: Crane Russak.

Tønnesson, Stein. 2017. *Explaining the East Asian Peace: A Research Story*. Copenhagen: NIAS Press.

Tran Nham, ed. 1996. *There Is Such a Country of Vietnam: Renovation and Development* (*Co Mot Viet Nam Nhu The: Doi Moi Va Phat Trien*). Hanoi: National Politics Publishing House.

Tran Quang Co. 1992. "The Post-Cold War World and Asia-Pacific". *IIR International Studies Review* (December).

Tran Uyen. 2003. "On Vietnam-ASEAN Relations". *Hanoi Moi*, 27 August 2003.

Trinh Xuan Lang. 1995. "Some Reflections on Our Policies toward ASEAN Countries and the USA from 1975 to 1979". *Proceedings of the Seminar on 50 Years of Vietnamese Diplomacy*. Hanoi: The IIR.

Turley, William, ed. 1985. *Confrontation or Coexistence: The Future of ASEAN-Vietnam Relations*. Bangkok: Institute of Security and International Studies, Chulalongkorn University.

Turley, William, and Mark Selden, eds. 1997. *Reinventing Vietnamese Socialism: Doi Moi in Comparative Perspective*. Boulder, CO: Westview Press.

Viet Chung. 2000. "The East-West Corridor Project". *Foreign Affairs Weekly*. Special Issues Marking the Fifth Anniversary of Vietnam's Joining ASEAN (July), pp. 34–35.

Vo Hung Dzung. 2000. Vietnam's Foreign Trades from 1991 to 2000: Achievements and Problems". *Economic Studies*, no. 11 (294), November 2002.

Vo Nguyen Giap. 2000. *The Headquarters in the Spring of Great Victory*. Hanoi: National Politics Publishing House.

Vu Duong Ninh. 2004. *Vietnam–ASEAN: Bilateral and Multilateral Relations* (*Việt Nam–ASEAN: Quan hệ song phương và đa phương*). Hà nội: Nhà xuất bản Chính trị quốc gia, National Political Publishing House.

———. 2005. "Vietnam-ASEAN: Ten Years of Companion on the Path of International Integration". (Việt Nam–ASEAN: Mười năm đồng hành trên chặng đường hội nhập quốc tế). *Southeast Asian Studies* (*Tạp chí nghiên cứu Đông nam Á*) 4: 22–40.

Vu Khoan. 1994. "Vietnam and ASEAN". *Communist Review* (November).

———. 1995. "Security, Development, and Influence in Foreign Relations". In *Integrating into the World and Preserving Our Characteristics*, edited by MOFA. Hanoi: National Politics Publishing House.

Wanandi, Jusuf. 1990. *ASEAN and Security Cooperation in Southeast Asia*. October. Jakarta: Center for Strategic and International Studies.

Westad, Odd Arne. 2018. *The Cold War: A World History*. New York: Penguin Book.

———, et al. 1998. *77 Conversations between Chinese and Foreign Leaders on the Wars in Indochina, 1964–1977*. Working Paper no. 22, Cold War International History Project. Washington, DC: Woodrow Wilson Center for Scholars.

———, ed. 2004. *The Third Indochina War: Domestic, Regional, and International Aspects*. London: Longman.

William, Michael. 1992. *Vietnam at the Crossroad*. London: Royal Institute of International Affairs.

Wolters, W. 1981. "Culture, History, and Region in Southeast Asian Perspective". In *ASEAN Identity: Development and Culture*, edited by R.P. Anand and

Purificacion V. Quisumbing. Hawaii: East-West Center Culture Learning Institute.

Womack, Brantly. 1996. "Vietnam in 1995: Successes in Peace". *Asian Survey* XXXVI, no. 1 (January): 73–82.

Wurfel, David. 1996. "The New World Order in Southeast Asia: Some Analytical Explorations". In *Southeast Asia in the "New World Order": The Political Economy of a Dynamic Region*, edited by David Wurfel and Bruce Burton. New York: St. Martin's Press.

———. 1997. "Doi Moi in Comparative Perspective". In *Reinventing Vietnamese Socialism: Doi Moi in Comparative Perspective*, edited by William Turley and Mark Selden. Boulder, CO: Westview Press, 1997.

———. 1999. "Between China and ASEAN: The Dialectics of Recent Vietnamese Foreign Policy". In *Vietnamese Foreign Policy in Transition*, edited by Carlyle Thayer and Ramses Amer. New York: St. Martin's Press.

——— and Bruce Burton, eds. 1996. *Southeast Asia in the "New World Order": The Political Economy of a Dynamic Region*. New York: St. Martin's Press.

Yahuda, Michael. 1998. *The International Politics of the Asia-Pacific, 1945–1995*. London: Routledge.

Yeong Mike. 1992. "New Thinking in Vietnamese Foreign Policy". *Contemporary Southeast Asia* 14, no. 3 (December): 257–68.

Zagoria, Donald. 1967. *Vietnam Triangle: Moscow, Peking, Hanoi*. New York: Pegasus.

———. 1995. "The United States and the Asia-Pacific Region in the Post-Cold War Era". In *East Asia in Transition: Toward a New Regional Order*, edited by Robert Ross. New York: M.E. Sharpe.

———. 1997. "Joining ASEAN". In *Vietnam Joins the World*, edited by James Morley and Masashi Nishihara, pp. 154–72. New York: M.E. Sharpe.

INDEX

Note: Page numbers followed by "n" refer to notes.

A
Abdul Razak, Tun, 15
American Affairs Department, 117
APEC Summit, 115–16
ASEAN
 basic documents, 84
 capitalist class in, 19
 chronology of joining, 135–40
 communist parties in, 50
 consultative forums, 81
 cooperative relations in, 82
 decision-making procedures, 146
 developmental models, 178
 foreign policy and principles,
  13–14, 19, 54, 180–81
 functional cooperation, 146
 Hanoi's view, 12, 14, 15, 22, 23,
  26
 and ideology, 203
 nation-building formula of, 175
 non-aggression treaty, 51
 non-recognition of PRG, 21
 opportunism, 22
 organizational structures and
  institutional arrangements of,
  134–35
 policy, 13
 self-seeking attitude, 22
 trade deficits, 155
 and US, 11, 102–14, 120
 Vietnam's membership in, 114,
  154–60
 war of liberation in Vietnam, 13
 working procedures and principles,
  169
ASEAN Chairmanship, 1, 7n1
ASEAN-China relations, 101
ASEAN-China Senior Officials
 Meeting, 112
ASEAN community, 1
 central role of ASEAN, 2
ASEAN Coordinating Committee,
 23
ASEAN Declaration on the South
 China Sea of 1992, 105–6, 109,
 111
ASEAN East-West Corridor Project,
 166n70
ASEAN Free Trade Area (AFTA),
 83, 156, 188
 ASEAN and, 145
 conduct studies on, 144
 and MOT, 148
 Vietnam and, 150–54

ASEAN Foreign Ministers' Meeting (AMM), 13, 23
ASEAN member states
  relations with, 11
  in US war, 18
ASEAN membership
  Hanoi decision on, 123
  and Vietnam's shifting national identity, 169–200
ASEAN National Committee (ANC) Office, 145
ASEAN National Secretariat (ANS), 147
ASEAN Regional Forum (ARF), 128n76
ASEAN Senior Officials' Meeting (SOM), 78
ASEAN-sponsored agreement, 44
ASEAN Summit, 25, 27, 136
ASEAN Treaty of Amity and Cooperation, 2
ASEAN-Vietnamese relationship, 171
Asia-3 Department Annual Report of 1980, 46
Association for Southeast Asian Studies (ASEAR), 92, 143
"Association mentality" in Vietnam, 187

B
Baker, James, 88, 89
Bali Treaty, 122, 138, 198n40, 209
  in ASEAN consultative forums, 76, 81
  ASEAN Declaration on the South China Sea, 105
  ASEAN membership, 136
  and Declaration, 106
  Fourth ASEAN Summit, 137
  Hanoi, 78, 106, 135
  MOFA, 82
  relations with Indochinese countries, 94
  Soviet bloc, 56, 203
  State Council, 181
  TAC, 25
  Vietnam and Laos, 120
Bandung Declaration, 85
Bangkok
  AMM meeting in, 15, 77
  Bangkok Post, 82
  bilateral talks with China, 113
  First ARF Meeting in Bangkok, 111
  Hanoi and, 40, 56
  Thai and Vietnamese embassies in, 40
  Vietnamese counterpart in, 100, 194n3
  Vietnamese Embassy in, 50
Bangkok Declaration, 91
Bangkok Post, 82
Brunei Darussalam, 77, 103, 109, 137, 140, 144

C
Cambodia
  Agreement on Cambodia, 67
  alliance with China, 31
  ASEAN membership, 2
  communist forces in, 89
  factions in, 90
  international agreement on, 79
  Paris Agreement on, 121, 194n3
  Thailand and ASEAN countries, 47
  troops to, 21
  Vietnam intervention, 2

and Vietnam relations, 93–94, 122, 177, 182
Cambodian communist parties, 89
Cambodian People's Party (CPP), 94
Carter, President Jimmy, 42
Central Committee Plenary Conference, 93
Central Committee Plenum, 80
Chatichai Choonhavan, 14, 33n22
Chengdu Summit, 88, 89
Chia Siow Yue, 153, 167n78
Chin Peng, 89
China
   bilateral agreements with, 111
   expansionism, 103
   hegemonism, 90
   leadership, 59
   National Offshore Oil Corporation, 105
   reactionary forces, 58
   socialism, 90
   Soviet Union and, 185
   strategy, 110
   threat to Vietnam, 53, 99–102
   troops, 102
Christopher, Warren, 95
Clinton, Bill, 115–16
"Cohesive and Responsive ASEAN", 1
Common Effective Preferences Tariffs (CEPT), 150
communist identity, 66, 186, 188, 201
communist ideology, 31, 88, 90, 92, 185, 187
communist parties in ASEAN countries, 50
Communist Party of Vietnam Congress, 2

Council of Ministers Document, 198n40
Council on Mutual Economic Assistance (CMEA), 43
CPV National Congress, 78, 87, 190
CPV Politburo, 94, 114, 136
Crestone Energy Corporation, 105–11
Cronin, Bruce, 185

D

Dang Dinh Quy, 159, 188
Dang Nghiem Hoanh, 107, 108, 114, 116
Dao Huy Giam, 154
Democratic Republic of Vietnam (DRV), 10, 31n4, 185
Deng Xiaoping, 42, 59
Diplomatic Academy of Vietnam (DAV), 6
Doi Moi, 2, 78
"domino theory", 21
Do Muoi, 77, 81, 90, 97, 138, 177, 178

E

equality-based regional organization, 210

F

fact-finding mission, 101, 143
Fatherland Organization National Congress, 196
Foreign Ministers' Conference (FMC), 48
foreign policy, 5–6, 18, 57, 205–6, 208–10
   ASEAN, 2, 19, 47
   Chengdu Summit, 89

Cold War and, 5
CPV National Congress, 190
design and conduct of, 3
of diversification and
   multilateralization, 84
Hanoi, 7, 17, 28, 41, 54, 64, 92,
   95, 170
implementation of, 31
objectives of, 180–85
of peace and neutrality, 12
post-Cold War Vietnamese foreign
   policy, 91
shift of Vietnam, 4
state identity in, 185–94
strategy, 63
Vietnamese diplomats in, 51
Vietnamese foreign policy, 6, 18,
   31, 57, 60, 65, 187–88, 191,
   201
Forum on the Comprehensive
   Development of Indochina, 96
Four Modernizations Programme, 99
Four-Point Position, 19, 23, 25–27,
   91
Free Trade Area, 83
Funston, John, 180

G

Geneva Agreements, 186
Geneva Conferences, 49
Ghazali Shafie, 55
Gilpin, Robert, 29
Golongan Karya (Golkar), 176, 179,
   197n34
Gulf of Thailand, 122

H

Hadi Soesastro, 166n77
Ho Chi Minh, 92, 127n51, 175, 185

Hoang Bao Son, 44, 68n17
Hong Ha, 77, 97, 182
human rights, 118, 183–84
Hun Sen faction, 89
Huxley, Tim, 21

I

IIR Southeast Asian Studies
   Division, 138
Indochinese alliance, 182
Indochinese countries, bloc of, 51
Indochinese revolutions, 25, 45
Indochinese socialist system, 47
Indochinese solidarity, 58
Indochinese Summit Meeting, 55
Indonesia, 104, 130n100
   ASEAN, 23, 206
   and China, relations between, 101
   diplomatic relations with DRV, 14
   economic assistance to Vietnam, 15
   overlapping sea zones, 122
   policy, 53
   post-Paris Agreement period, 22
   rice production, 157
   sea boundaries, 40
   Sino-Vietnamese conflict, 52
   Southeast Asia policy, 80
   Soviet Union, relations with, 17
   "substantive dialogues" with
      Vietnam, 54
Institute for Southeast Asian Studies,
   12, 174, 210n4
Institute of Southeast Asian Studies,
   Singapore, 153
Institutional arrangements, 147–50
International Commission, 22
international community, 23
International Conference on Human
   Rights, 183

Index

International Conference on
   Kampuchea (ICK), 56
international politics, in Third World,
   170
intra-ASEAN cooperation, 86
intra-ASEAN disputes, 121

J
Japan-Vietnam relations, 96–98
Jiang Zemin, 88, 96, 115
Johnson South Reef, 103
Joint Declaration of the Sixth
   ASEAN Summit, 161n2

K
Kampuchea
   and ASEAN states, 100
   China and, 44, 45, 56, 58
   issue, 45
   and Laos, 24–25, 36n57, 64, 66,
      115
   revolution in, 72n58
   self-determination of, 44
   and Southeast Asia, 49, 52
   Vietnam-ASEAN relations, 15–16
   Vietnamese troops, 41, 55
Khmer Rouge, 64
   and anti-Phnom Penh factions, 55
   Beijing and, 41, 42, 64
   issue, 41
   regime, 41
   troops, 45
Kim Ninh, 92, 126n49, 179, 210n4
Kissinger, Henry, 2930
Kuala Lumpur Declaration, 13

L
Lao People's Revolutionary Party
   (LPRP), 94

Le Cong Phung, 109, 137
Le Duan, 20, 34n38, 36
Le Duc Anh, 77, 107, 113, 131n126,
   140, 164n38, 177, 178
Le Duc Tho, 29
Le Mai, 104, 183
Le Thi Bang Tam, 151
Le Van Bang, 98, 113, 115, 117
Lee Kuan Yew, 101, 130n112, 176,
   177, 194n3
Li Peng, 89, 107
Lim Jock Hoi, 2
Luu Doan Huynh, 68n17, 75n99,
   126n49, 182, 196n22, 198n45
Luu Van Loi, 62

M
Mahathir Mohamad, 107–8, 171,
   177, 196n21
Malayan Communist Party (MCP),
   21, 89
Malaysia, 11
   bilateral agreements with China,
      111
   formal diplomatic relations with, 21
   political dialogues, 56
   technological cooperation, 15
Manila Declaration, 112
Maoist communist groups, 50
Marxist and Leninist doctrines, 206
"Matrix of dynamics", 202
Ministry of Public Order (MOPO),
   145
Ministry of Public Security, 96
Mischief Reef, 111–14, 116, 117
MOFA American Affairs Department,
   115
MOFA ASEAN Department Report,
   183

MOFA ASEAN Department Review, 98
MOFA Media Coverage Plan, 182
MOFA North America Department Report, 95
MOFA Southeast Asian and South Pacific Affairs Department, 76, 135
MOFA Suggested Media Plan, 198n46, 207, 208
Morris, Stephen, 58, 73n79
Moscow, 57, 59, 62, 105
Multilateral Trade Department, 149

N

Naisaing Marangkoun, 33n22
NAM Summit, 21, 26
National Center for Social Sciences and Humanities, 127n51, 145
National Committee for International Economic Cooperation (NCIEC), 148
National Liberation Front (NLF), 22, 27
National Party Congress, 51
National Security Act, 197n35
Ngo Tat To, 108
Nguyen Co Thach, 47, 48, 52–55, 59, 72n59, 88, 124n16, 171
Nguyen Dy Nien, 210n5
Nguyen Duy Hung, 137
Nguyen Duy Quy, 143
Nguyen Duy Trinh, 15, 25, 40
Nguyen Hoai Son, 152
Nguyen Hoang An, 164n48
Nguyen Manh Cam, 77, 81, 92, 96, 97, 101, 110, 130n112, 136, 140, 181, 196n22, 196n26, 200n67
Nguyen Manh Hung, 101, 130n112

Nguyen Minh Vu, 151
Nguyen Ngoc Son, 143, 163n38
Nguyen Thanh Huy, 149
Nguyen Trung Thanh, 112
Nguyen Xuan Phuc, 1, 2, 7n1
Nhan Dan, 13, 25, 28, 36n58, 110, 140
Nixon Doctrine, 16–17, 21–23, 34n38
non-aggression treaty, 48
  with ASEAN countries, 51
Non-Aligned Movement (NAM), 21, 44
non-socialist political systems, 174

O

"on-the-job training" process, 143
open-door reforms programme, 2

P

Papua New Guinea, 136–37
Paracels, 30, 98, 102,
Paris Agreement, 9, 121
  on Cambodia, 194n3
  DRV and PRG, diplomatic relations with, 10
  and Hanoi, 9, 11, 17
  implementation of, 12, 63–64
  Saigon government, 21
  South Vietnam, 37n70
  Thailand, 14
  in Vietnam-ASEAN relations, 11
  Vietnamese revolution, 21
Paris Conference, 49
Paris Peace Talks, 14
People's Action Party (PAP), 176, 179, 197n34
Pham Chi Lan, 152, 166n72
Pham Duc Duong, 92

Pham Nguyen Long, 174
Pham Van Dong, 15, 30, 33n22, 41, 44
Phan Hien, 26, 28, 35n50, 37n71, 39n86, 40, 45, 49, 54, 71n51
Phan Van Khai, 124n16, 148, 174, 208
Philippines, 14, 22, 24, 26, 54, 104
    ASEAN support for, 113
    economic assistance to Vietnam, 15
    and South China Sea, 117
    US bases in, 17
    US forces in, 16
Phnom Penh, 41, 44, 45, 47
Pike, Douglas, 62, 74n95, 192
Politburo, 84–85, 94, 114, 146, 183, 207
    ASEAN membership, 76
    Bali Treaty, 138
    MOFA Memo, 101
    Thirteenth CPV Politburo Resolution, 78, 86, 87, 93, 100, 173, 201
Pol Pot faction, 89
Porter, Gareth, 171
post-Cold War, 95
    Vietnamese foreign policy, 91
    Vietnamese leadership in, 120
Provisional Revolutionary Government (PRG), 9, 12, 37n70
    Paris Accords and recognition of, 22

Q
Qian Qichen, 100
Quang Thai, 13, 32n16
Quang Xuan, 117

R
Research Unit on AFTA (RUA), 151
rice, 15, 157
Roth, Stanley, 117

S
Saigon regime, 9, 11, 14, 24, 102
Severino, Rodolfo, 107
Singapore, 11, 17, 21, 54–56, 104, 136, 144, 153, 176
    ASEAN membership, 24, 194n3
    friend of Vietnam, 211n13
    one-party rule system, 179
    trade with, 73n76
    Vietnamese companies in, 14–15
Singh, Ajit, 112
Sino-Philippines dispute, 116
Sino-Soviet rift, 186
Sino-Soviet war, 60
Sino-US normalization, 42
Sino-US relations, 115, 116
Sino-Vietnamese alliance, 90, 92
Sino-Vietnamese borders, 42, 99
Sino-Vietnamese communist alliance, 203
Sino-Vietnamese conflict, 104
Sino-Vietnamese military clashes, 103–5
Sino-Vietnamese relations, 42, 87–92
    Vietnam's ASEAN membership, 95–96
Sino-Vietnamese Summit, 88, 89, 100
socialism, 89
    in Vietnam, 179
socialist internationalism, 205
socialist international relations, 186
soft infrastructure, 158
South China Sea
    Chinese expansion in, 117

disputes in, 102–14
Philippines and, 117
US-Vietnamese relations, normalization of, 119
and Vietnam, 116
Southeast Asia, 26
  expansionism in, 30
  expansionist policies in, 50
  Indochina and, 30
  international conference on, 48
  international relations in, 14
  Maoist communist groups in, 50
  opposing systems in, 51
  peace and stability in, 80
  Zone of Peace, Freedom, and Neutrality (ZOPFAN) in, 13
Southeast Asian and South Pacific Affairs Department, 136, 138, 176
Southeast Asian communist parties, 50
Southeast Asian economic "tigers," 160
Southeast Asia Treaty Organization (SEATO), 16, 18
South Vietnam, 9, 15, 16, 37n70, 186
Soviet aid to Vietnam, 1976–86, 61
Soviet bloc, 87
Soviet Union, 3, 58, 62–63
Soviet-Vietnamese alliance, 3
Soviet-Vietnamese cooperation, 60
Soviet-Vietnamese Treaty of Friendship and Cooperation, 42, 59
Spratly, 87, 98, 102–5, 107, 110–11, 116–17
Spring-Summer Offensive, 22
State Committee for Social Sciences, 12

State Planning Commission, 143
Sunthorn Hongladarom, 44
Supreme National Council, 90

T

Thai Communist Party, 21
Thailand
  and ASEAN countries, 47
  "bamboo diplomacy", 182
  civil aviation agreement with, 15
  diplomatic relations with Vietnam, 15
  domestic affairs, 51
  modern diplomacy, 57
  Paris Agreement, 14
  technological cooperation, 15
  US bases in, 17
  US military forces in, 16, 28
  Vietnam and, 28, 104, 122
Thayer, Carl, 90, 94
Tiananmen Square incident, 88, 89, 116
Tran Duc Luong, 147
Tran Le Duc, 103
Tran Quang Co, 142, 173
Treaty of Amity and Cooperation in Southeast Asia (TAC), 3–4, 25
  and ASEAN, 86
  proposal for Vietnam, 40
Treaty of Friendship and Cooperation, 41–43, 46, 59
  with Moscow, 56
  Soviet Union, 192
  Vietnam and China, relations between, 3
Trinh Xuan Lang, 27
Truong Chinh, 51, 71n56
Truong Dinh Tuyen, 153
Tu Chinh (Vanguard Bank), 105–11

U

UN Convention on the Law of the Sea, 119
United Malays National Organization (UMNO), 176, 179, 197n34
United States of America
  ASEAN and, 102–14
  China policy, 115
  and Chinese schemes, 30
  foreign policy, 95
  lackeys, 24, 118
  military organizations, 43
  Nixon Doctrine and, 21, 23
US-Philippines security treaty, 117
US-Vietnamese relations, 95
  normalization of, 119

V

Vietnam-ASEAN relations, 2–4, 6, 15–16, 23, 56, 65
  in 1975–78, 40
  in 1995, 5
  decision to join ASEAN, 7
  deterioration in, 97
  four-point policy, 77
  implications for, 87–92
  improvement of, 81, 202
  Nixon Doctrine, 17
  Paris Agreement in, 11
  perceptions and priorities in, 28
  relations with major powers, 94–95
  Southeast Asia issue in, 18
  trade, 154
  trends in, 11
Vietnamese diplomacy, 56
Vietnamese institutions, weakness of, 157
Vietnamese leadership, in post-Cold War era, 120
Vietnamese media, sections of, 59
Vietnam-US relations, normalization of, 42
Vietnam War, 3, 13, 117
  ASEAN countries in, 30
Vo Van Kiet, 82, 90, 110, 131n115, 136, 137, 181
Vu Duc Dam, 141, 148, 149, 189, 200n67, 207
Vu Khoan, 101, 121, 131n126, 132n143, 137, 143, 173, 181, 182
  ASEAN membership, 85, 182
  in Singapore, 136–37
  State Planning Commission, 143
Vu Quang Diem, 101, 102, 107, 112, 113, 117
Vu Tien, 44

W

Wong Polnikorn, 44

Z

Zhang Dewei, 89
Zone of Peace, Freedom, and Neutrality (ZOPFAN), 13, 26, 28, 48

The Author
Nguyen Vu Tung is a professor at the Diplomatic Academy of Vietnam. He gained a PhD degree in Political Science from Columbia University (New York) and serves as Vietnamese diplomat in the United States of America and the Republic of Korea.

www.ingramcontent.com/pod-product-compliance
Lightning Source LLC
Chambersburg PA
CBHW050326020526
44117CB00031B/1807